Mavericks
at Work

P9-ELX-638

Mavericks at Work

WHY THE MOST ORIGINAL MINDS IN BUSINESS WIN

William C. Taylor & Polly LaBarre

HARPER

HARPER

an imprint of HarperCollins*Publishers*
77–85 Fulham Palace Road,
Hammersmith, London W6 8JB

HarperCollins' website address is: www.harpercollins.co.uk

First published by William Morrow, an imprint of HarperCollins*Publishers* 2006
This edition 2007

1

© 2006 William C. Taylor and Polly LaBarre

William C. Taylor and Polly LaBarre assert the moral right to be
identified as the authors of this work

A catalogue record of this book is
available from the British Library

ISBN-13   978-0-00-724406-5
ISBN-10   0-00-724406-1

Designed by Susan Yang

Printed and bound in Great Britain by
Clays Ltd, St Ives plc

All rights reserved. No part of this publication may be
reproduced, stored in a retrieval system, or transmitted,
in any form or by any means, electronic, mechanical,
photocopying, recording or otherwise, without the prior
written permission of the publishers.

This book is proudly printed on paper which contains wood
from well-managed forests, certified in accordance with
the rules of the Forest Stewardship Council.
For more information about FSC,
please visit www.fsc.org

Mixed Sources
Product group from well-managed
forests and other controlled sources
www.fsc.org Cert no. SW-COC-1806
© 1996 Forest Stewardship Council

FSC

To Chloe, Paige, and Grace—
mavericks at home
WCT

To my parents—
who held me close, but never fenced me in
PL

Contents

. . . .

What ideas is your company fighting for? • *Can you play competitive hardball by throwing your rivals a strategic curveball?* • *Changing the channel: The one-of-a-kind network that transformed television.*

Can you be provocative without provoking a backlash? • *Why strategic innovators develop their own vocabulary of competition.* • *Winning on purpose: The values-driven ad agency that carves its beliefs into the floor.*

Why "me-too" won't do: Make-or-break questions about how you and your organization compete.

PART TWO

REINVENTING INNOVATION

Chapter 4

Ideas Unlimited: Why Nobody Is as Smart as Everybody

How to persuade brilliant people to work with you, even if they don't work for you. • *Why grassroots collaboration requires head-to-head competition.* • *Eureka! How one open-minded leader inspired the ultimate Internet gold rush.*

Chapter 5

Innovation, Inc.: Open Source Gets Down to Business

Have you mastered the art of the open-source deal? • *Why smart leaders "walk in stupid every day."* • *Bottom-up brainpower: How a 170-year-old corporate giant created a new model of creativity.*

Chapter 6

Maverick Messages (II): Open-Minding Your Business

Shared minds: The design principles of open-source leadership.

PART THREE

RECONNECTING WITH CUSTOMERS

Chapter 7

From Selling Value to Sharing Values:
Overcoming the Age of Overload

If your products are so good, why are your customers so unhappy? • *How to build a cult brand in a dead business.* • *"Our customer is our category"—the retailer that sells a sense of identity.*

Chapter 8

Small Gestures, Big Signals: Outstanding Strategies to Stand Out from the Crowd

Do you sell where your customers are—and your competitors aren't? • Warm and scuzzy: How Howard Stern became the world's most unlikely teddy-bear salesman. • Why the company with the smartest customers wins.

Chapter 9

Maverick Messages (III): Building Your Bond with Customers

Brand matters: The new building blocks of cutting-edge marketing.

PART FOUR

REDESIGNING WORK

Chapter 10

The Company You Keep: Business as if People Mattered

Can you attract more than your fair share of the best talent in your field? • How to find great people who aren't looking for you. • Building the character of competition: Why the world's friendliest airline unleashes the "warrior spirit" in its workforce.

Chapter 11

People and Performance: Stars, Systems, and Workplaces That Work

The first law of leadership: "Stars don't work for idiots." • How free agents become team players. • From bureaucracy to adhocracy: The many merits of a messy workplace.

Chapter 12

Maverick Messages (IV): Practicing Your People Skills   **253**

Hiring test: Is your design for the workplace as distinctive as your designs on the marketplace?

APPENDIX

Maverick Material   **263**

The Maverick Promise

We've always believed that the first step in any successful venture—starting a company, launching a product, even writing a book—is to establish a clear definition of what it means to succeed. Our definition of success for this book begins and ends with its impact on you. We will consider *Mavericks at Work* a success if it opens your eyes, engages your imagination, and encourages you to think bigger and aim higher. Most of all, we will consider it a success if it equips you to act more boldly as a leader and win more decisively as a competitor. We will measure our success by how much we contribute to yours.

That said, this is more than a how-to book. It is also a what-if book. Business needs a breath of fresh air. We are, at last, coming out of a dark and trying period in our economy and society—an era of slow growth and dashed expectations, of criminal wrongdoing and ethical misconduct at some of the world's best-known companies. But NASDAQ nuttiness already feels like time-capsule fodder, the white-collar perp walk has become as routine as an annual meeting, and the triumphant return of me-first moguls like Donald Trump feels like a bad nostalgia trip, the corporate equivalent of a hair-band reunion. We've seen the face of business at its worst, and it hasn't been a pretty sight. This book is intended to persuade you of the power of business at its best.

Which speaks to our second goal for *Mavericks at Work*—to restore the promise of business as a force for innovation, satisfaction, and progress, and to get beyond its recent history as a source of revulsion, remorse, and recrimination. Indeed, despite all the bleak headlines and blood-boiling scandals over the last five years, the economy has experienced a period of realignment, a power shift so profound that we're just beginning to appreciate what it means for the future of business, for how all of us go about the business of building companies that work, and for doing work that matters.

In industry after industry, executives and organizations that were once dismissed as upstarts, as outliers, as wild cards, have achieved positions of financial prosperity and market leadership. There's a reason the young billionaires behind the most celebrated entrepreneurial success in recent memory began their initial public offering (IPO) of shares with a declaration of independence from business as usual. "Google is not a conventional company," read their Letter from the Founders. "We do not intend to become one."

Nor does the unconventional cast of characters you will encounter in this book. From a culture-shaping television network with offices in sun-splashed Santa Monica, California, to a little-known office furniture manufacturer rooted in the frozen tundra of Green Bay, Wisconsin, from glamorous fields such as advertising, fashion, and the Internet to old-line industries such as construction, mining, and household products, they are winning big at business—attracting millions of customers, creating thousands of jobs, generating tens of billions of dollars of wealth—by rethinking the logic of how business gets done.

Alan Kay, the celebrated computer scientist, put it memorably some

35 years ago: "The best way to predict the future is to invent it." The companies, executives, and entrepreneurs you'll meet in the pages that follow are inventing a more exciting, more compelling, more rewarding future for business. They have devised provocative and instructive answers to four of the timeless challenges that face organizations of every size and leaders in every field: setting strategy, unleashing new ideas, connecting with customers, and helping their best people achieve great results.[1]

There's nothing quite so exhilarating as being an eyewitness to the future. We felt that sense of exhilaration throughout our travels as we immersed ourselves in organizations that have shaped the course of their industries by reshaping the sense of what's possible among employees, customers, and investors. We spent countless hours with leaders at every level of these organizations, from CEOs to research scientists, who understand that companies with a disruptive presence in the marketplace also need a distinctive approach to the workplace.

We went deep inside these organizations, looking to understand the ideas they stand for and the ways they work. We participated in a filmmaking class at one of the world's most successful movie studios. We attended a closed-to-the-public awards ceremony at Radio City Music Hall, where employees of what has to be the world's most entertaining bank sang, danced, and strutted their stuff. We sat in on a crucial monthly meeting (the 384th such consecutive meeting over the last 32 years) in which top executives and frontline managers of a $600 million employee-owned company shared their most sensitive financial information and most valuable market secrets. We walked the corridors of a 120-year-old research facility where a team of R&D executives is changing how one of the world's biggest companies develops new ideas for consumer products. We walked the streets of Manhattan with employees from a hard-charging hedge fund who were sizing up ideas about marketplace trends and stock market picks.

This book is our report from the front lines of the future—an account of what we saw, what it means for business, and why it matters to your company, your colleagues, and your career. It is not a book of best practices. It is a book of *next* practices—a set of insights and case studies that amount to a business plan for the 21st century, a new way to lead, compete, and succeed.

Our basic argument is as straightforward as it is urgent: when it comes to thriving in a hypercompetitive marketplace, "playing it safe" is no longer playing it smart. In an economy defined by overcapacity, oversupply, and utter sensory overload—an economy in which everyone already has more than enough of whatever it is you're selling—the only way to stand out from the crowd is to stand for a truly distinctive set of ideas about where your industry should be going. You can't do big things as a competitor if you're content with doing things only a little better than the competition.

Another well-known bit of philosophy, made famous by Hall of Fame basketball coach Pete Carril, captures the competitive spirit at the heart of this book. During his 29-year tenure, Carril's Princeton Tigers regularly squared off against (and often beat) teams whose players were bigger, faster, and more physically gifted than his team. "The strong take from the weak," his coaching mantra went, "but the smart take from the strong."[2]

This book is devoted to the proposition that in business, as in basketball, the smart can take from the strong—that the best way to outperform the competition is to outthink the competition. Maverick companies aren't always the largest in their field; maverick entrepreneurs don't always make the cover of the business magazines. But mavericks do the work that matters most—the work of originality, creativity, and experimentation. They demonstrate that you can build companies around high ideals and fierce competitive ambitions, that the most powerful way to create economic value is to embrace a set of values that go beyond just amassing power, and that business, at its best, is too exciting, too important, and too much fun to be left to the dead hand of business as usual.[3]

Who are these mavericks? The core ideas in this book are rooted in the strategies, practices, and leadership styles of 32 organizations with vastly different histories, cultures, and business models. Half of them are publicly traded companies or business units inside public companies. The other half are privately held companies, venture-backed start-ups, or even not-for-profits. Some of them are giants, with thousands of employees and billions of dollars in sales. Some of them are pip-squeaks, with a few hundred employees and sales in the tens of millions of dollars. But the distinctiveness of their ideas and the power of their practices make all of them true business originals. They are rethinking competition, reinventing innovation, reconnecting with customers, and redesigning work. Together, they are creating a maverick agenda for business—an agenda from which every business can learn.

No one can promise that every company you meet in these pages will thrive, without setbacks or reversals, for years to come. The realities of competition are too treacherous for that. We can't promise that every technique or business practice we highlight will work just as well in your organization. There's a difference between learning from someone else's ideas and applying them effectively somewhere else.

What we can promise is a book that is as eye-opening, as energetic, as flat-out useful as we know how to make it, a book that aims to be true to the maverick spirit of the agenda it champions and the leaders it chronicles. To that end, we've added four sections we call "Maverick Messages"—which distill the ideas we explore and the stories we tell into a set of action-oriented takeaways. We end the book with a valuable collection of resources (called "Maverick Material") that will help you keep learning long after you've finished reading.

We hope we've delivered on the maverick promise. Please visit us on the Web, learn more about the ideas, themes, and case studies in this book, and share your own stories and lessons about what it takes to be a maverick at work.

William C. Taylor
Polly LaBarre
www.mavericksatwork.com

PART ONE

Rethinking Competition

Chapter One

. . . .

Not Just a Company, a Cause: Strategy as Advocacy

One reason we're in Wilmington, Delaware, is because this is home to so many credit card companies. Every morning, when I drive to work, I see their signs and it makes me angry. They provide the opium of consumerism in American finance. There are restaurants in town that won't take my reservation, because they know I might offend people. But that's what keeps me motivated. That's what gets me charged up to do battle.

—ARKADI KUHLMANN, PRESIDENT AND CEO, ING DIRECT USA

At times, Arkadi Kuhlmann can sound a lot like consumer activist Ralph Nader or crusading reformer Eliot Spitzer. He rails against the banking industry's exorbitant fees. He expresses contempt for the needless complexities and hidden charges that infect the home mortgage business. And don't even get him *started* on credit cards. He's fed up with a financial culture that encourages people to save too little, invest too recklessly, and spend too much.

"In the beginning, people loved credit cards," Kuhlmann declares. "Customers were proud to pull them out of their wallet. Today people *hate* credit cards—the nonstop marketing, the sky-high interest rates, companies pushing cards at kids in college. Everybody knows that credit card excess isn't good. That's not a popular message here in Wilmington, of course. As I explained to the local newspaper, 'It's sort of like preaching, and why not preach among the heathens?'"

But Kuhlmann is not a consumer activist or a politician, and he's certainly not a preacher. He's a banker. In fact, he's the founder of one of the fastest-growing retail banks in the country, which happens to be a subsidiary of ING Group, a 150-year-old company headquartered in Amsterdam that ranks as one of the largest financial services conglomerates in the world. His operation, ING Direct USA, opened for business in September 2000. At the end of 2005, it had signed up 3.5 million customers, attracted nearly $40 billion in deposits, and begun generating consistent (and rapidly increasing) profits. During its first two years, the start-up absorbed losses of $56 million as it banked on future growth. Over the next two years, it posted profits of $127 million. In 2004, with just 1,000 employees, the operation generated profits of $250 million.*

Sometimes it seems that righteous indignation can pay handsome dividends. But Arkadi Kuhlmann is more than a banker with a brash attitude. He is a hard-charging maverick with a full-throated message about the future of his industry. He and his colleagues insist that they are not just building a bank. They are challenging the common (and misguided) practices of the whole banking business—a business that they believe is ripe for change and renewal. "People want to do business with companies that share their values," Kuhlmann says. "We speak with a new voice—a different kind of voice for business."[1]

Expressing that voice often puts Kuhlmann's company at odds with its bigger, richer, more traditional rivals. We paid one of our many visits to Wilmington in June 2005, two months after President George W. Bush signed the laughably misnamed Bankruptcy Abuse Prevention and Consumer Protection Act of 2005. The law, the most sweeping revision of U.S. bankruptcy procedures since the 1970s, cracked down hard on cash-strapped individuals and families seeking protection from creditors. Its passage was met by howls of protest from consumer groups, law

---

*Because ING Direct USA is a wholly-owned subsidiary of ING Group, it reports financials on a pretax basis. Thus, these profit figures reflect pretax results.

professors, even many bankruptcy judges, but inspired squeals of delight from banks, credit card companies, and giant retailers—powerful organizations whose executives and lobbyists had marched in lockstep for years on Capitol Hill. Virtually everyone who was anyone in the financial services sector applauded their glorious political victory.

Everyone, that is, except Arkadi Kuhlmann. He was the only CEO of a U.S. bank to oppose the bill publicly, comparing it to "using a cannon to kill a mosquito." He submitted written testimony to a U.S. Senate committee, participated in a press conference with liberal Senate stalwarts Ted Kennedy and Russ Feingold, and took out a full-page ad in the *Washington Post*. Time and again, he raised the ire of his industry colleagues by raising a host of uncomfortable questions about their pet project on Capitol Hill. What about the tens of thousands of families who go bankrupt because of catastrophic illnesses and huge medical bills? What about the 16,000 military personnel who declared bankruptcy in 2004? What about the credit card industry's stubborn refusal to curb its most aggressive marketing practices?[2]

"To the banking establishment, I'm sort of the bad guy," Kuhlmann declares with undisguised relish. That reputation applies far beyond its challenge to the industry's political strategy. Indeed, it's at the heart of ING Direct's *business* strategy. "Before we launched the company, we looked around and said, 'The banking industry is bust. The consumer always loses.' Then we said, 'How can we do something radically different? How do we re-create and re-energize an industry? How can we build a company around a big new idea?' "

That big idea involves using the future-forward power of the Internet to champion the timeless virtues of thrift and financial security. ING Direct USA, essentially an Internet-based savings bank, is a direct-to-the-customer operation. (Customers can also bank by mail or phone, but more than 70 percent use the Web.) Everything about its operations emphasizes speed, simplicity, and low overhead. ING Direct has no brick-and-mortar branches, no ATM machines, no highly paid commercial bankers or smooth-talking financial advisers. It also charges no customer fees, requires no minimum deposits, and avoids paper like the plague. Most importantly, the bank offers a limited number of easy-to-understand product offerings: old-fashioned savings accounts (with no minimum balances), a selection of CDs (with no minimum deposits), nine easy-to-understand mutual funds (which can be combined into portfolios described as conservative, moderate, and aggressive), and no-frills home mortgages with an online application that takes less than ten minutes to complete.

The intentional simplicity of the company's products and business model keeps ING Direct's costs extremely low: in some parts of the business, they are one-sixth the costs of a conventional bank. Low costs enable ING Direct to guarantee higher interest rates to depositors (with some basic savings products, as much as four times the industry average) and charge lower rates to its mortgage customers. The end result is an online money machine that adds 100,000 customers (40 percent of whom are referred by word of mouth) and $1 billion in deposits every month. Indeed, by the end of 2004, ING Direct had become the country's largest Internet-based bank, the fourth-largest thrift bank, and one of the forty largest banks of any sort.

But the bank's animating spirit isn't about low costs or fast growth. It's about an agenda for reform. Kuhlmann and his colleagues declare that they are "leading Americans back to savings"—presenting a clearcut business alternative to the excesses and shortcomings of how the financial sector does business. "Everything we do starts with our big idea," the CEO says, "which is to bring back some fundamental values: self-reliance, independence, having a grubstake. One way or another, most financial companies are telling you to spend more. We're showing you how to *save* more. What's better than apple pie, the little guy, fighting for the underdog? We want to own that space."

WHAT IDEAS DO YOU STAND FOR?
STRATEGY THAT MAKES A STATEMENT

For decades, a well-defined set of parameters governed the logic of business competition. Strategy was about delivering superior products: Is your company's automobile or appliance or computer cheaper, better, nicer to look at? Strategy was about selecting attractive markets: What demographic segments or customer categories matter most to your organization? Strategy was about mastering economics: What advantages in scale, costs, margins, and pricing allow your company to deliver superior performance in productivity, profitability, and shareholder returns?

Which is why, truth be told, so much of strategy has been about *mimicry*. Big companies in most industries have been content to compete from virtually identical strategic playbooks and to vie for advantage on the margin: Whose products can be a little better? Whose costs can be a little lower? Whose target markets can be a little more attractive? Think General Motors versus Ford, CBS versus ABC, Coke versus Pepsi. Every once in a while, of course, something genuinely new alters the trajectory of an industry: the rise of sport utility vehicles or zero percent financing in the auto business, the creation of reality programming in the television business, the ubiquity of bottled water and natural drinks in the beverage business. But inevitably (and almost immediately), innovation gives way to duplication. Every big player is quick to copy the original creative impulse (or acquire one of the creators), so that strategy returns to its familiar and predictable formulas.

In the 1990s, with the explosion of the Internet and the rise of a generation of ambitious, venture-funded start-ups, business competition took on a more heated, more frenetic, less copycat tone. Strategy was about designing radically new business models that would overthrow decades of perceived wisdom on how specific industries worked: Who could apply high-speed computers and networked communications to slash production costs, vastly increase consumer choice, and otherwise do violent harm to established economic models? Who could, in the dot-com-driven lingo of the era, "Amazon" their rivals or "Napsterize" their industry?

No book better summed up this revolutionary fervor than the aptly titled *Leading the Revolution* by Gary Hamel, the celebrated strategy guru. Hamel is one of the most influential business thinkers of his generation, a brilliant speaker, consultant, and professor who's been affiliated with the London Business School and the Harvard Business School. Hamel's core constituency is senior executives in the world's most powerful companies, and his book took these power players to task for the groupthink that afflicts so many of them in the executive suite. "Most people in an industry are blind in the same way," Hamel warned. "They're all paying attention to the same things, and not paying attention to the same things."

So what's the solution? Revolution! Hamel urged aspiring "corporate rebels" and "gray-haired revolutionaries" to "start an insurrection" in their industries. "You can become the author of your own destiny," he thundered to his readers. "You can look the future in the eye and say: I am no longer a captive to history. Whatever I can imagine, I can accomplish. I am no longer a vassal in a faceless bureaucracy. I am an activist, not a drone. I am no longer a foot soldier in the march of progress. I am a Revolutionary."[3]

Phew! Of course, this period of explosive innovation ended the way most revolutions do—badly and bloodily, choked on its own excesses. Some of the most celebrated business revolutionaries of the 1990s— Enron and Worldcom leap to mind—became some of the most notorious corporate outlaws of the early 21st century.

This is the backdrop for the emergence of a new generation of maverick companies and the arrival of what we believe is the next frontier for business strategy. The logic of competition has evolved from the imitative world of products versus products to the revolutionary fervor of business models versus business models to, now, the promising realm of value systems versus value systems. Call it strategy as advocacy: Who can redefine the terms of competition by challenging the norms and accepted practices of their business before disgruntled customers or reform-minded regulators do it for them? Who has the most persuasive and original blueprint for where their business can and should be going—not just in terms of economics but also in terms of expectations? Who can unleash a set of ideas that shapes the future of their industry and *re*shapes the sense of what's possible for customers, employees, and investors?

To be sure, these questions are hardly without precedent. More than a decade ago, Jim Collins and Jerry Porras published *Built to Last,* which became one of the best-selling business books of all time. As Collins and Porras examined the success of venerable companies such as Johnson & Johnson, 3M, and Procter & Gamble, they discovered a sense of purpose at each of the companies, a "set of fundamental reasons for a company's existence beyond just making money." And this sense of purpose, they added, tends to be timeless and enduring—"a good purpose should serve to guide and inspire the organization for years, perhaps a century or more."[4]

Each of the maverick companies you'll meet in the next two chapters exudes an undeniable sense of purpose. But it's a sense of purpose that provokes: each company's strategy tends to be as *edgy* as it is enduring, as *disruptive* as it is distinctive, as *timely* as it is timeless. In an era defined by the business, cultural, and social hangover from the excesses of the nineties boom—a period of Wall Street scandal, CEO misconduct, and unprecedented levels of mistrust between companies and their customers and employees—the most powerful ideas are the ones that set forth an agenda for reform and renewal, the ones that turn a company into a cause.

Roy Spence, cofounder and president of GSD&M, the free-spirited ad agency based in Austin, Texas, is a colorful and charismatic voice on the future of business strategy. Spence has been a guiding force behind some of the most visible brands and high-impact organizations in America, from Wal-Mart to the PGA Tour to the U.S. Air Force. But the client that first put his agency on the map was Southwest Airlines. According to Spence, Southwest's remarkable climb to industry leadership (it carried more domestic passengers in 2005 than any other airline) is not just about low-cost economics or high-touch service. Ultimately, it's about the edgy and disruptive sense of mission that drives every aspect of how it does business.[5]

Southwest has become such a mass-market icon that it's easy to lose sight of the utter distinctiveness of its approach to the airline business. The company's direct point-to-point route system avoids the high costs and endless delays of the hub-and-spoke system around which the mainstream industry is built. The company has never offered first-class service or assigned seating or in-flight meals, and it was a late (and reluctant) participant in frequent-flier programs. Southwest's no-frills approach to interacting with customers keeps fares low and makes for easy-to-understand offerings.

Yet low fares don't mean sullen service. Quite the opposite: the company's gate agents, flight attendants, even its pilots, are famous for their flashy smiles, showy personalities, and corny sense of humor. Anyone who has flown Southwest on Halloween, an almost-sacred holiday at the fun-loving airline, and marveled at the costumes worn by everyone from baggage handlers to mechanics, understands that this is an airline that flies on a different kind of fuel from its competitors. Indeed, Southwest may be the most colorful and instructive example ever of the power of strategy as advocacy. This is a company whose distinctive value system, rather than any breakthrough technology or unprecedented business insight, explains its unrivaled success.

GSD&M signed on with Southwest in 1981, back when the ten-year-old airline, cofounded and run by Herb Kelleher, a gutsy, chain-smoking, whiskey-swilling adopted Texan (one of the Lone Star State's most legendary entrepreneurs was born in New Jersey), was considered a flighty sideshow to the blue-chip companies that ruled the sky. Today, in an industry that hovers on the brink of disaster (the old guard lost a collective *$30 billion* from 2001 to 2004), Southwest soars alone as a consistent moneymaker and fast-growing enterprise. A few years back, *Money* celebrated its 30th anniversary by identifying the best-performing stock over the magazine's three-decade history. The winner wasn't General Electric, IBM, Merck, or some other revered name. It was Southwest Airlines, a maverick force in one of the least attractive industries in the world. (It does pay to be a maverick. According to *Money,* a $10,000 investment in Southwest shares in 1972 was worth more than $10.2 million 30 years later.)[6]

Spence is adamant about the strategic lessons behind his client's remarkable flight path. Southwest didn't flourish just because its fares were cheaper than Delta's or because its service was friendlier than the not-so-friendly skies of United. Southwest flourished because it reimagined what it means to be an airline. Indeed, Spence insists that Southwest isn't in the airline business. It is, he argues, in the *freedom* business. Its purpose is to *democratize the skies*—to make air travel as available and as flexible for average Americans as it has been for the well-to-do.

That unique sense of mission is what drives Southwest's business strategy, from the cities it serves to the fares it charges right down to whom it hires and promotes. There is, Spence argues, a direct connection between the economics of Southwest's operating model, the advertising it aims at its customers ("You are now free to move about the country"), and the messages it sends to its 30,000-plus employees ("You are now free to be your best"). Spence explains the connection this way: "Business strategies change. Market positioning changes. But purpose does not change. Everybody at Southwest is a freedom fighter."

Obviously, all this talk of freedom is in part an exercise in product marketing and employee morale-boosting. But anybody who's flown Southwest understands that there's more to the airline's performance than low costs and high productivity. There is, in fact, a genuine sense of purpose (and a one-of-a-kind sense of humor) that animates the company. Libby Sartain spent 13 years in the People Department at Southwest, the last 6 in charge of the department as its vice president. (We'll meet her again in chapter 7, where we explore her new agenda as Chief People Yahoo—the senior HR strategist at one of Silicon Valley's flagship companies.) Sartain is adamant that the advocacy mission that defined Southwest in the marketplace reflected, and was driven by, an equally palpable sense of purpose in the workplace. "We examined the company at the most detailed level," Sartain explains, "and asked, 'From the minute you think of working here to the minute you leave, what makes this experience unique? What is it about our workforce that separates us from the competition?'"

In the workplace, employees took up a battle cry designed to connect the company's disruptive business strategy to daily life inside the organization: "At Southwest, Freedom Begins with Me." Sartain and her team went so far as to identify the "Eight Freedoms" that defined the working experience at the airline—from "the freedom to learn and grow" to "the freedom to create financial security" to "the freedom to work hard and have fun" to "the freedom to create and innovate"—and she created a traveling "freedom exposition" to recruit employees to the cause behind the company.

Over time, the Eight Freedoms "got to the very core of what the experience of working at Southwest is about," Sartain says. "The message was, 'You're not just loading a bag in the belly of that plane, you're not just serving cocktails, you're not just creating a budget or writing software. *You are giving people the freedom to fly*. It's your efficiency and ingenuity that allows us to keep offering low fares and keeps our planes in the sky.'"[7]

What ideas is your company fighting for? What values does your company stand for? What purpose does your company serve? Those are the questions that Roy Spence seeks to answer for every organization with which he works. "Anybody who's running a business has to figure out the higher calling of that business, its purpose," he insists. "Purpose is about the difference you're trying to make—in the marketplace, in the world. If everybody is selling the same thing, what's the tie-breaker? It's purpose."

There's no doubt that Spence is a master at using clever language to define and position companies in compelling ways. (He's in the ad business, after all, and his nickname inside the agency is "Reverend Roy.") Language, as we'll explore in chapter 2, counts for a lot when it comes to strategy. How you *talk* about your company speaks volumes about how you *think* about your business. And ultimately, how you think about your business determines how well it performs.

"Sure, you could say that Southwest Airlines really wants to get more people to fly," Spence explains. "Or you can say that the company is in the business of democratizing the skies. Would you rather be in the airline business or the freedom business? Language is what creates the edge—and operating on the edge leads to more creativity in the business."

GSD&M's best-known bit of language may well be "Don't Mess with Texas," which has become the unofficial slogan of the agency's famously maverick home state. Remarkably, GSD&M coined the phrase in 1985 as the centerpiece of an anti-litter campaign it devised for the Texas Department of Highways. Over the years, the message was adopted by musicians, good old boys, and politicians and became a rallying cry on a par with "Remember the Alamo." "We took them out of the litter business and put them in the pride business," says Spence. "It became a big, macho, Texan kind of deal. That's an edgier place to play. And that edge is why litter went down so much. We made it anti-Texan to litter."

Roy Spence is so committed to the power of purpose (his agency defines its business as purpose-based branding) that one of his GSD&M colleagues, Haley Rushing, actually has the title of "Chief Purposologist." Rushing, who is trained in cultural anthropology, immerses herself in the history, economics, values, and practices of existing and potential clients to unearth the advocacy agenda (or lack thereof) at the heart of their strategy.

"We don't create the purpose of an organization," Spence says. "Our job is to bring it to life and create the language of leadership. In the nineties, we saw that a rising tide lifts all boats. Now we see that a changing tide tests the strength of your anchor. What you stand for is as important as what you sell."

INNOVATION THROUGH AGITATION—
STRATEGY ON THE EDGE

You don't need to convince Arkadi Kuhlmann of the power of purpose or tell him that the values you stand for are as important as the products you sell. "I love our advocacy position," he exults. "It differentiates us. Most companies, especially in an industry like banking, are truly boring. If you do things the way everybody else does, why do you think you're going to do any better?"

In many respects, ING Direct USA is to banks what Southwest is to airlines—an aggressive, low-cost competitor with a brash attitude and a clear point of view. That's why the company, much like its founder, is feisty, combative, colorful. Its headquarters complex, composed of five beautifully renovated buildings on or near the Christina River in downtown Wilmington, is a blast of color in an otherwise drab, sleepy city. The distinctly American complex also pays homage to the Dutch origins of ING Direct's parent company. Sales and customer service operate out of a sparkling office tower once owned by Chase Manhattan that's been renamed the Spaarport ("piggybank" in Dutch). In the lobby of the Spaarport, crackling with energy, is an ING Direct café, an ultramodern coffee shop that offers up cappuccino, sandwiches, CNBC on flat-screen TVs, and free Internet access. Marketing operates out of a onetime railroad office, built in 1904, that's been renamed the Orangerie.

(ING Direct's flagship product is the "Orange" savings account, and orange colors every aspect of the company's public presence.) The top executives work in a 19th-century leather tannery renamed the Pakhuis ("warehouse" in Dutch), which was renovated in 2000 and remodeled in 2005 to accommodate the company's torrid growth.

It's a point of pride for Kuhlmann that many of the people who work in these buildings have been recruited from outside the banking business. "If you want to renew and re-energize an industry," he advises, "don't hire people from that industry. You've got to untrain them and then retrain them. I'd rather hire a jazz musician, a dancer, or a captain in the Israeli army. They can learn about banking. It's much harder for bankers to *unlearn* their bad habits. They're trapped by the past. Remember, resurrection has only worked once in history."

Well, maybe twice. Kuhlmann himself is a three-decade veteran of the banking industry whose career began as a fast-track executive with the ever so proper Royal Bank of Canada. "It's amazing when I think back to those days," says Kuhlmann, seated at his no-frills workspace in the company's open-office setting. "At age thirty-three, I was made vice president of commercial banking. I had a private office with the nicest curtains. I had a private dining room. I had a chauffeur who picked me up at seven-thirty in the morning and a guy who came by my desk at eight-thirty to polish my shoes. I remember what happened after the board meeting where I got named vice president. Someone came out and said, 'Congratulations on your red hat.' I asked one of my colleagues, 'Red hat, what did he mean?' He said, 'You know, like the cardinals wear.' I had true corporate power in the old-fashioned sense. Today I've got none of those trappings of power."

Indeed, Kuhlmann makes it a point to remind his colleagues that ING exists precisely to challenge that style of power. On the sidewalk outside the Pakhuis, for example, is a thick white line painted directly in front of the entrance. The not-so-subtle message: cross that line and you've left the sleepy environs of downtown Wilmington (and the financial services establishment) to enter a different kind of place. Employees leaving the Pakhuis see a sign posted right before the exit. It reads, DID TODAY REALLY MATTER?

"We keep increasing the intensity, the passion, the goals," Kuhlmann says. "We're doing a billion dollars a month of new deposits right now. I just announced that we are going to step that up to two billion dollars. It's scaring the hell out of everybody, but we'll do it. It's very hard to be an employee here and not ask yourself, 'Am I up for this or not?' It's not about getting people stressed. It's about getting them full of conviction."

Outside its home base, ING Direct is a master of bold publicity stunts and brash PR moves. To increase its visibility in southern California, the bank paid for free fill-ups at Shell stations in Manhattan Beach, Santa Monica, and Burbank. The lines of cars stretched for miles, and motorists waited for hours—the scenes became a fixture on the TV news. In northern California, Kuhlmann, a motorcycle enthusiast, personally led 700 Harley-Davidson owners on a 60-mile "Freedom Ride," culminating in an ear-splitting concert by the classic rock group Kansas. In Boston, ING Direct paid for all subway lines on the MBTA (known as the "T" among Bostonians) to be free one morning to rush-hour commuters—a high-profile stunt that the company dubbed the "ING Direct Boston T Party."

To be sure, the first order of business for ING Direct is about bread-and-butter substance, not bells-and-whistles stunts—creating financial products that make it easy and financially rewarding for customers to save. But just as big a part of its strategy is identifying products it *won't* offer. As aggressive as ING Direct has been in its target markets, it has shown just as much restraint in avoiding potentially lucrative markets that are off-target. ING Direct doesn't issue credit cards, market auto loans, or even provide checking accounts—lines of business that most bankers would launch in a heartbeat if they were in Kuhlmann's shoes.

But those services encourage customers to spend rather than to save, so they're not part of the model.*

ING Direct has also resisted the temptation to enter online broker-age, an obvious bit of diversification that any self-respecting MBA stu-dent would urge the company to embrace. Millions of customers already bank with ING Direct over the Web, so why not let them trade stocks as well? "Because if you are truly committed to helping people change their financial lives, and to doing it step by step, then you should not encourage them to do things that could lead them to lose money," explains Jim Kelly, the bank's chief customer service officer, who also oversees marketing, sales, and operations.

That's instructive: companies that compete on a disruptive point of view are defined as much by the opportunities they choose *not* to pur-sue as by the businesses they do enter. Roy Spence remembers the early days of Southwest Airlines, when it faced one of many bare-knuckle challenges to its advocacy mission. In 1981 a start-up called Muse Air, launched by Lamar Muse, a disgruntled cofounder and former CEO of Southwest, mounted an assault on Herb Kelleher and his other onetime colleagues by offering an airline with planes that were sleeker, seats that were roomier, and service that focused on luxury rather than down-home humor. (Industry wags nicknamed Muse's company Revenge Air.) Southwest was rattled; many executives urged Kelleher to buy his own fleet of new planes, especially when surveys showed that cus-tomers, by a huge margin, preferred the Muse aircraft to Southwest's dowdier planes.[8]

But Kelleher resisted the temptation—not because he was eager to disappoint customers, but because he was determined to stay true to the

---

*Obviously, mortgages are a form of lending, not savings. But, as Kuhlmann and his colleagues are quick to point out, building equity in their homes is the most important way that Americans in-vest in their financial future—so it's a natural fit with the company's pro-saving strategy.

airline's mission. "Everybody was stunned that we didn't go with this beautiful new plane," Spence recalls. "But Herb said, 'If we go with this new plane—and granted, it's prettier and customers like it better—we'll have to train our pilots to fly two different kinds of aircraft and train our mechanics to service two different kinds of aircraft. That will increase our costs, which we'll have to pass on to our customers. We're not going to do it, because that's not the purpose of our airline. That's not how you democratize the skies.' "*

In other words, companies that compete on a distinctive set of ideas are comfortable rejecting opportunities and strategies that more traditional players would rush to embrace. ING Direct even rejects *customers* that it considers out of sync with its advocacy message. A case in point: Kuhlmann himself turned down a $5 million deposit from one high roller who wanted to do business with the bank. It was nothing personal, the CEO insists, but if ING Direct is building an institution that promotes the financial interests of the little guy, then it doesn't need to (and shouldn't) cater to power brokers. "Rich Americans are used to platinum cards, special service," he says. "The last thing we want in this bank is to have rich people making special demands. We treat everybody the same."

Indeed, ING Direct is one of the few financial institutions that has no deposit minimums for customers but imposes (unofficially) deposit *maximums*. You want to start a savings account with one dollar? No problem—ING Direct will even deposit an additional $25 as a welcome-to-the-bank gesture. You want to open a savings account with a million dollars? *No thanks.* "We are about Main Street, not Wall

---

*The Muse Air saga ended badly for everyone. Lamar Muse never could get the better of his former colleagues, and Southwest wound up buying his company four years after it got off the ground. Southwest renamed the airline TranStar and operated it as an independent subsidiary. But TranStar found itself in brutal fare wars with Texas Air and its take-no-prisoners boss Frank Lorenzo, who would eventually become the most hated man in the airline business. TranStar ceased operations in 1987.

Street," explains customer service chief Kelly. "Our most important role is to help people who need help the most save money. People who are going to deposit a million dollars—they don't need a lot of help. And let's be realistic. That customer is going to want more from us— 'I've got a lot of money in your bank, I need this *now*.' They'd expect us to do things for them that we just don't do. I would much rather have a thousand accounts with one thousand dollars each than one million-dollar account. I can touch more people that way."

It is an undeniably upside-down strategy for building a bank— placing a premium on customers with *less* money to deposit than on those with *more* money to deposit. But it's a strategy with a clear economic rationale—executing a low-overhead, low-cost, low-margin, high-volume business model. It's true to the value system that has shaped ING Direct's identity in the marketplace. It's a strategy that makes a statement—a point of view that resonates with customers and employees, that changes the conversation about the future of financial services, and that attracts more than its fair share of attention from the media and other commentators.

"Re-creating an industry is about creating a story around customers, around employees, around products," Kuhlmann says. "Banking is about money, and money is about who you are, how you think about your future, looking out for the ones you love. We are trying to make savings cool. We're creating a story that carries a sense of mission, a story that shifts people to a new point of view."

For example, Kuhlmann and his team love to think of themselves as advocates for their customers. But just as Kuhlmann turned down that $5 million deposit, there's little tolerance for customers who don't fit the model—whether those customers are Joe Millionaire or Joe Six-Pack. Every year the company "fires" more than 3,500 customers who, one way or another, don't play by the bank's rules. Maybe they made too many calls to customer service, maybe they asked for too many exceptions to the bank's carefully designed procedures, maybe they made big transfers for short periods of time to skim off some interest. Whatever the infraction, ING Direct doesn't hesitate to close the account and automatically transfer the customer's funds to its backup bank. ("Our china shop is too fragile for us to let bulls run around," quips Kelly.)

Firing thousands of customers every year is a controversial business practice, CEO Kuhlmann concedes, which is why he believes it's good business. "It's good because it agitates everybody," he says. "It agitates the marketplace. It agitates the customers who don't belong. But we want to sort them out. The customers who are right for you, they love you. They become evangelists. The customers who you close out, they hate you. But you know what they do when they hate you? They tell everybody about you—and that's good. It creates dialogue. There's nothing like differentiation."

WHY "ME TOO" WON'T DO— ### STRATEGY AS ORIGINALITY

There is an undeniable populist strain to the organizations we've encountered thus far. For 35 years, Southwest Airlines has pursued a flight plan to recast the economics of travel and "democratize the skies." For more than five years, ING Direct has banked on a critique of the worst practices in financial services and vowed to "lead Americans back to savings." GSD&M's Roy Spence, an unapologetic Texas progressive, urges clients not just to sell products but to express the "higher calling" of their business.*

But disruptive points of view come in all shapes, sizes, and sentiments. Advocacy is about strategic *clarity,* not the business world's

*Spence is serious about the pursuit of a higher calling. In 2004 a dismayed "Reverend Roy" responded to the election victory of fellow Texan George W. Bush by embarking on a road trip. He visited 112 churches trying to understand the religious divide that became such a big part of the presidential campaign. The result is *The Amazing Faith of Texas* (www.amazingfaithoftx.com), a book of photojournalism that highlights five values common to most religions.

version of political correctness. The make-or-break issue isn't fighting for the little guy. It's fighting the competitive establishment with insights that challenge its me-too mind-set.

In their no-nonsense competitive manifesto *Hardball: Are You Playing to Play or Playing to Win?* strategy experts George Stalk and Rob Lachenauer urge executives to stop pussyfooting around with "softball" issues such as corporate governance and stakeholder management and to focus on what matters most in business—"us[ing] every legitimate resource and strategy available to them to gain advantage over their competitors." Stalk and Lachenauer celebrate tough-as-nails companies that "focus relentlessly on competitive advantage" and "unleash massive and overwhelming force" against vulnerable rivals.[9]

We admire hard-charging companies too. But we're convinced, based on the cast of fiercely competitive mavericks we've come to know, that the most effective way to play hardball is to build an agenda for growth around a strategic *curveball*—to prosper as a company by championing fresh ideas about the future of your business. Originality has become the litmus test of strategy.

Nowhere is the power of strategic originality more evident than at the West Coast headquarters of HBO, the powerhouse (and superprofitable) cable network that is the most original force in the numbingly me-too world of mass entertainment. HBO headquarters is anything but a place of populist pretense. The building, near the beach in Santa Monica, is a potent mix of Hollywood power and a laid-back California lifestyle. The eager valet attendants and the phalanx of headset-wearing receptionists provide visitors with a tingle of celebrity. In the cavernous lobby, young actor-writer types fidget on boldly patterned furniture. Gleaming white walls, green glass, and splashes of hot pink give the space a futuristic feel—in sharp contrast to the beige-toned inner sanctum with its views of palm trees, tennis courts, and lush green lawn.

The calm of the executive suite is ruffled only slightly by the daily turmoil of show business. In one corner office, Nancy Lesser, HBO's high-powered publicist, is finalizing seating arrangements with the producers of the Golden Globes award show for a delegation of celebrities, including Sarah Jessica Parker, Matthew Broderick, and Mark Wahlberg, who are flying in to attend the gala. (HBO's programs and stars were nominated for 20 Golden Globes in 2005, more than twice as many as any other network.) Meanwhile, in another corner office, Chris Albrecht, HBO's chairman and CEO, is finishing a call, headset on, eyes focused intently on the middle distance: "Fifty million?" he asks. "*Sixty* million? Okay, if it has to be sixty million, it's sixty million." Click.

Wrangling for prime seats at an awards show or haggling over big-budget productions comes with the territory in Hollywood. But almost everything else about HBO breaks the mold. Indeed, the company announces its maverick status right at the door. A giant LED display marks the entrance to the lobby. The words on the screen, which run in a continuous loop, may be the most disruptive message in recent television history: "It's not TV. It's HBO."

Television—has there ever been an industry that's so glamorous and so desperate for fresh thinking? This is a business where strategy is based almost *entirely* on mimicry. Think back to June 1994, when NBC's *Today* show unveiled its new-look broadcast from a glass-walled studio in Rockefeller Center. Within a year or two, virtually *every* morning show had a windowed studio somewhere in New York City. A decade later, when Donald Trump attracted big ratings for NBC with *The Apprentice,* rival networks raced to sign their own billionaires, from Internet bad boy Mark Cuban (ABC) to British magnate Richard Branson (Fox). And so it goes in the vast wasteland: *Survivor* begets *Big Brother,* which begets *I'm a Celebrity, Get Me Out of Here!* Or *The Osbournes* begets *The Simple Life,* which begets *Growing Up Gotti.* All of which beget a sense of resignation among viewers and an air of desperation among TV executives: how does anyone win when everyone is playing the same game?

And then there's HBO. There's no denying the network's glittering financial performance over the past decade. With a subscriber base of nearly 28 million households, HBO dwarfs any and all of its pay-cable rivals. Its parent, Time Warner, doesn't break out detailed financial results for the unit, but Wall Street analysts report the company's average earnings growth at 20 percent per year since 1995, and estimated *profits* of $1.1 billion in 2004 (more than any other network, cable or broadcast) on roughly $3.5 billion in revenue. HBO alone has an estimated market value of some $20 billion.

What has truly distinguished HBO is not its profitability but its programming. As anyone within reach of a TV clicker knows, the network shaped the pop-culture conversation of the early 21st century with a trio of hits: *Sex and the City* (an antic mix of sex, shoes, restaurants, and relationships that ran from 1998 to 2004), *The Sopranos* (David Chase's unstintingly original series about an angst-ridden New Jersey mob boss debuted in 1999), and *Six Feet Under* (the darkly comic chronicles of a dysfunctional family of undertakers from Oscar-winning screenwriter Alan Ball that ran from 2001 to 2005). The "3S's," in HBO parlance, drew prime time–sized audiences to a network that reaches only one-quarter of all TV households, planted fear in the hearts of broadcast executives, and won universal acclaim from critics. At the 2004 Emmys, the highpoint of HBO's hold on pop culture, it received an unprecedented 124 nominations and won 32 awards.

Even with the retirement of two of the three S's, HBO's lineup has remained without peer in its invention, emotion, and overall excellence. In addition to its new-generation weekly series (including *Entourage* and *Big Love*), HBO has produced a stream of miniseries, made-for-TV movies, and theatrical releases. The network's $120 million miniseries *Band of Brothers* (produced by Tom Hanks and Steven Spielberg) premiered on September 9, 2001, and drew a total audience of nearly 59 million people in the weeks following the September 11 terrorist attacks. The network has committed more than $300 million to two more mega-projects: Tom Hanks's series about John Adams and a Pacific war series from *Band of Brothers* producers Spielberg and Hanks. Meanwhile, HBO's much-acclaimed documentary group, run since 1979 by Sheila Nevins, has won 15 Oscars, 81 Emmys, and 25 Peabody Awards.*

HBO's track record isn't just a matter of commissioning smarter scripts or landing better actors than its rivals. It's rooted in a distinctive point of view about how to create value in the entertainment business—the strangely disruptive proposition that quality and originality, not mediocrity and mimicry, drive long-term prosperity. With HBO, what you see on the screen reflects what the company stands for in the marketplace—ideas that reset the expectations of the viewing audience and set the network apart from decades of conventional wisdom in New York and Hollywood.[10]

Technically speaking, of course, HBO and the networks are not competitors. HBO sells itself to viewers; the networks sell their viewers to advertisers. But broadcast networks, pay channels, and basic cable are all clamoring for attention in an increasingly cluttered, competitive, and fragmented entertainment marketplace. In a business where originality is often viewed as a risk rather than an asset, HBO's ability to connect with a big audience, elevate its expectations, and keep pushing cultural boundaries is more than a breakthrough for the network. It changes the game for everyone.

"The name of the game [at the broadcast networks] is whatever gets the largest number of people to watch," says Alan Ball, a self-described refugee from the network TV "gulag" and the creator of *Six Feet Under*. "What is that? It's a car wreck. It's *Fear Factor*. It's getting *Playboy* playmates to eat sheep's eyeballs. They're proud of that! 'Look at the numbers we got! Supermodels puked on each other and people tuned in!'"

---

*Thanks to DVD sales and syndication rights, original programming is the gift that keeps on giving. Industry analysts estimate that HBO's *Band of Brothers* DVD generated sales of $186 million, while the *Sex and the City* DVDs pulled in $250 million and *The Sopranos* DVDs topped $300 million. A&E bought rights to *The Sopranos* for a reported $162.5 million for 65 episodes. That's $2.5 million per episode—a record for a drama sold into syndication.

Talk to CEO Chris Albrecht about how he and his colleagues evaluate programming and he almost never mentions target demographics or overnight ratings. (And he has never raved about sheep's eyeballs.) "We ask ourselves, 'Is it different? Is it distinctive? Is it *good*?'" he explains. "Ultimately, we ask ourselves, 'Is it *about* something?' By 'about something' I mean not just the subject, or the arena, or the location, but really *about* something that is deeply relevant to the human experience. *The Sopranos* isn't about a mob boss on Prozac. It's about a man searching for the meaning of his life. *Six Feet Under* isn't about a family of undertakers so much as it is about a group of people who have to deal with their feelings about death in order to get on with their own lives. The next question is, 'Is it the very best realization of that idea? Is it true to itself?'"

The truth about HBO is that it took years to hone its competitive strategy and programming formula—and honing the strategy required making an explicit decision to reject the business assumptions and performance metrics that guide traditional TV executives. The network, which began life in Wilkes-Barre, Pennsylvania, in 1972 as a pay channel that featured boxing, theatrical films, and stand-up comedy, had experimented with a touch of original programming from early on. Some of it was truly memorable, like Robert Altman and Garry Trudeau's campaign mockumentary *Tanner '88*. Some of it was downright horrible: the first "original program" on HBO was actually a polka festival special.

The strategic inflection point came in 1995. After a decade of holding different leadership posts at HBO, Chris Albrecht became president of original programming while Jeff Bewkes took over as HBO's boss. (Bewkes is now president and COO of Time Warner Inc. Albrecht has run HBO since mid-2002.) At that time, HBO's original programming was confined to two half-hour comedies, *Dream On* and *The Larry Sanders Show*, which the network touted as "the best hour of comedy on television." (Company insiders joked that they should have called it "the *only* hour on HBO.")

Albrecht and Bewkes convened the network's executive committee and key original programming executives. The question before the group: are we who we say we are? The answer came back: not really. "The words we always used to talk about ourselves were 'different,' 'worth paying for,' '*better*,'" says Albrecht. "In that meeting, we came to the conclusion that we weren't quite there yet, but that it was a great thing to strive for. The only way to move forward and win is to take chances and to be distinctive."

At HBO, "distinctive" had meant "not on network TV." At the 1995 meeting, says Bewkes, the leadership team chose to "jump fully off this cliff." It was a big leap. The unit didn't have hoards of cash to invest in programming, and there was no way to measure return on investment for any particular show. "It was a real mess," he recalls. "But we just said, 'Forget about it—let's just do good stuff and we'll solve it later.' We decided to take the high road." As it turns out, taking that road led to a decade of artistic creativity and financial prosperity unlike anything in television history.

Of course, even the high road has its share of potholes and detours. Success on the scale of HBO invariably gives rise to recrimination, imitation, and pressures for duplication—obstacles that confront successful mavericks in any industry.* During our final visit to HBO's West Coast headquarters, you could sense the pop-culture conversation shifting. Critics who couldn't stop celebrating HBO were beginning to castigate the network: Is there life after *Six Feet Under*? What's the offspring to *Sex and the City*?

---

*Commentators call it the "HBO effect"—in an industry of copycats, it was only natural for other networks to mimic HBO. Pay-cable rival Showtime is openly borrowing from HBO's playbook with such edgy series as *The L Word* (*Sex and the City* for the lesbian set) and highbrow movies (*The Lion in Winter* with Glenn Close and Patrick Stewart). FX is making claims to being the "HBO of basic cable" with programs like *The Shield, The Thief,* and *Nip/Tuck,* and the 2005 breakout hit *Desperate Housewives* on ABC is unfailingly billed as an heir to *Sex and the City*.

Albrecht and his colleagues openly acknowledge the perils of success, and that is why they have been engaged in an ongoing strategic conversation to define the future—a future that remains rooted in the network's core mission ("It's not TV. It's HBO") while moving it in new directions. They are determined to reproduce their business results without repeating themselves in the marketplace.

"We're very aware that the biggest hurdle to our success is our own success," Albrecht says. "Are we ever going to get 124 Emmy nominations again? Not going to happen. That's fine, so long as we keep challenging our own thinking. We hear the questions: How are you going to follow *The Sopranos*? What are you going to do after *Sex and the City*? Those are the wrong questions! We don't think about staying where we are, and we don't worry about topping ourselves. 'TV' is a finite idea. 'It's not TV' is an *infinite* idea. Our little slogan is taking on a whole new meaning. Before, it was a kind of rebel yell. Now it's an organizing principle for our strategy, which is to not limit ourselves by the idea of TV."

One way to move beyond TV is to move from the small screen to the big screen. HBO is positioning itself to shape the market for great independent films, much as it shaped great TV fare. The network's recent slate includes the award-winning *The Life and Death of Peter Sellers* and *Lackawanna Blues*, Paul Newman's adaptation of Richard Russo's Pulitzer Prize–winning novel *Empire Falls*, along with theatrical releases such as the singular *American Splendor*, the wrenching *Maria Full of Grace*, the documentary *Spellbound*, and Gus Van Sant's *Last Days*. In September 2004 the *Los Angeles Times* surveyed HBO's offerings and concluded, "There's new hope for maverick movies, and, in an odd twist, it's coming not from some new studio or well-heeled cineaste but from TV." In May 2005 HBO formed a joint venture with New Line Cinema, called Picturehouse, to distribute eight to ten films a year.

Colin Callender, president of HBO Films, recalls that when he and Chris Albrecht took over film production in 1999, "we looked at the landscape and said, 'Everyone is copying us.' The cable movie, which we invented, was a genre everyone is doing. So we need to reinvent what we're doing. We had started making movies that filled a gap in the television landscape, and now we saw a massive gap within the moviemaking landscape. No one was making sophisticated, intelligent, entertaining, grown-up movies anymore. So we now look at HBO movies as filling that gap."

Ultimately, Chris Albrecht argues, the opportunity to maintain the competitive gap with imitation-minded rivals is as much about computer programming as original programming. The new game isn't merely to create new shows but to find new ways to package and deliver shows in the emerging digital landscape of mobile, personal, disaggregated entertainment choices—a landscape shaped by TiVo, the iPod, and other disruptive technologies that keep much of the TV establishment awake at night, even as they delight the audience.

"Some traditional companies may view these changes as the enemy," he explains. "We view them as our friend. This new wave of technology plays to our strengths. We got to where we are by riding a new technology with a product that was compelling, groundbreaking, and game-changing. The cable industry was built on the back of HBO. Now we get to do it again."

So it goes for companies that compete on the originality of their ideas. It's not enough for leaders to challenge the prevailing logic of their business; they also have to rethink the logic of their own success. Sure, Albrecht and his colleagues would love to introduce another pop-culture TV phenomenon like *Sex and the City*. But they're not going to invent the network's future by trying to replay its past. Their plan is to take the phrase "it's not TV" literally—to make shows available on a wide range of devices, in all kinds of settings, 24 hours a day. That's why HBO has pushed ahead with subscription video on demand (viewers in about 8 million households can now watch HBO programs at whatever time they choose), and why Albrecht has set in motion a range of other content-delivery experiments.

"We have to be *more* aggressive and take *bigger* risks than before," he says. "We're actively looking for new cliffs to jump off. We're doing things nobody else will do, because they can't chase us into those spaces. We didn't get here by playing by the rules of the game. We got here by setting the rules of the game."

Chapter Two

Competition and Its Consequences: Disruptors, Diplomats, and a New Way to Talk About Business

We admit it: we're suckers for entrepreneurs and company builders who relish the chance to shake up the establishment and champion a different and better future for their industry. In a business world defined by too much strategic mimicry and too many lowest-common-denominator competitive formulas, it's exhilarating to get immersed in a brash young company like ING Direct USA, to follow the unorthodox flight to leadership of a breakthrough innovator like Southwest Airlines, or to watch the creative and financial performance of HBO. If the new arena of competition is value system versus value system, there's nothing quite like companies and executives who step into the arena convinced of the virtue of their values—and prepared to communicate their confidence in no uncertain terms.

We also recognize that it can be unnerving. Business history is littered with the corpses of hard-charging Davids who weren't afraid to look squarely into the eyes of slow-moving Goliaths, but who couldn't contend with the inevitable response. Fanning the flames of competition is a great way to energize a marketplace and generate attention for your strategic agenda. It's also an invitation for a fierce competitive backlash. To put it in the "hardball" vernacular of George Stalk and Rob Lachenauer, tossing your industry a strategic curveball just might earn you a damaging beanball from bigger, richer, harder-throwing rivals.

Marc Andreessen and Mike McCue learned this lesson the hard way in one of the most famous David-versus-Goliath stories in modern business history—the rise, retrenchment, and eventual sale of Netscape Communications. Andreessen, of course, was the twentysomething programming genius who launched Netscape and became an A-list celebrity when the company went public in 1995. McCue joined Netscape in 1996 as the company's vice president of technology after his outfit, Paper Software, was bought by Andreessen. The two were lead protagonists as Netscape grew explosively. They carried the hopes and dreams of a generation of programmers and entrepreneurs determined to challenge Microsoft's chokehold on the computer business, but then watched helplessly as Bill Gates responded with a blistering counterattack, driving a chastened Netscape into the waiting arms of America Online.*

Today, Andreessen and McCue are leading new companies, both of which are well funded, aggressive, ambitious—and decidedly more circumspect than Netscape. At first blush, McCue, a thirtysomething technologist with a quick, lopsided grin, a flop of brown hair, and fresh-scrubbed pink cheeks—looks every bit the poster boy for the eternally youthful face of Silicon Valley. He could easily be mistaken for one of the young techies gliding around his company's parking lot on a Segway scooter. As cofounder of Tellme Networks, McCue has raised nearly $250 million from the world's top venture capital firms to pursue

---

*Not that Netscape should be thought of as a failure. The acquisition by AOL, when finalized, was valued at $10 billion—not a bad price for a company that was less than five years old.

a strategic plan that he calls Dial Tone 2.0—the prospect of marrying telephones and the Internet to reinvent how people use the phone and how companies communicate with and market to their customers. Imagine picking up the phone, McCue says, but rather than dialing ten digits or navigating a maze of frustrating prompts and menus, just stating your business: "Call Mom at home," or, "Is my flight on time?" or, "Has my FedEx package arrived?"

There's no denying the scale of Tellme's business goals, especially in a world where people place one trillion phone calls a year, more than 100 billion of which go to 1-800 services. "We have a lot of ambition," McCue says. "We talk about placing and answering every single phone call on earth."* But this bold agenda does not inspire brash rhetoric: McCue sounds more like a diplomat than a disruptor, like someone who has a clear point of view about how to reshape his industry but is not prepared to demean, diminish, or even decode what his rivals are doing.

"At Netscape, the competition with Microsoft was so severe, we'd wake up in the morning thinking about how we were going to deal with them instead of how we would build something great for our customers," McCue says. "Basically, we 'mooned' Microsoft. And man, did we pay for it."

What lessons has McCue taken from Netscape to his new company, which is growing at blazing speed, generating healthy profits, and dealing with many of the familiar perils of success? "What I realize now is that you can never, ever take your eye off the customer," McCue replies. "Even in the face of massive competition, don't think about the competition. Literally don't think about them. Every time you're in a meeting and you're tempted to talk about a competitor, replace

---

*Tellme has a long way to go to achieve its ambitions, but it's registered some impressive achievements. Its high-powered clients include American Airlines, Merrill Lynch, and Cingular. Already Tellme powers more than *one billion* 411 calls per year and boasts the world's biggest voice-over-Internet deployment.

that thought with one about user feedback or surveys. *Just think about the customer.*"

Andreessen, now in his early thirties, has emerged as an unlikely elder statesman in high-tech circles, a voice of experience and reason in an industry that still revels in grandiose claims and overcharged rhetoric. His post-Netscape company, Opsware, has already gone public, with a market value in February 2006 of more than $750 million and a sharp focus on the arcane world of data-center automation. Andreessen appreciates the power (the necessity even) of business strategies and value systems that challenge the industry's established points of view. He's just lost his taste for the fight-to-the-death spirit that tends to accompany these change-the-game aspirations.

"My view is that the only new companies that end up succeeding are those founded on ideas that were considered pretty crazy at the time they were started," Andreessen says. "Big established companies are really good at executing on the ideas that make a lot of sense. So if you're going to start a company, you better have an idea so radical that most people think it's crazy. Dell sounded crazy—a personal computer company started in the teeth of an enormous recession in the industry. People thought the idea behind Netscape was nuts—everybody told us we'd never amount to anything. Google sounded like a crazy idea— *another* search engine, started in 1998, growing right through the dot-com meltdown. It seemed like complete lunacy. Of course, the problem is that a lot of ideas that sound crazy *are* crazy. So for every Dell, Netscape, and Google, you get 300 companies with crazy ideas that fail."

The other problem, Andreessen says, is that all too often companies with crazy ideas end up in crazed competition with the powers-that-be. Indeed, he watches with morbid fascination as the latest David-versus-Goliath showdown takes shape in Silicon Valley—a struggle with eerie echoes of his own battles at Netscape. "Google is being led through the nose into a direct confrontation with Microsoft," Andreessen warns. "I've seen this before! Everybody loves the fight, everybody lines up for these all-out battles. It's not clear to me why *both* companies can't win. But ingrained behavior pushes both sides toward all-out war. The one thing it does is draw attention to you—a lot of people know your name. But one of the hardest parts of business is when everybody knows *too much* about your business."

Early on in the growth of his new company, Andreessen encapsulated what he'd learned from his Netscape days in a document called "Ten Reasons We're Going to Go Out of Business." It was, he told an interviewer at the time, "a list of the ten most serious threats" to the company. "It definitely focuses the mind as much as the prospect of an imminent hanging." Andreessen told us that he no longer maintains the list ("We're on much firmer footing than at any point in the last five years"), but that he does work to instill and maintain the strategic modesty that the list implies. "Now we get to worry about lots of other things," he says.[1]

The moral of the stories told by McCue and Andreessen: you don't have to be a pugnacious leader or a combative organization to recognize the power of strategy as advocacy. The point is not to have sharp elbows. It's to develop a sharp-eyed point of view about your industry and to present crisp and persuasive alternatives to business as usual. Sometimes the innovators with the most compelling strategic twists choose to broadcast them with a whisper rather than a shout.

COMPETING BY *NOT* COMPETING—THE BUSINESS VALUE OF "NERD VALUES"

Jim Buckmaster, president and CEO of Craigslist, the online bulletin board that has become a darling of Internet users, will never be mistaken for the hard-charging Arkadi Kuhlmann, the silver-tongued Roy Spence, or the twentysomething version of Marc Andreessen. He is soft-spoken, reserved, and minimalist in his rhetoric and demeanor. But his low-key personality (along with that of founder Craig Newmark) is a perfect fit for the disruptive idea at the heart of this one-of-a-kind company—to provide a no-frills "public service" in an industry filled with overblown claims, intrusive marketing, and a grow-at-all costs mind-set.

"I don't want to bad-mouth corporations," Buckmaster says. "We're a corporation. But there's room for a lot more diversity in the approach companies take. We're trying to stake out one modest example for corporate America, for people to see if it's applicable to what they do."

Craigslist, based in San Francisco, has attracted worldwide acclaim by virtue of what Buckmaster calls its "nerd values." The company, which took shape in 1995, operates Web sites from San Francisco (the original) to Sydney, Australia, from Boston to Berlin, from Atlanta to Amsterdam. But there's no talk here of monetizing eyeballs, maximizing click-throughs, or building a backlog of banner ads—the universal business language of the Internet. On Craigslist, users swap messages, sell goods and services, search for apartments, and look for jobs on a site that charges no monthly fees, accepts no advertising, and uses virtually no graphics.

Its bare-bones form and function give Craigslist a simple, almost simplistic, feel. (One writer cracked that the site has "the visual appeal of a pipe wrench.") Yet that very simplicity is the heart of a forward-looking business strategy. The company is built around an explicit commitment to serve as an alternative to business-as-usual on the Internet. Craigslist doesn't have an elaborate mission statement (that would be too showy for this low-key crew), but the site does offer a brief statement of purpose. Craigslist is about "giving each other a break, getting the word out about everyday, real-world stuff." It is committed to "restoring the human voice to the Internet, in a humane, noncommercial way." It focuses on "keeping things simple, common sense, down-to-earth, honest, very real."

But here's what's so instructive: these authentically anticommercial values have unleashed a pop-culture sensation and a hot commercial property. Independent filmmaker Michael Ferris made a documentary,

24 Hours on Craigslist, that captures the strange and wonderful passions of the people who rely on the site. (The tagline for one of the trailers for the film: "There are Web sites about films. Now see a film about a Web site.") *USA Today* described the Craigslist phenomenon this way: "Some call the site a public forum. Others call it a classified market. Many call it an obsession."[2]

Experts on Internet strategy call it something else—one heck of a business. It's no multibillion-dollar behemoth like Google or Yahoo— and that's precisely the point. It's a fabulously successful small company whose reach extends around the world and whose influence extends across the Internet. Craigslist operates 190 Web sites in all 50 states and 34 countries—sites that add 6.55 million new classified ads and receive more than 3 billion page views from 10 million visitors each month. Financial analysts have estimated that Craigslist, which has never raised a dime of venture capital and employs fewer than 20 people, who work out of a Victorian house in San Francisco's Inner Sunset neighborhood, could fetch as much as $100 million if it were put up for sale—a valuation of more than $5 million per employee.*

Fortune magazine, the unofficial voice of the big-business establishment, has marveled at the small company's hugely impressive business results. In an article titled "Guerrilla Capitalism," the magazine estimated Craigslist's 2005 revenues "in the neighborhood" of $20 million, with annual expenses that "cannot possibly run to" more than $5 million. The magazine's conclusion: "The company that is indifferent to money, therefore, gushes profits."

CEO Buckmaster revels in his company's unorthodox path to prosperity—what he calls "the ironies of unbranding, demonetizing, and

---

*As impressive as these figures seem, they'll be out of date by the time you read them. Craigslist is growing so fast, in so many places around the world, that it's almost impossible to publish data about the operation that isn't obsolete by the time it appears in print. Fortunately, the site itself maintains reasonably up-to-date statistics for those who are interested.

noncompeting." Together, these three "ironies" represent sharp (and sharply effective) departures from the commercialism that infects so much of the Web—which is precisely why the site attracts such a fervent following and has become such a strong business. "By paying no attention to these areas—or by trying to do the opposite of what other organizations do—we end up being strong in each of them," he explains.

Craigslist certainly has an unconventional approach to investing in its brand—it doesn't. "We pay zero attention to brand," Buckmaster says. "We never use that word internally. We do zero advertising. We don't have a logo. We've never done a focus group. We don't care about any of that. And now we're told we have the strongest brand ever for a company our size. That's pretty ironic."

Craigslist has a fresh approach to competition—it doesn't believe in it. "We have no interest in competing with anyone," Buckmaster says. "We consider our mission to be one of public service. We're just trying to create something as useful as possible. If people want to use it, great. If they don't find it useful, that's great too. Yet we keep reading that we're one of the newspaper industry's deadliest competitors." Indeed, one respected analyst has estimated that, in the San Francisco area alone, newspapers are losing $50 million to $65 million in annual classified-ad revenue because of Craigslist.

Above all, Craigslist has a distinctive approach to economics—it keeps finding reasons *not* to charge customers. It imposes modest fees on companies that post job listings in Los Angeles, San Francisco, and New York City. There's long been talk of imposing a $10 fee for apartment listings in New York City—an effort to pare back on the 500,000 listings it receives per month, many of which are duplicates. Newmark and Buckmaster have also discussed plans to charge for job listings in a few other cities, including Boston, San Diego, and Washington, D.C., in an effort to reduce the number and increase the quality of the posted openings. Other than that, though, the site is free. Yet Craigslist generates healthy profits, and Internet titan eBay bought a 25 percent stake in

2004 so it could learn more about the company and its mastery of classifieds.

That's the ultimate irony of Craigslist—and the powerful logic of strategy as advocacy. By building a company around a unique set of anticommercial values and practices, Craigslist has built a flourishing commercial property. "We have to run a strong business, we have to have cash reserves, we want to be here over the long run," Buckmaster says. "But we don't view the Internet as being subject to a 'land grab' or 'first-mover advantage.' Companies that want to dominate in a hurry— they're the ones that spend all the money. We're definitely oddballs in the Internet industry, and we always have been. Lots of people made fun of us, especially at the height of the dot-com boom. Most of those people are out of business now."

WHAT YOU THINK SHAPES HOW YOU TALK— CREATING A STRATEGIC VOCABULARY

Listen closely to maverick entrepreneurs like Arkadi Kuhlmann and Jim Buckmaster, and you quickly realize that they don't sound like traditional executives. They almost never use conventional jargon to explain how they do business. They almost always describe their strategies and practices—the ideas that animate their companies—in ways that sound unique, authentic, even a bit strange. How many bankers tout the virtues of "agitating" their customers? How many Internet CEOs discuss "the ironies of unbranding, demonetizing, and noncompeting"?

One sign that a company is pursuing a truly original competitive strategy is that it has created its own vocabulary. Not buzzwords, acronyms, and the other verbal detritus of business-as-usual, but an authentically homegrown language that captures how a company competes, how its people work, why it expects to succeed, and what it means to win. You can't judge a book by its cover, but you can evaluate a company by its language. Because they *think* about their business differently, maverick organizations almost always *talk* about their business differently. They devise a strategic vocabulary that distinguishes them from their rivals and sets expectations in the marketplace and for everyone in the organization.

The best way to appreciate the power of language in business (and to evaluate how your own vocabulary stacks up) is to visit a company that speaks a language all its own. Consider our visit to the Seattle headquarters of Cranium, a seriously important young player in the deeply troubled world of toys and games. It's a bit overstated (but only a bit) to suggest that Cranium is to board games what Pixar is to animated films—a maverick newcomer that has produced a string of hits by infusing a tired industry with fresh energy and a different perspective on how to compete. Since November 1998, Cranium has released a stream of games aimed at adults, preschoolers, and just about every age in between. The games have won rave reviews and millions of loyal fans. Cranium, its namesake title and the Toy Industry Association's 2001 Game of the Year, ranks as the fastest-selling independent board game of all time. (It is now available in 10 languages and 20 countries and has sold a staggering 5 million copies.) Cadoo, the company's second title, won Game of the Year in 2002, and Hullabaloo was Game of the Year in 2003 and again in 2006.

All told, in less than seven years, Cranium has won more than 80 industry awards, sold more than 15 million copies of its products, and attracted an estimated 30 million players for at least one of its games. This is, quite simply, a performance without precedent in a $20 billion industry that is actually shrinking, torn apart by kids' fascination with computers, the Internet, video games, and all forms of electronic entertainment and by Wal-Mart's stranglehold over the distribution of traditional toys and games, which has resulted in the bankruptcy of fabled retailer F.A.O. Schwarz, the humiliation of Toys "R" Us, and other devastating shocks to the retail system. There hasn't been much fun in toyland for an awfully long time—unless, that is, you work at Cranium.

In the media, Cranium's track record has been a source of both celebration and mystification. Is it the latest in a line of press-savvy consumer companies that have mastered the art of good PR? (When Julia Roberts appeared on *Oprah* and declared herself a Cranium enthusiast, the game's popularity went into overdrive.) Is its unrivaled sales record a testimony to the power of clever packaging and smart design? (All of the company's artwork, from the games themselves right down to its business cards, feature distinctive illustrations by Gary Baseman, creator of the TV series and feature film *Teacher's Pet.*)

Or is the Cranium phenomenon about something deeper, an emerging New Age ethos gripping society? In a long essay for the *New York Times Magazine,* writer Clive Thompson deconstructed Cranium's unparalleled performance in the marketplace and concluded that the company's games have become an emblem of "America's insatiable thirst for self-esteem." Why has the company won in the marketplace? Thompson asks. Because, he argues, "Cranium appears to have discovered the paradox that gets kids and families playing together: a game where no one loses."[3]

Richard Tait, Cranium's cofounder and "Grand Poo Bah" (yes, that's the title on his business card), is adamant that at the heart of the company's consistent growth is a disruptive business strategy—and that at the heart of the strategy is a homegrown language that communicates the ideas that define the company. How Cranium *thinks* about its business shapes how everyone at the company *talks* about the business, both among themselves and to the outside world. And the fact that everyone at the company talks about the business in the same way allows it to keep introducing new games, targeting new slices of the market, even venturing outside board games to book publishing, television, and other fields, without straying from its core values.

"This wasn't about games at the beginning," explains Tait, who was a rising star at Microsoft (where he won Employee of the Year honors) before he and cofounder Whit Alexander (also a decorated Microsoft veteran) decided to trade the rigors of software for the fun of games. "We wanted to provide an alternative to the entertainment choices people have, to create a movement around that alternative. So much of entertainment is destructive and demeaning. Look at television: 'You're fired!' 'You are the weakest link.' Who's going to sleep with whose girlfriend on the island? Our disruptive moment was when we said, 'We're going to create lighten-and-enlighten experiences, a unique combination of laughter and learning that gives everyone a chance to shine. People will laugh and feel and connect, but at the same time they are going to be getting smarter. That was our disruptive idea."

The language of "lighten and enlighten" and "shine"—reflecting a genuine sense of mission and a feel for the interplay between seriousness of purpose and flat-out fun—infuses every aspect of how Cranium operates. Life here just *sounds* different from life at most companies. Executives have job titles that make perfect sense to their colleagues, but not to many other people. Whit Alexander is Cranium's "Chief Noodler." The business card of Jack Lawrence, the company's CFO, identifies him as "Professor Profit." Catherine Fisher Carr, the person responsible for the content of the games, has the title "Keeper of the Flame." Customers aren't just customers, they're *Craniacs*—game players who share the passion and values that animate the company that makes the game. "I get e-mails from customers that say, 'Proud to be a Craniac,' 'I am a Craniac,'" says Richard Tait. "This really is a movement."

Even hard-core business operations are described in unusual ways. Scattered around Cranium headquarters are "Pulse" stations—fun, colorful, visual representations of key financial indicators, including sell-through numbers at retailers, operating profits, and on-time delivery of products. These stations (which measure the "pulse" of the company) are updated regularly and keep everyone posted on the guts of Cranium's business results. Meanwhile, the watchwords of the product development process are "Gather-Grow-Glow." *Gather*—which friends or family members are expected to play the game? *Glow*—what are the moments of success and celebration (of "shine") that the game is meant to unleash? *Grow*—what are the players going to learn from the game?

To outsiders, Cranium's offbeat titles and homegrown vocabulary may sound forced, hokey, even off-putting. But for Richard Tait this vocabulary is vital to the company's business strategy and operating success. "Every great company has a distinctive culture," Tait says, "and every culture has a language, a shared sense of values. We've established a culture in the company that is impregnable. We defend it, we rally around it, we refine it. And as part of that culture, there is a vocabulary. Everyone you meet at Cranium can talk to you about lighten and enlighten, about shine, and about what it means to bring that into people's lives."

Everyone you meet at Cranium can also talk about CHIFF, perhaps the centerpiece of the company's strategic vocabulary. CHIFF stands for Clever, High-quality, Innovative, Friendly, and Fun. The acronym is meant to explain the games' personality and performance—how they should look, how they should be built, and how the product brochure should read. In fact, if you spend any amount of time at Cranium headquarters, you can't help but chafe under the relentless drumbeat of CHIFF. Do the company's new TV ads feel CHIFF? Do the latest changes to the Web site look CHIFF? Are the instructions for the newest game CHIFF enough?

The company has a senior executive, Jill Waller, whose title is actually "CHIFF Champion." Her job is to make sure that the product development process stays true to this crucial element of Cranium's vocabulary. Waller's CHIFF checklist involves a detailed methodology that shapes everything from how to vet ideas for new games (a process called "the Cranium Cuisinart") to how to make detailed production plans ("the Manufacturing Mindmeld") to how to revise games once they're in the market ("Operation Big Ears"). "Everyone knows what a game has to be like, what the experience of playing it has to be like," Waller says. "Everything we do has to be CHIFF."

Some readers may be rolling their eyes at the colorful language spoken at Cranium. This is, after all, a young, offbeat (albeit phenomenally successful) company that is literally in the business of fun and games. But time and again, as we immersed ourselves in companies with original, break-the-mold business strategies, we discovered an only-spoken-here strategic language, a vocabulary of competition designed to capture what the company stood for and how its people worked together to advance its agenda.

Go back to Austin, Texas, and Roy Spence's ad agency, a creative place to be sure, but a hard-nosed competitor as well, one whose clients include some of the world's most powerful companies and best-known advertisers. As we've seen, Spence believes that his agency's purpose-based strategy is distinctive enough that his bustling firm, with annual billings of $1.3 billion, needs an executive with the title "Chief Purposologist." (She is, in some respects, GSD&M's version of Cranium's "CHIFF Champion.")

But that title is just a tiny part of the agency's strategic vocabulary, and that vocabulary is what keeps new generations of employees connected to the 35-year-old agency's original and unwavering purpose. Spence's colleagues have gathered a collection of "Royisms" that they believe define how GSD&M operates—the genetic code for the agency's competitive spirit. "We are curious and restless—a safe haven for misfits that somehow fit here," reads one. "We like who we are. We like people who like us. When people come in to change our core culture, the body rejects them," reads another. "We are not like the big boys, and we don't want to be," reads a third. "We must never play by their rules—it's a trap."

Expressive language, to be sure. But where GSD&M's business vocabulary most comes to life is in the design and personality of the agency's headquarters building. If what you think shapes how you talk, the logic goes, then where you work should reflect how you think as well. Spence and his colleagues are true believers when it comes to the power of disruptive business ideas, and their beliefs are evident the

moment you arrive at the GSD&M offices. The strikingly original facility, called Idea City, has become a defining landmark of the Austin
business scene and a source of fascination among business commentators around the world. Nothing about the place is standard-issue office
building. The three-story, 137,600-square-foot headquarters is overflowing with offbeat art and wild decor. There's also a movie theater, a
classic diner, and a bookstore.

But the most telling aspect of Idea City is that it is actually organized
as a city—on the theory that the energy, diversity, and barely controlled
chaos of urban environments produce the most exciting ideas. The
complex is divided into districts, each of which has its own personality.
There's the Financial District, where the agency's business types con-
gregate. There's Greenwich Village, where the agency's creative types
work. Each major client gets its own neighborhood, sort of an immersion zone for the company's products, personality, and purpose. There
are War Rooms, Hot Shops, Idea Teams—ways of describing how and
where people work that are unique to GSD&M.

In the middle of it all is the Rotunda, the town square through
which the 540 residents of Idea City pass on a daily basis. (Company
wags call it the Roytunda, an homage to their silver-tongued president.)
And on the floor of the Rotunda, written in concrete, are the values
that animate the agency: community, winning, restlessness, freedom and
responsibility, curiosity, integrity. These words appear in plenty of other
places at GSD&M headquarters as well—the building is overflowing
with visual reminders of what makes the agency tick.

Some people wear their hearts on their sleeve. Why does GSD&M
carve its values into the floor? "It sounds hokey, but it's not," explains
Spence. "People understand that these values are not temporary. They
are literally etched in the concrete of the town square. Those values are
the common drivers of our purpose. People want to work at companies
that know what they stand for. Everybody at this company knows what
we stand for."

WHAT IT MEANS TO SUCCEED—BUILDING THE FUTURE BY REBUILDING AN INDUSTRY

It's a long way from Austin, Texas, to Redwood City, California, and there's a vast gulf separating the freewheeling spirit of the ad business from the backbreaking demands of the construction business. But when you walk into the offices of DPR Construction, Inc., and visit with cofounder and president Doug Woods, it feels like you've traveled 1,800 miles to arrive at another Idea City—and another company that speaks its own language.

Doug Woods doesn't sound like a nail–pounding, lunch pail–toting construction boss. But he's spent his entire career building office complexes, high-tech factories, and research labs. DPR's enviable track record of success (it generates annual revenues of more than $1 billion and wins raves from construction industry gurus as a best-in-class operation) has been driven by an explicit commitment to *re*-building an out-of-date, dysfunctional sector of the economy. From day one, DPR has embraced the power of strategy as advocacy: it aspired to grow as a company by becoming a disruptive force in its industry.

"This industry hasn't changed the way it does business a whole lot in the last hundred years," says Woods, sitting in the Patsy Cline conference room at company headquarters. (DPR headquarters, which exudes the slick feel of its Silicon Valley neighbors, is filled with rooms named after pop-culture notables.) "From the very beginning, we wanted to be quantifiably different and better. We wanted to be a truly great construction company."

Indeed, back in 1990, before Woods and his cofounders, Peter Nosler and Ron Davidowski (the "P" and "R" in DPR), hammered their first nail, they hammered out a "core ideology" designed to set them apart from their peers—and to announce their intention to challenge convention in their industry. "We exist to build great things," the ideology declares. "We must be different from and more progressive than all other construction companies. We stand for something."*

What DPR stands for is an approach to the business that takes on and remedies some of the most notorious pitfalls of construction, the designed-in headaches that give the industry such a bad name: unreliable price estimates, endless cost overruns, delays and slipped schedules, completed projects with a never-ending list of fixes, and lawsuits and recriminations between builders and clients. Woods and his colleagues have been unblinking in their critique of what's gone wrong with the industry to which they have devoted their professional lives. They have also made it clear that they would not look to the powers-that-be in their industry for ideas or inspiration about how to fix what ailed the business. "We've tried to emulate some of the high-tech companies and what propelled them," Woods says. "Silicon Valley has been a proving ground for people who created new ways of doing business. That's what we wanted to do in construction."[4]

Little wonder, then, that DPR, by virtue of its technology-inspired approach to the business, has become the contractor of choice for many of the country's technology darlings. For example, it built Pixar Animation Studio's lavish headquarters, the dream factory where Steve Jobs and his colleagues turn out blockbusters like *Finding Nemo* and *The Incredibles*. It has built big corporate campuses for some of the biggest names in Silicon Valley. It has built vast computer-chip factories across the country. And it has become a leading force in biotechnology and pharmaceuticals, building offices, laboratories, and state-of-the-art manufacturing complexes. These are all buildings that require fierce

---

*Fans of Jim Collins's will notice the obvious influence of his ideas at DPR. The company's founders spent time with the celebrated business guru early on in the company's history and worked to apply many of the ideas from *Built to Last* as they built their organization. It's a fascinating case study—translating timeless ideas honed at blue-chip companies, from 3M to Disney, to a young company in the rough-and-tumble world of commercial construction.

attention to detail, have huge budgets, and allow no margin for error. For Charles Schwab, DPR built a mission-critical data center inside an existing building while stock-trading operations continued on the floor above. For Motorola, it built a state-of-the-art semiconductor plant in Austin, Texas, without interrupting operations at the other ultrasensitive chip lines that surrounded the new factory. For Pixar, it transformed the site of a run-down Del Monte cannery into an exquisitely stylish film-making complex that is downright breathtaking in its blend of high-tech wizardry and quirky personality. (We'll visit the Pixar complex for other reasons in chapter 11.)

DPR didn't just build its business (and these buildings) in accordance with its aim-high ideology. The founders also established "tangible images" and "vivid descriptions" of the future—rich, easy-to-visualize portraits of what success would look like if the company lived up to its ideology. Early on, success meant being recognized as a different kind of company, a change-minded maverick in a slow-moving industry. "Our families will say we work for a great company," reads one of the company's first 12 descriptions. "Our friends back East will mention that they have heard about DPR's greatness," says another.

As DPR grew and prospered, its strategy and ideology remained constant, but its definitions of success grew decidedly more ambitious. "Over the next 30 years," reads one of its more recent "vivid descriptions" of the future, "our people practices will be recognized as being as progressive and influential as Hewlett-Packard's were over the last 50 years." Reads another, "When it comes to quality and innovation, we will do for the construction industry what Toyota did for the auto industry." And another: "Like Microsoft and Sun Microsystems, our people and company will be known for being aggressive and 'bullet smart.'"

A construction company that aims to be thought of in the same breath as Toyota, Microsoft, and some of the legends of Silicon Valley? This is hardly conventional language in a business whose stereotype image includes the salty language of its employees—and that's the point.

"I've never wanted to be like everybody else," says Woods. "I don't want DPR to be like everybody else. We wanted to create a new culture, a new way of doing business in this industry."

Like Roy Spence's ad agency, DPR is a company that believes firmly in the power of language and symbols. Painted on the walls of its offices in Redwood City are the slogans and rallying cries that get repeated at all the company's offices around the country. "We exist to build great things," one wall declares. "Smarter, faster, better, safer," exclaims another. "Exceed all expectations," urges a third.

This strategic vocabulary is about more than just talk. One of the company's core values is "ever forward"—basically, a commitment to keep pushing to get better, whether or not the marketplace demands it. "We believe in continual self-initiated change, improvement, learning, and the advancement of standards for their own sake." To help translate that core value into an operating reality, the company named two "Ever Forward Champions"—staffers whose job is to measure DPR's performance along its target goals, to share those results widely, and to keep developing new ways to improve the scores. The Ever Forward Champions play a key role in DPR's "Global Learning Group," an ambitious training program that steeps all 2,000 employees in both technical skills—budgeting, planning and scheduling, project management—and the fine points of DPR's culture. Each employee is expected to spend at least 80 hours per year in these courses—again, not exactly standard operating procedure at most construction companies.

It's hard to overstate just how richly descriptive DPR is about virtually all aspects of its business and day-to-day work practices. It seems to have invented a piece of vocabulary to describe every nook and cranny of its strategy and future. DPR's latest future-defining exercise is Mission 2030—a vivid picture of what the company will look like in 25 years—and a clear set of benchmarks along the way, defined as Base Camp 2010. (DPR will establish other interim Camps on the path to 2030.) One of the most ambitious goals: to increase each year the percentage of business

DPR lands "without competition"—that is, clients who consider no other company to build their project. At present, that percentage stands at 33 percent of DPR's business, a striking figure in an industry where competitive bids are as routine as coffee breaks.

Why invest so much energy in building a vocabulary as opposed to just, say, building factories and laboratories for clients? "Because at the heart of every great company is a clear sense of purpose," answers Peter Salvati, a senior DPR executive who works out of the company's San Diego office and has played a lead role in Mission 2030. "One of the things I always have fun with—and I've probably done this with a hundred clients—is to suggest that they ask other construction companies, 'Why does your company exist?' You ought to be able to answer that about your own company. But so many people just look at one another, shrug their shoulders, and say, 'To make money, I guess.' It's different for us."

Being different has made all the difference at DPR. There's no question that the company has prospered by unleashing a disruptive business strategy in its industry. But the ultimate gauge of its performance, says Doug Woods, is how much influence it has on the rest of the industry. It all goes back to strategy as advocacy. Indeed, another goal for Base Camp 2010 is for DPR's internal scorecard—detailed metrics about schedules, budgets, change orders, and the like—to become a generally accepted benchmark for the construction business as a whole.

In other words, DPR wants its definitions of success to be adopted by its rivals as standard operating procedure. "If you really are building great things," says Peter Salvati, "then people ought to be benchmarking themselves against you. They ought to be trying to emulate what you do." Adds Doug Woods, "This is not about something internal at DPR. This is about being a force for transformation. We want to lead the industry to a different place."

That's the essence of strategy and the logic of competition at every company we've visited in these two chapters—from ING Direct's campus in Wilmington, Delaware, to Cranium's fun-and-games head-quarters in Seattle, to HBO's building near the beach in Santa Monica, to our many stops in between. Sure, it may seem safer, more prudent, more *conventional,* to devise a game plan for your company that con-forms to the generally accepted rules of how your industry works. But if that's such a winning formula, why are so many industries in such dire straits? That simple question speaks to the long-term futility of a business formula based on strategy as mimicry. Back in chapter 1, ING Direct's Arkadi Kuhlmann said it best with a question of his own: if you do things the way everybody else does them, why do you think you're going to do any better?

Chapter Three

Maverick Messages (I):
Sizing Up Your Strategy

Few companies consciously set out to be just another me-too player with another ho-hum business model, following a bland formula that's hard to distinguish from everyone else's. But in industry after industry, that's precisely how most companies wind up competing, which is why competition feels so unforgiving.

In his hugely influential book *The Innovator's Dilemma,* Clayton M. Christensen awakened business to the power of "disruptive technologies"—digital breakthroughs that reshaped the governing economics of entire product segments, sometimes whole industries. We believe that a new wave of strategic innovation is being built around disruptive *points of view.* Maverick leaders don't just strive to build high-performance companies. They champion high-stakes agendas. They create a competitive edge around an edgy critique of their industry. They present a fresh take on the world that clicks with customers, energizes employees, and shapes their business, from the markets they target to the customers they serve and the messages they send. They understand that the only sustainable form of market leadership is thought leadership.[1]

Roy Spence of GSD&M calls his ultimate goal "positioning beyond defeat"—being so clear about a company's purpose and so relentless about turning that purpose into a collection of business strategies and operating practices and a set of messages to the marketplace that traditional competitive responses are rendered largely ineffective. "People don't have time for companies to be confused," he argues. "Neiman Marcus knows it's for rich people. Deal with it. Nike is in the business of crushing the competition. So be it. The companies that get in trouble are the ones that are mushy about who they are."

As you work on positioning beyond defeat—as you think about the values you stand for as an organization and as a leader—ask these five questions about your company's strategy.

1. Do you have a distinctive and disruptive sense of purpose that sets you apart from your rivals?

That's the defining question at the heart of these first two chapters, and it's what separates the mavericks we've highlighted from their me-too competitors. The founders of DPR Construction were determined, from the moment they started the company, to reckon honestly and openly with the designed-in flaws of their industry and to build an organization that would prosper by fixing those flaws. The founders of Cranium didn't launch their company because they had one good idea for a single board game. Instead, they had a wide-ranging critique of what was wrong with family entertainment— and an unapologetic sense of mission about providing a clear alternative, through board games but also through book publishing, TV shows, and other lines of business that Cranium has begun to enter after its runaway success with games.

Even when their company was a tiny start-up, the Cranium founders believed and acted as if they were playing for high stakes—

not just thinking about games, but rethinking how parents could relate to their kids and how families could relate to one another. "We've always acted as if we're a much bigger company than we really are," says Grand Poo Bah Richard Tait. "We're still a fairly young player in our industry, but we conduct ourselves as if we are a global movement. This isn't a job. It's the pursuit of a dream, to give everyone a chance to shine. It's a big, ethereal goal, but we won't stop until we're convinced that we're making progress against that goal."

High ideals, to be sure. But don't confuse high ideals with modest ambitions. Companies with the most values-based critiques of their industries often turn out to be the savviest and most aggressive competitors. The stock market value of fun-loving Southwest Airlines exceeds the stock market value of every other U.S. airline *put together*. Quality-obsessed HBO was the first network in TV history to generate more than $1 billion in annual profits. ING Direct holds assets of more than $40 million per employee; the average for U.S. banks is about $5 million per employee. In other words, Arkadi Kuhlmann's outfit is eight times more productive than the competition at generating assets. Who says high-minded values can't drive cutting-edge performance?

2. Do you have a vocabulary of competition that is unique to your industry and compelling to your employees and customers?

And we mean a real, honest-to-goodness, only-spoken-here business language. Commerce Bank, a fabulously successful financial services company that we'll visit in chapter 7, has such a unique strategy, and such a homegrown vocabulary, that it actually publishes a dictionary of "Commerce Lingo." New employees learn the meaning of "One to Say Yes, Two to Say No": "The rule that states all employees can say 'yes' to a customer, but must first check with their supervisor before saying 'no.'" They learn the essence of "retailtainment": "The art of engaging customers and creating moments of magic so that every customer leaves Commerce with a smile." And on it goes for pages, explaining terms that eventually become second nature and ultimately make Commerce a one-of-a-kind competitor.

Or consider the most exciting and fast-growing company in one of the world's dullest and slowest-growing businesses. Much as Southwest Airlines has registered gravity-defying performance in a deadweight industry, Whole Foods Market has brought a fresh model of competition to a stale business mired in copycat strategies. The famously high-end grocer (nickname: Whole Paycheck) opened its first store in 1980 and went public in 1992. As of 2005 it had 170-plus stores, 33,000 employees, $4 billion in revenue—and a stock market performance that looks more like Google's than that of its notoriously low-return rivals in the grocery business. (Investors who put $100,000 into the IPO had $3.5 million 13 years later.)

But the success of Whole Foods isn't just about organic produce or high-priced fish. It's about a truly original business strategy that sets it apart from the competition and shapes what the company sells and how it operates. Whole Foods chairman and CEO John Mackey has developed a business ideology that blends a taste for libertarian politics, a commitment to selling healthy foods and ensuring the compassionate treatment of animals, an eagerness to share financial information and decision-making authority up and down the organization, and a true zest for growth.[2]

That competitive ideology shapes how the company communicates with employees, customers, and even investors. Whole Foods has issued a "Declaration of Interdependence" that will never be confused with the bland, generic-sounding mission statements that most companies paste on cubicle walls and forget immediately. The Declaration, which was developed in 1985 and revised in 1988, 1992, and 1997, is a richly worded, painstakingly crafted document that is both aspirational and candid.

Indeed, the statement ends with the rare (and refreshing) admission that the company, like any organization, doesn't always live up to the ideals it espouses. The Declaration "reflects the hopes and intentions of many people," it reads. "We do not believe it always accurately portrays the way things currently are at Whole Foods Market so much as the way we would like things to be. It is our dissatisfaction with the current reality, when compared with what is possible, that spurs us toward excellence and toward creating a better person, company, and world."

Companies that think differently about their business invariably talk about it differently as well. What language does your company speak?

3. Are you prepared to reject opportunities that offer short-term benefits but distract your organization from its long-term mission?

At every company we've explored in these first two chapters, the road to prosperity has been determined in part by the road not taken—choices not to pursue markets that looked seductive but were at odds with the company's advocacy agenda, decisions to turn down customers who could pay the bills but didn't fit the strategic bill.

Scott Bedbury, a marketing wizard who played a key role in brand-building for Nike and Starbucks, and whom we'll meet again in chapter 8, likes to say that some of the best moves he ever made were the growth opportunities he passed up. He calls it the "Spandex Rule of Branding," and it applies to strategy as well as marketing: "Just because you can doesn't mean you should."

The Spandex Rule helps to explain why ING Direct passes on business opportunities that would make traditional bankers salivate. It explains why Craig Newmark and Jim Buckmaster of Craigslist are determined to keep looking for reasons not to charge visitors, even though the site's devoted users, both buyers and sellers, are certainly prepared to pay for some services. It explains why Southwest Airlines has never adopted some of the most common practices of its rivals.

"The 'invisible' decisions that you make to stay on purpose can be ten times more important than your visible decisions," argues Roy Spence. "Nothing's more difficult than saying no to an attractive opportunity. And nothing's more important."

4. Can you be provocative without provoking a backlash?

One key test of any would-be disruptor is whether he or she can also be a convincing diplomat. That insight may be the most enduring contribution of the rise and fall of Netscape, the company that single-handedly defined the revolutionary fervor of the dot-com boom. Eventually, waving a red flag at Bill Gates and his colleagues is Redmond, Washington, forced Netscape to wave the white flag as an independent company.

Even a fire-breathing maverick like Arkadi Kuhlmann appreciates the virtues of diplomacy. Not with his competitors, mind you, but with his colleagues. After all, ING Group operates in many of the businesses that Kuhlmann loves to critique, from home mortgages to credit cards. So he is careful to reassure his Dutch brethren that he's a team player as well as an industry reformer. Back in the 1990s, when he launched ING Direct Canada, Kuhlmann named the conference rooms at bank headquarters after Dutch villages—a symbolic gesture that received a warm welcome in Amsterdam. Indeed, Kuhlmann's diplomatic skills are so well developed that when *Fortune* surveyed the parent company's American presence, it concluded that the operation that felt most Dutch was ING Direct USA.[3]

5. If your company went out of business tomorrow, who would really miss you and why?

We first heard this question from advertising maverick Roy Spence, who tells us that he got it from strategy guru Jim Collins. Whatever the original source, the question is as profound as it is simple—and worth taking seriously as you evaluate your approach to strategy and competition.

Why might a company be missed? Because it's providing a product or a service so unique that it can't be provided nearly as well by any other company. Because it's created a workplace so dynamic that most employees would be hard-pressed to find a similar environment somewhere else. Because it has forged a uniquely emotional connection with customers that other companies can't replicate. Precious few companies meet any of these criteria—which may be why so many companies feel like they're on the verge of going out of business.

HBO is not one of those companies. In today's 500-channel cable universe, it's hard to argue that TV viewers would be left staring at blank walls (or, *gasp,* reading a book) if HBO were to disappear from the small screen. But one vital constituency would suffer irreparable harm—the ever-growing collection of writers, directors, actors, and producers who believe they have no other outlet on television for their most daring work. "They say, 'We want your voice. We want your vision. We want the story that you see.' And they mean it," marvels *Six Feet Under* creator Alan Ball. "That might seem obvious, but at the networks every decision is second-guessed by every single executive. At HBO they leave you alone for the most part and trust your instincts." (Instead of returning to film after *Six Feet Under* went, well, six feet under, Oscar-winner Alan Ball has re-upped with the network on two major projects.)

Forget HBO's programming library and technology strategy. The network's hardest-to-duplicate advantage (and thus, the piece of its business that would be most sorely missed) is its ability to attract and unleash Hollywood talent that once shunned TV. "People always fixate on the content freedoms at HBO as a kind of unfair advantage," says Carolyn Strauss, a network lifer who is president of

HBO Entertainment, "but the freedoms that are really important aren't the freedom to swear, or to be naked, or to blow somebody's head off. They're about expressing a distinct point of view and allowing the creator's voice to come through in as unencumbered a way as possible."

Those freedoms, carefully guarded by Strauss, Chris Albrecht, and the network's leadership team, are why some of the world's biggest stars and most-respected filmmakers—from Paul Newman to Tom Hanks to Mike Nichols—bring their passion projects to HBO. Albrecht understands that there is a "limited supply of supremely talented people who can create successful television," and that most of them "have a better chance of getting rich and famous elsewhere." So he focuses on making the experience of working with HBO memorable—the kind of experience that writers, directors, and actors would miss if it went away. "If you're interested in the work itself," he says, "there are very few other places in the broadcast business where you can call your own shots as a creator." These creative freedoms are an essential part of HBO's competitive strategy.

Can you identify one piece of how your company operates that, if it were to disappear, would be sorely missed in the marketplace? If not, can you identify one good reason why your company is not at risk of disappearing?

PART TWO

Reinventing Innovation

Chapter Four

Ideas Unlimited:
Why Nobody Is as Smart as Everybody

Gold mining is an old industry, a tired industry. The pace of change is gla-
cial. Traditionally, mining companies have worried about how strong
your back is, not how big your brain is. We wanted to do something that
no one in the industry had done, to tap into the intellectual capital of the
whole world.

—ROB MCEWEN, FORMER CHAIRMAN AND CEO, GOLDCORP, INC.

R ob McEwen was running out of ideas—and out of patience. It
had been more than five years since he'd made a gamble that
most executives in his business thought was fool's gold, acquiring
a mine with a history of low productivity, bare-bones investment, and
bitter labor relations. But McEwen's mine was in the Red Lake district
of northwest Ontario, which, since the discovery of gold there in the
1920s, has produced more than 24 million ounces, nearly 10 percent of
gold-rich Canada's total output. And this out-of-favor property
bumped up against the reliably productive Campbell Lake mine, which
had churned out 9 million ounces over the years.

There had to be rich deposits of ore somewhere below his 55,000-
acre site, McEwen reasoned. *But where?* So he raised the stakes and
provided his geologists at Goldcorp, Inc., with a fresh $10 million to
spend on exploration at the capital-starved Red Lake mine, situated more
than 1,300 miles from company headquarters in downtown Toronto.
Soon, the geologists reported some tantalizing news: in nine of the

exploratory holes they had drilled, the average concentration of ore was 30 times richer than what Red Lake was currently producing. Eureka! Goldcorp had discovered gold. But the discovery raised as many questions as answers. *How big was the deposit?* McEwen and his geologists didn't know. *Where were the best spots to transition from exploration to deep drilling?* The team couldn't say. *How much time and money would it take to figure it out?* No one was prepared to offer a firm estimate.

Another year went by as Goldcorp struggled to make sense of its promising find and to understand just what it was sitting on. Tired, frustrated, and eager for a break from the grind, McEwen, an unabashed science and technology enthusiast, decided to spend a week at MIT with a delegation of presidents and CEOs from other companies, learning about trends in information technology. Part of the weeklong program focused on Linux and open-source software—computer code written by programmers scattered all over the world, people who are passionate enough about their craft, or who have a strong enough stake in the success of the project on which they work, to volunteer their time and expertise to write software that no company owns but millions of people can't live (or at least work) without. For years open-source programs such as Apache, Perl, and Sendmail have been the unseen, mission-critical backbone of the Internet. It's a taken-for-granted part of life among the Internet cognoscenti, but something of a mind-bender for us civilians: the world's most important technology platform relies on ideas and computer code generated largely by a decentralized corps of volunteer programmers, most of whom have never met one another and few of whom work together in any formal setting.*

----

*That said, open source doesn't mean not-for-profit. Open-source software has inspired a flood of venture capital investments in companies that package, service, and otherwise commercialize this grassroots code. In 2004 alone, according to the *New York Times*, venture investors poured $149 million into start-ups built around open-source systems. This is the second wave of open-source investing. In 1999 and 2000, according to the *Times*, venture capitalists invested $714 million in 71 open-source companies.[1]

In the case of Linux, a worldwide collection of grassroots, self-directed teams have built an operating system that powers a fast-growing share of the world's computer servers—and has become a power player in the software industry. Some of the biggest technology companies in the world, including IBM, Hewlett-Packard, and Intel, devote hundreds of programmers and major financial resources to the Linux cause. But the real action is with the grassroots volunteers who cook up features, write code, fix bugs—and share their ideas with everyone else on the project.

The more McEwen learned about the open-source phenomenon, the more intrigued be became. People didn't have to work *for* his company, he realized, in order to work *with* his company. He could prospect for drilling strategies from the farthest reaches of the world. "All of a sudden a light went on," he recalls. "It was like a flash: this is the template I've been searching for! I went running back to Toronto convinced that we had to change how Goldcorp thought about mining. I wanted us to create a new approach to exploration at Red Lake."

McEwen sketched the outlines of his idea to Goldcorp's geologists and executives. The company would use the Internet to post all of its data on the mine—50 years worth of maps, reports, and raw geological information—along with software that displayed the data both in two dimensions and three dimensions. It would then invite scientists and engineers from anywhere in the world to download the data, analyze it as they saw fit, and submit drilling plans to Goldcorp, which would convene a blue-ribbon panel of judges to evaluate the submissions. The goal would be to help the company find its next 6 million ounces of gold.* Unlike the early days of Linux, this wouldn't be a labor of love or a symbol of geek rebellion. There would be a reward—prize money of $500,000, to be divided among 25 semifinalists and 3 finalists chosen by the judges.

---

*It was a somewhat arbitrary goal—basically, the difference between the 9 million ounces of gold that Campbell Lake had produced and the paltry 3 million ounces produced by Red Lake.

McEwen was ecstatic. Many of his colleagues were horrified. How could Goldcorp share its most proprietary data with the outside world? It was as if Coca-Cola decided to open the vault and publish the secret formula for Coke. That's comically out-of-date thinking, McEwen rebutted. "We all have the nineteenth-century image of a prospector with his mule and a pickax who won't tell anyone where he found his gold," he says. "Lots of people in the industry still think that way, even though it makes no sense. Our executives said, 'What if someone decides to buy all the land around us?' I said, 'We've got 55,000 acres. Let's worry about that first.'"

The bigger worry, though, was what the outside world would think of Goldcorp: Why couldn't its executives and geologists find the gold on their own? "Just before we launched," McEwen says, "the resistance really built up: Isn't the rest of the world going to think that we're stupid? Or at least that Rob McEwen thinks we're stupid?" The boss turned these all-too-human concerns on their head. Many of Goldcorp's geologists already had their favorite targets, places where they believed the company would hit the mother lode. Goldcorp kept those targets to itself but was curious to see if outsiders would reach similar conclusions. "If three-quarters of the people who submit plans think your target is a good place to drill, that third-party confirmation does you wonders," he told the skeptics. "And we're all going to be here if we make the big discovery, so we're all going to win from this infusion of brainpower. I turned every objection into a benefit."

Thus was born "the Goldcorp Challenge." At his industry's annual high-profile event, the spring conference of the Prospectors and Developers Association, McEwen unveiled the open-source contest. Most of the executives and financial analysts in the crowd were puzzled, if not downright hostile. ("Everyone thought we were crazy," McEwen recalls. "They totally dismissed the idea.") But as word got out to the worldwide fraternity of scientists and geologists in the mining industry, the reaction was enthusiastic—a virtual gold rush. More than 1,400 qualified participants ("online prospectors," in the language of the Challenge) downloaded Goldcorp's treasure trove of data. More than 140 of them crunched the numbers, ran the data through software programs, and submitted detailed drilling plans. More than half of the targets identified by the award-winning submissions were new to Goldcorp—sites the company had not considered drilling. Several years after the completion of the Challenge, Goldcorp was *still* drilling targets identified by the winners. Inspired by the success of Linux and open-source software, the company had discovered a new way to discover gold.[2]

Rob McEwen continues to marvel at the energy and far-flung brainpower the contest unleashed. (The submissions came from 51 countries, and the semifinalists were from Canada, Australia, Russia, the United States, and Spain.) But more striking than the *number* of ideas that streamed into Toronto were the diversity and originality of the ideas. Goldcorp was tapping into vastly different technical fields and receiving proposals from scientists with whole new perspectives on how to analyze the data. Thanks to the Challenge, Goldcorp got access to fields of research and styles of thinking to which it would never have had access otherwise.

"I expected to see lots of geologists using their standard tools—geophysical analysis, geochemical analysis," McEwen says. "But we also had people using applied math, advanced physics, intelligent systems, computer graphics. When I opened up one of the entries [which would be named the first-place winner], I almost fell out of my chair. It was a visual depiction of our ore body that communicated so powerfully what was happening underground. I had never, *ever* seen graphics like this in our industry."

The industry, meanwhile, had rarely, if ever, seen anything like the surge in Goldcorp's operating performance and stock price. Today Red Lake is considered the richest gold mine in the world, as measured by the concentration of gold per ton of rock that Goldcorp unearths. (The mine site has expanded to 100,000 acres.) It has proven reserves and resources of 6.6 million ounces, reserves that keep growing as Goldcorp does more drilling. It is producing so much ore at such a low cost that Goldcorp is the only company that stockpiles gold in anticipation of higher prices down the road. Indeed, at the end of 2004 Goldcorp was holding on to more bullion than the central banks of 45 of the world's countries, including giants like Canada and Mexico.

Small wonder its share price has glittered on the New York Stock Exchange.* For years the company's Web site proudly displayed a stock ticker that compared its performance since 1993 (when McEwen transformed Goldcorp from a closed-end investment fund into a publicly traded operating company) with the performance of some of the most famous names in the world. A $100,000 investment in Microsoft in 1993, the ticker reported, was worth $895,000 in late 2005. A $100,000 investment in Warren Buffet's Berkshire Hathaway was worth $748,000. A $100,000 investment in Goldcorp was worth more than *2.9 million*— a nearly thirtyfold appreciation.

To be sure, Goldcorp's global brainstorming was far from the only factor behind this performance. There was the good luck of the original discovery at Red Lake. There were Rob McEwen's talents as an evangelist for the investment virtues of gold in general and of Goldcorp stock in particular. ("Remember," he often ended his communications with shareholders and the media, "gold is Money and Goldcorp is Gold!") There was the rising price of gold itself, which crossed the $500-an-ounce threshold and reached an 18-year high in late 2005.

---

*At the end of 2004 Goldcorp announced that it would acquire Wheaton River Minerals, a gold-mining company based in Vancouver, in a share swap valued at $2.3 billion. The "new" Goldcorp ranks as the world's lowest-cost producer of at least one million ounces of gold per year. Rob McEwen served as chairman of the combined entity until he stepped down in October 2005 to renew his passion for exploration. He acquired a major position in and became CEO of US Gold, which controls promising (but unproven) territory in gold-rich Nevada, next to high-output mines owned by some industry giants.

But the Challenge was a pivotal event in the history of the company. It was a breakthrough innovation that turbocharged the process of turning a find into a fortune, and it gave Goldcorp a reputation for creativity and originality in a business that lacks both. "This is an industry mired in inertia," McEwen says. "It's populated by people who are linear in their thinking, incremental in their progress. We wanted to build a 21st-century mining company."

THE SMARTEST GUYS (AREN'T) IN THE ROOM— THE BEST IDEAS FROM THE MOST PEOPLE

Where do great ideas come from? The traditional answer is the stuff of entrepreneurial folklore, the creation myth of the creative process. Big ideas come from big thinkers: the eccentric genius, the inspired founder, the visionary CEO. Business history is filled with heroic tales of breakthroughs fueled by unique imagination and individual determination. Alexander Graham Bell and the telephone. Henry Ford and the assembly line. Edward Land and instant photography. Walt Disney and the magic of Disneyland.

Bill Gates, the richest man in the world and by most accounts one of the great business geniuses of all time, offers a perfect image of the lonely leader's guide to innovation. In March 2005 the *Wall Street Journal* ran a front-page account of Gates's secretive, twice-a-year "Think Weeks" in which the Microsoft cofounder heads off by himself, in total seclusion, to a remote cabin in the Pacific Northwest. Armed with white papers penned by Microsoft staffers, fueled by orange soda and two meals a day, Gates reads, reflects, and thinks big thoughts. Among the business ideas to receive a green light from the boss after these retreats, the *Journal* reports, were Microsoft's Web browser, its Tablet PC, and its online videogame business.[3]

As unique a ritual as it is, Think Week reflects a widely shared executive mind-set. For decades most leaders assumed that because they had the loftiest title, the most stock options, and (in theory at least) personal accountability for bottom-line results, they had to come up with, sign off on, and certainly be responsible for all the ideas that shaped the future of their organization. It was their job, as the raised-eyebrow expression goes, to be the smartest guy in the room.

But what happens when competitors become so numerous, when markets become so unpredictable, when technologies evolve so quickly, when problems become so intractable, that no individual leader—*not even Bill Gates*—can think of everything?* Then it becomes necessary to invent a new model of invention, to create a new set of ideas about the creative process. That's what Rob McEwen sensed at MIT, and why his introduction to a new, more open, more grassroots approach to exploring for gold felt so liberating. No matter how long he sat or how hard he pondered, he wasn't going to outthink the collective intelligence of hundreds of geologists from around the world.

Now consider a different kind of leadership ritual, this one shaped by a different mind-set about the best way to unearth important ideas or combine small observations into big insights. Tom Brown is no Bill Gates (who is?), but he's awfully good at what he does. For years, Brown was one of the most heralded banking analysts on Wall Street, a fiercely opinionated researcher whose up-or-down calls could make or break stocks, a perennial member of *Institutional Investor*'s All-America Research Team. Today, like so many movers and shakers on Wall Street, Brown runs a hedge fund. His firm, Second Curve Capital, manages hundreds of millions of dollars by making big, long-term bets on banks and financial services companies (the only kinds of stocks he

---

*Indeed, while there's much to admire about Gates's immersion in ideas about the future of Microsoft, his Think Weeks also seem like cram sessions for a makeup exam. Many of the outcomes of these retreats, at least as reported in the *Journal,* are responses to technology breakthroughs that originated elsewhere or to long-festering problems, like software security, that outsiders identified years earlier.

buys or sells) that Brown and his colleagues believe in and shorting companies they believe get more credit from investors than they deserve.

Needless to say, Brown spends much of his time hobnobbing with CEOs, bantering with CFOs, making guest appearances on CNBC—working in the rarified world of hedge fund managers hunting for their next great investment decision. But once a year Brown, as the leader of Second Curve Capital, organizes a different kind of hunt, dubbed "the Branch Hunt," in which he unleashes the collective intelligence of the whole firm to see things he can't see by himself. On the day of a Branch Hunt, every member of Second Curve Capital—the receptionist, the IT specialist, the compliance officer, all the analysts, and Brown himself—reports for work in the Chrysler Building high above midtown Manhattan, not in power suits and high heels but in track suits, T-shirts, jeans, and sneakers. The firm divides up into teams, each team is assigned an avenue, and each member of the team spends the better part of the day visiting every retail bank along that avenue—a stroll that goes on for what seems like endless blocks and countless hours.

There's a method to this blister-inducing madness, and we tagged along in June 2005 to see it in action. Each member of the team left Second Curve headquarters with five crisp $100 bills. They used the money to open checking accounts at two of the banks they visited, suffering through the often tedious process (which took as long as 40 minutes in some branches) and reporting in detail on the experience. Each participant in the Branch Hunt also carried a stack of forms that allowed him or her to give quick-but-thorough grades at every stop. (The day's "Rules of Engagement" were on the top form: "NO going through the motions. IGNORE preconceived notions. LOOK for Wow! at every location.") One member of each four-person team also carried a digital camera and was charged with snapping photos that captured the experience of visiting the banks—the good, the bad, the ugly, and the unintentionally hilarious.*

But the real treasure of the Branch Hunt came at the end of the day, when the firm reconvened to discuss everyone's experiences. It was like a spirited seminar on the past, present, and future of retail banking. Much of what people saw was a function of who they were and where they sat in the organization. Some of Brown's colleagues had a keen eye for customer service (or lack thereof) and staff morale at the branches. A couple of the firm's analysts talked about each branch's "rate board" the way baseball junkies dissect the box scores. Everyone had an eye for the absurd. Each team hooked up its digital camera to a projector and regaled colleagues with their pictures—many of which were worth more than a thousand words. (Everyone's favorite: a sign in a Chase branch warning customers about suspicious behavior, including "someone [who] squirts mustard or ketchup on you.") Brown himself was both the distinguished professor and the class cutup, handing out $500 awards for the best anecdote, the best photo, the best sign, and so on.

By the end of the day, Brown and his colleagues had produced a wealth of street-savvy insights, begun to identify questions for their next round of meetings with bank executives, and reached some new conclusions about the relationship between big-picture CEO claims and day-to-day realities in one of the country's most competitive retail bank marketplaces—not to mention shared some great war stories and a renewed sense of camaraderie. It was a learning experience to be remembered, filled with insights that might not have emerged any other way.

Does one day of well-designed peer-to-peer interaction transform the investment decisions of a major New York hedge fund? Of course

---

*Memo to anyone trying this at home: always take photos at the *end* of your visit. Security officers don't look kindly on strangers taking snapshots at branches, and they are likely, as they did on this day, to give chase to figure out if you're casing the joint. Memo to anyone actually casing a bank: tell the security officer you're "on a branch hunt," and he or she will let you go on your merry way.

not. But by organizing the Branch Hunt year after year, turning more people loose on the marketplace every time, and getting more systematic about processing their observations, Brown manages to generate collective intelligence about where the retail banking market is heading, what certain companies are doing right, what others are doing wrong— intelligence more powerful than anything he could come up with on his own.

There's an expression in open-source circles: "Many eyes make bugs shallow." Translation: the more smart people you can persuade to look at a software glitch, the more likely it is to get fixed. The same goes for leadership in general. Many eyes, all trained on a specific market or a well-defined business problem, will invariably find opportunities that elude the gaze of a few honchos at the top. Why settle for being the smartest guy in the room when it's so clear, in so many different settings, that nobody is as smart as everybody?

That's the guiding theme of the next two chapters. If you agree, as we argued in chapters 1 and 2, that originality has become the essence of strategy—that a disruptive point of view combined with authentic values is what separates fast-growing industry leaders from companies stuck in the middle of the pack—then it becomes urgent for you, as an entrepreneur or an executive, to unearth and identify the new ideas and points of view that can shape the future of your business. *But that doesn't mean you have to do it yourself.* Just because you're in charge doesn't mean you have to have all the answers. One of the defining responsibilities of a 21st-century leader is to attract the best ideas from the most people, wherever those people might be.

Linux, of course, is the ultimate emblem of this new logic of leadership and innovation—the radically grassroots, come-one-come-all alternative to the smartest-guy-in-the-room model. By now, the basic outlines of the Linux story are familiar to almost every programmer in the world, and the software itself is firmly established in the mainstream of the computer industry. Back in 1991, Linus Torvalds, a graduate student at the University of Helsinki, was inspired to create a new computer operating system styled on the long-established Unix language. (Linus plus Unix equals Linux.) One of his first steps was to announce his plan to the world—and to invite anyone and everyone to help. Over time, this call for collaboration galvanized a volunteer army of programmers, who organized themselves into groups, made their code-writing contributions transparent for everyone else to see, fixed bugs, added features, debated revisions—and together, working in a decentralized, peer-to-peer community, built an open-source operating system that now ranks, along with Google, as Microsoft's most nettlesome strategic challenger.[4]

But Linux is about more than the future of computer systems. It is a metaphor for the future of innovation itself. The world is teeming with smart, skilled, passionate people who are eager to demonstrate how much they know and how good they are—people who just might contribute anything from a killer idea to a whole collection of small innovations that will set you apart from the competition. These people don't have to work for you in order to work with you. But you do have to invite them into your organization and persuade them to give you their best effort.

In a report issued by Demos, an influential British think tank, researchers Charles Leadbeater and Paul Miller studied open-source methods as a technological and sociological phenomenon. Like every expert in the field, Leadbeater and Miller look to Linux as the sine qua non of grassroots innovation. But they argue persuasively that the open-source model is reshaping numerous other realms of science and society, from open-source astronomers, who have made major contributions to their field, to Internet-enabled social activists who collected 24 million signatures in support of the Jubilee 2000 campaign, which inspired the forgiveness of $36 billion in developing-country debt.[5]

Leadbeater and Miller have their own label for this rising tide of distributed creativity. They call it "the Pro-Am Revolution." Pro-ams, they explain, are "amateurs who work to professional standards." They are "knowledgeable, educated, committed, and networked by new technology." They also represent a vast pool of talent that is ready, willing, and able to contribute to projects and organizations that encourage them to do so. Innovation in the 20th century, Leadbeater and Miller argue, "was shaped by large hierarchical organizations with professionals at the top." The Pro-Am Revolution is "creating new distributed organizational models that will be innovative, adaptive, and low-cost."

J. C. Herz, a leading authority in computer games (and an adviser to the Pentagon on how gaming technologies influence military strategy), sees the open-source, pro-am phenomenon at work in her field. In an eye-opening white paper called "Harnessing the Hive," she documents what happens when skilled enthusiasts literally take their favorite games into their own hands, modify and improve what happens, and share their innovations with fellow players—a phenomenon she calls "massively networked innovation."

Herz points out that the popularity (and immense profitability) of *The Sims,* one of the most beloved and successful computer games ever, relies heavily on the contributions of rank-and-file enthusiasts who craft (and share) props, characters, and buildings to populate the virtual world. She estimates that more than 90 percent of the content of *The Sims* has been produced *by the players themselves* rather than by Maxis, the company (owned by industry juggernaut Electronic Arts) that sells the game. By providing programming tools and encouraging players to create and swap content, Maxis turned its customer base into a volunteer product development department—and enhanced its leadership position in a brutally competitive market.

The top-down model of innovation can't possibly compete with the global brainpower of this distributed community, Herz argues. The new creed of creativity, she believes, is: let a thousand flowers bloom, so long as they sprout in our garden. Companies can't ignore "the collective intelligence of the network—the fact that a million people will always be smarter than twenty people."

Tim O'Reilly, founder of O'Reilly Media, the computer-book publisher and host of the annual O'Reilly Open-Source Convention, argues that sustained innovation is no longer just about who has the most gifted scientists or the best-equipped labs. It's about who has the most compelling "architecture of participation." Which organizations make it fun, interesting, and rewarding for far-flung engineers and pro-am enthusiasts to contribute an idea or solve a problem? Which companies treat their offerings as a "perpetual beta"—products and services that can always (and easily) be modified, enhanced, and upgraded by customers who have a stake in (and get satisfaction from) making things better and more useful?* In a world being reshaped by massively net-worked innovation, the strategic challenge is to design products that "get smarter the more people use them"—and to design companies with which smart people want to interact. Ultimately, O'Reilly argues, the companies that are most likely to dominate their business are the ones most adept at harnessing the collective intelligence of everyone with whom they do business.

Of course, companies will always compete to recruit the most talented full-time employees and to put those talented employees to the highest possible use. As we'll explore in chapter 7, the best leaders have a crisp answer to the question: why would great people want to work for us? Indeed, perhaps the most powerful indicator of a company's future share of the product market in its industry is its current position in the talent market for that industry: *is it attracting more than its fair share of the best people?* But in an era in which great ideas can come from anywhere in the world—and anyone in the world—there are new questions as well: Is yours the kind of organization that smart people are eager to

---

*Tim O'Reilly's May 2004 online paper "The Open-Source Paradigm Shift" is the rare essay that changes how you see the world the moment you read it. In the spirit of the ideas the essay champions, it is freely available on the Web (http://tim.oreilly.com). A subsequent essay, "What Is Web 2.0?" expands O'Reilly's earlier arguments and is just as compelling.

work with? Is it a magnet for brainpower, wherever those brains may be located? Organizations with compelling answers to these questions are the ones that will build the most enduring competitive advantage in the years ahead.

COLLABORATION . . . COMPETITION . . . COMEDY?
DESIGNING AN ARCHITECTURE OF PARTICIPATION

When Tim O'Reilly explains the architecture of participation, he, like so many of his fellow technology evangelists, roots his ideas and case studies in search, photography, music, and other forms of computer software and digital media. He also emphasizes the creative breakthroughs that can result when millions of people collaborate, formally and informally, in the "many-to-many" style of the Web. As *BusinessWeek* put it in an ecstatic cover story called "The Power of Us," the "nearly 1 billion people online worldwide—along with their shared knowledge, social contacts, online reputations, computing power, and more—are rapidly becoming a collective force of unprecedented power. For the first time in human history, mass cooperation across time and space is finally economical."[6]

True enough. But it's possible to misunderstand (and thus misinterpret) much of what is happening with grassroots innovation. Two points merit special emphasis. First, so much of peer-to-peer collaboration, it turns out, is fueled by an intense (and intensely personal) spirit of *competition*—a spirit that comes naturally to business settings of all kinds. One of the most powerful ways for lots of people to work together as a group is to compete against one another as individuals. Second, while it's the technology pundits who tend to dominate the conversation about the new logic of creativity, there is nothing that limits these ideas to the virtual space of the Internet or the borders of Silicon Valley. Embracing open-source innovation is as much a leadership mind-set as it is a product development methodology, and open-minded leaders can apply these ideas in fields far beyond the realm of cutting-edge geekdom.

But first let's hear from the geeks. If you want to appreciate the competitive underpinnings of open-source collaboration, pay a virtual visit to TopCoder, Inc., a for-profit, all-business twist on Linux, Apache, and other grassroots approaches to creating high-performance software. Founder Jack Hughes describes TopCoder as "open source meets capitalism"—and the moment you see his business model in action, you understand what he means. This is, indeed, a geek's paradise. The company, based outside Hartford, Connecticut, was founded in April 2002, and has been on a rocket ship ride ever since. As of February 2006, Top-Coder had attracted nearly 75,000 individual programmers from nearly 190 countries as registered members. A big chunk of the company's business is writing sophisticated software for blue-chip clients such as ABB, Philip Morris, and ING. TopCoder signs a contract to build a computer application for one of these big-name companies, divides up the application into a collection of discrete software components, and then turns its members loose to create the code in an open-source style, with everyone eligible to contribute and everyone's work visible to everyone else. (The identities of the client companies almost always stay secret, however.)

But here's the twist: these programmers collaborate to produce great code by vying fiercely in head-to-head competitions. Their work is organized as a series of online matches (as well as live, on-site tournaments) in which TopCoder members battle deadlines (and one another) to design and write the most elegant components and impress a jury of their peers. These competitions are dripping with geek machismo: members boast about their technical prowess, talk trash about their rivals, and aren't afraid to express outrage (and file appeals) when they don't win.

"Competition is at the core of this company," explains CEO Hughes, who exudes a hard-charging, take-no-prisoners attitude. "Great performers tend to be naturally competitive. They want to know where they stand, they want to know how good they are. They also want to be challenged, to improve their skills. If you ask any top person in any field, 'How do you improve?' they will tell you, 'By working with people who are better than me.' So the question for them becomes, 'How do I get a chance to work with, and compete against, people who are better than me?' " Hughes's answer, of course, is for them to join TopCoder.

What are these programmers competing *for,* exactly? Money is one obvious prize. The sprawling TopCoder community includes a remark-able number of young programming guns from low-wage countries (China, India, Romania, Poland) who have earned tens of thousands of dollars (in some cases, more than $100,000) by winning software-writing competitions. (As of mid-2005, TopCoder had distributed more than $2 million in prize money.) Recognition matters too. The TopCoder Web site tracks the performance of individual programmers the way the *Bill James Handbook* grades baseball players. All members get a personal statistics card (visible to all other members) that lists every competition they've entered, how often they've won, and how much money they've made. Ultimately, all that data get boiled down to a nu-merical rating that captures how an individual member stacks up against every other member of the community. If you're not confident (even a little cocky) about your abilities, TopCoder is not for you.

Adic (that's his TopCoder handle), a twentysomething programmer born in Bistrita, a small town in Romania, is a classic example of who thrives in TopCoder's ultracompetitive open-source environment. He's a talented software designer working on his second master's degree, and he's won lots of competitions (including 21 of the 26 Java design challenges he's entered). All told, he's earned nearly $71,000 from TopCoder—serious money by Romanian standards—all of which he has banked to buy a house.

But money, Adic insists in an e-mail interview, is not what keeps him writing code for TopCoder. The two big draws are the sheer energy of competing against other programmers and the opportunity to improve his skills. "Of course," he adds, "without the money I couldn't afford to spend all the time [I spend on TopCoder]." So "I guess money is important, but it's not *why* I do it. It's what *allows* me to do it."

Wishingbone (that's his TopCoder handle) is another twentysomething graduate student. He's based in Hangzhou, China, and he's won nearly $20,000 from TopCoder competitions—again, serious money in his part of the world. For Wishingbone, the most memorable part of the experience has been the recognition he's received. Over e-mail, he explains how meaningful it was to win the competition that made him a "red member" of TopCoder (that is, a programmer with a rating greater than 2200). "I was the first red member from my school," he says, "and I think I was the first red member from China. In the past, people would say, 'Wishingbone has solved thousands of [software] problems, or Wishingbone is the chief judge for a programming contest at Zhejiang University. Now they just say, 'Wishingbone is a TopCoder.' "*

It's hard to overstate the competitive zeal on the "component" side of TopCoder's business—that is, the business of writing commercial software for big-company clients. But that zeal can't compare with what happens on the "algorithm" side, a high-profile business that has put Top-Coder at the center of the most competitive frontier of technology—the competition for top-flight programming talent.

With algorithms, as with components, big-name companies (including Yahoo, Google, Microsoft, Intel, and Sun Microsystems) pay TopCoder to unleash its grassroots army of programmers. Unlike with components, though, these programmers don't compete to write commercial applications for a specific client. They compete *simply to compete*—to solve digital brainteasers under tight deadlines, great pressure, and the intense

---

*The imagery here is so delicious, it's impossible to resist the obvious comment: we now live in a world where being "red" in Red China says as much about your programming prowess as your Communist credentials.

scrutiny of their peers. Sponsors like Yahoo and Google watch the competitions carefully, valuing the chance to get their name in front of some of the world's most talented young programmers—and to offer jobs to competitors who stand out.* In 2005, for example, TopCoder organized Google's first-ever "India Code Jam," which attracted 14,000 first-round registrants. There was plenty of prize money at stake, but the 50 finalists won something even more valuable—job offers from the hottest company in the world.

The so-called Competition Arena, where the weekly online software-writing tournaments take place, is itself an impressive piece of software. The site contains a practice area, chat rooms, and real-time leader boards. Participants and spectators alike thrive on the rush of simultaneously competing, analyzing the competition, and practicing against the competition in a completely transparent environment.

Even the most intense competitors, Hughes says, love to explain themselves to other TopCoders. "The competition arena is designed to facilitate interaction and education," he explains. "In the chat rooms and discussion forums, members talk endlessly about the last match—who won, who didn't, and why. We put an analysis of every match written by a member up on the site. And the arena is always full of trash talk and discussion during a match. That's what pulls the members together. When we have the on-site matches, they're all dying to get together to meet one another."

The on-site matches (called "the TopCoder Open" and "the Top-Coder Collegiate Challenge") pump up the drama even higher. The top-seeded coders meet face to face, onstage, under bright lights. Film crews and a rowdy audience watch as the contestants furrow their brows and strut their stuff. Some of them are draped in the flag of their home

---

*Talk about a global talent pool. The 2005 TopCoder Collegiate Challenge, sponsored by Yahoo, brought to Santa Clara, California, 24 finalists from 10 countries, including the Netherlands, China, Poland, Croatia, Norway, Australia, and the Slovak Republic.

country; others clutch good-luck charms. Everyone is on the edge of their seats. The tension spirals with each round, as the world's top young programmers inch forward and slide back in the rankings based on the quality of their code and their skills at picking apart code written by the competition.

These are the exciting images and wrenching emotions that have made TopCoder such a high-profile force in the computer industry. (Indeed, it's hard to find a big-name software company that isn't a sponsor of a TopCoder tournament.) But the reality, says Hughes, is less dramatic. "The vast majority of the time spent on the TopCoder site is in the *practice* rooms," he explains. "Thousands of our members never compete, never get a rating. They're just trying to improve their skills. From a member perspective, the site is built around education as well as competition."

That's the essential link between collaboration and competition, between collective innovation and individual initiative. By competing *against* one another in a thoroughly transparent environment, talented programmers are learning *from* each other—and building software together in the process. It is an architecture of participation that works on several levels simultaneously, which may be why it is working so effectively in the marketplace. "At our core," says CEO Jack Hughes, "we are a talent management company. I'm a huge believer in open source, but I'm also a huge believer in capitalism. Everything we do is designed to allow software designers and programmers to capture the value they create. We are enablers of the individual."

But enough about competition among high-testosterone geeks. How about an open-source approach to music, or comedy, or even Shakespeare? This speaks to our second point of emphasis about designing an effective architecture of participation: *it's not just an online phenomenon.* To look for evidence of how that mind-set can reshape the creative landscape in fields far beyond science and technology, look no further than the green fields and rugged landscape of Scotland.

Every August, artists, producers, talent scouts, and ticket holders flock to Scotland for the annual Edinburgh Fringe Festival, a dawn-to-dusk display of artistic talent. The festival was born in 1947 when a few gate-crashers decided to perform on the "fringe" of the world-famous Edinburgh International Festival. Nearly 60 years later, the fringe dwarfs the main event. In 2005 the Fringe Festival sold 1.25 million tickets to a three-week gathering that offered nearly 27,000 performances involving more than 16,000 performers in 1,800 shows hosted by nearly 250 venues.[7]

This onetime symbol of artistic rebellion is now the largest arts gathering in the world, although it's lost little of its capacity to amaze and confound. Sure, there's plenty of Shakespeare, both traditional and avant-garde, theatrical revivals, and a fair share of sketch comedy. But the heart and soul of the festival is work that is daring, experimental, and sometimes downright weird. During the 2004 Fringe, the *New York Times* marveled at the range of offerings in Edinburgh. A well-reviewed show called *A Mobile Thriller* literally took place in the backseat of an Audi, playing to three audience members at a time. One of the hottest tickets, noted the *Times,* was to a one-man show called *Jackson's Way,* a brutal comic take on an American motivational speaker. Meanwhile, a short walk away, Christian Slater was starring to mixed reviews in a theatrical remake of the Jack Nicholson film *One Flew Over the Cuckoo's Nest.*

Paul Gudgin, the Fringe's artistic director since 1999, calls the festival "the world's greatest artistic incubator." What happens at the Fringe affects the arts scene worldwide. Every year the best-received dramas and musicals get scooped up for runs in New York, London, and other major cities. In 2005 some 2,000 journalists and critics chronicled the hits, misses, and offbeat performances of the three-week extravaganza. Winning the festival's most prestigious prize, the Perrier Award for comedy, often called the Oscar of comedy, can be a fast-track ticket to stardom.

But the Fringe is more than performance art. It is a colorful symbol of the performance of open-source innovation. Making the Fringe come to life is a massive business challenge in terms of both creative decisions and logistics. Who gets to perform? What's the right blend of comedy and drama, music and theater? Who performs in which venue? Who markets each event? Yet here's the amazing part: *no one is in charge of the Fringe*—certainly not in the conventional sense of that word. Although his title is artistic director, Gudgin doesn't decide who performs or where, and he doesn't influence the overall mix of performances. "We have no artistic guru, no committee, no guiding body of any kind," he explains. "Yet an extraordinary cluster of performers turns up every year to move the mix in a new direction."

So what makes the Fringe function? A carefully designed architecture of participation that blends wild-eyed creativity with the spirit of unblinking competition. Gudgin and his colleagues lead the largest and one of the most influential arts gatherings in the world by making the festival as compelling as possible to as many participants as possible—and then letting the participants themselves decide what happens. "The analogy with [open-source] software is interesting," Gudgin says. "In the arts, everyone wants to be the curator or the creative director—it's the ultimate auteur position. At the Fringe, we have to be the exact opposite. Our job is to get the circumstances absolutely right, to sell the whole experience, to make it as inviting as possible to anybody who could possibly contribute. We can't curate new ideas into existence."

Essentially, the Fringe is a self-organizing system governed by the self-interested calculations of four key constituencies: the performers, the venues, the audience, and the press. Any troupe or individual artist is eligible to perform; the challenge is to persuade one of the 250 venues to host your show. There is a well-understood hierarchy of venues in Edinburgh—certain theaters have more status than others—and different venues use different criteria to evaluate performers. Once you're in, the challenge is to separate yourself from the crowd—to persuade visitors to attend your show as opposed to one of the hundreds of others taking place at the same time—and to persuade the critics that yours is a show worth reviewing. "You have to hit the ground running at the Fringe," Gudgin says. "The audience has to make so many choices so quickly— you have to be a true standout if you want them to choose you. But if you can make your show work among the 1,700 shows at the Fringe, chances are it'll work in the wider marketplace."

There are no hard-and-fast rules to competing for attention. The most obvious way to generate buzz is to win a major award early in the festival. In 2005 Kahlil Ashanti opened his one-man show *Basic Training* to a literally empty house. (In the show Ashanti plays 23 different characters as he chronicles his tough life and unlikely stint in the U.S. Air Force, where he joined the Tops in Blue entertainment brigade.) But by the end of the festival, after winning a prestigious Fringe First award, he was performing to sold-out crowds and found himself featured in a *New York Times* account of that year's proceedings. Some performers spend big money on marketing their shows. Others rely on outrageous stunts—such as guerrilla theater in the streets of Edinburgh. Still others rely on truly counterintuitive strategies. One of the fastest-selling tickets at the 2003 Fringe was a "secret show" by Johnny Vegas, a British comedian. In a marketing twist that would make Yogi Berra proud, everyone wanted to attend the Johnny Vegas stand-up comedy performance because nobody knew about it.

"It's very difficult to *impose* success at the Fringe," Gudgin says. "It has to happen organically. It's very much like a market—or like going to a horse race. Everyone is collecting tips about which shows to bet on. People spend quite a bit of time standing in line, waiting to get tickets, talking about what they've seen. There's a hugely efficient grapevine that goes on in Edinburgh." Even the festival's artistic director can't put his finger on how any particular show manages to get heard through the grapevine: "If [a performance] grips the imagination and excites conversation, it's a success. But it's quite brutal. If you turn up with last year's story, you won't attract any attention."

The real genius of the Fringe—and its key lesson for business and innovation—is not which kinds of shows work, but how the entire festival manages not only to work but to get bigger and more important every year. The Fringe's architecture of participation centers on the answer to that age-old dramatic question: what's my motivation? Gudgin and his colleagues have a keen understanding of the reasons why so many artists are so eager to present their best work in Edinburgh. They understand the rules of attraction that make the Fringe a magnet for top-flight performers.

For some, it's important to be part of an occasion bigger than themselves. "Real artists are artists to the core," Gudgin says. "To be even a small part of this extraordinary gallery, with 17,000 other performers, means something." For others, it's important to embrace competition in its purest form. "If you're a true athlete, you want to be at the Olympics," Gudgin says. "Even if you know you're not going to win the gold medal, you want to see where you rank against the peers. The same goes for the performers who come to the Fringe."

Finally, and perhaps most universally, the Fringe presents a one-of-a-kind chance for performers to make a splash, turn heads, be discovered. "You rarely make money in Edinburgh," Gudgin says. "But you can make your career. We've got thousands of journalists at the festival. You have a better chance of getting your work reviewed here than anywhere else in the world. This is a proving ground, a way to raise your profile, a place to get noticed."

From the point of view of the audience, the Fringe looks like a free-wheeling, uproarious, basically altruistic arts festival. From the point of view of the performers, it is a demanding, high-stakes, brutally intense competitive arena—which is why they are likely to deliver their most inspired work. What works every summer in Edinburgh has worked in so many of the situations we have encountered in this chapter—an architecture of participation through which head-to-head competition leads to group collaboration. To make your organization as competitive as possible, maximize the opportunities to collaborate with as many smart people as possible outside your organization. To maximize the effectiveness of this grassroots collaboration, encourage participants to compete with one another—and learn from one another in the process. To maximize what *you* learn from the process, minimize the natural leadership instinct to control what happens among the participants.

That last point may be the toughest to embrace. As a leader, Paul Gudgin is constantly preaching the virtues of self-restraint—*to himself.* Every year, no matter how successful the Fringe has been, outside criticisms and second-guesses inevitably arise—too much comedy, not enough avant-garde drama, too few super-popular shows (or *too many* super-popular shows, which means the Fringe is playing it safe). And every year Gudgin and his colleagues fight the temptation to use their authority to fine-tune either the performances or the mix.

"Our job is to do the absolute minimum necessary to make this event happen," he says emphatically. "The *worst* thing we could do is to decide what kind of festival Edinburgh should be, to engage in what I call programming through the back door. My most important responsibility is to make sure that the people who decide what the festival should be are the artists and the audience. What we have to do at all times is to make as few rules as possible."

Chapter Five

Innovation, Inc.:
Open Source Gets Down to Business

We understand that to tough-minded executives who are on the line to deliver reliable short-term performance and create long-term economic value, open-source innovation can feel messy, chaotic, even strange. Self-managed, volunteer hackers who pool their skills and wind up competing with the most powerful technology company in the world? Thousands of solo programmers who compete head to head to build software that's bought by companies with which they have no contact (and whose identities they don't even know)? Tens of thousands of actors and singers and comedians who converge on a city in Scotland to create an arts festival that nobody runs but for which more than a million people buy tickets? It's nothing if not a mind-shift.

But we're convinced that the outside-in logic of transparent, decentralized, grassroots creativity is poised to reshape strategy and executive leadership just as dramatically as it's reshaping science and the arts. Indeed, leading open-source evangelists are making the connection between the roots of their software and the future of corporate innovation. Meanwhile, influential figures from an array of big, important global companies are incorporating principles and practices from open source into how they organize R&D and launch new products. Two worlds are colliding—and not just in the pages of a sci-fi novel. In this chapter, we explore what happens when open-source innovation gets down to business.

Eric Raymond is a provocative writer, an engaging speaker, and an accomplished programmer. He is also one of the most visible proponents of the power of open-source innovation. If Linus Torvalds is the George Washington of Linux, the movement's founding father and trusted general, then Raymond is its Tom Paine—a controversial pamphleteer and polemicist who rallies the faithful, rails against perceived foes, and explains the cause to outsiders.* Raymond's 1997 online essay "The Cathedral and the Bazaar," which was later published as a book, remains the movement's defining manifesto. It is to the open-source revolution what *Common Sense* was to the American Revolution.[1]

Raymond is amazed, and more than a little amused, by how a set of ideas hatched on the periphery of the computer world is now at the center of a worldwide conversation about the future of creativity itself. "Five years ago, I was a nutty radical," he chuckles. "Now I'm in the mainstream. And watch for this model to ramp up exponentially as people figure out how effective it is."

Raymond is reluctant to draw sweeping conclusions about broader applications of open-source programming to business and innovation. ("When I step too far away from software," he worries, "I weaken my case. I'm very cautious about speculating about other fields.") But there

---

*True to the hacker spirit, Raymond is as offbeat as he is accomplished. In addition to open-source software, his other great passion is firearms. He runs a Web site called "Geeks with Guns" and has organized firearms-training sessions at Linux conventions. "Geeks and guns are a natural match," he has said. "Open-source software is about getting freedom; personal firearms are about keeping it."

are a few conclusions he is prepared to draw—conclusions that leaders who are serious about innovation must take seriously.

"The open-source movement clearly demonstrates that the more smart people you can persuade to work on a problem, the more likely it is to get solved," he says. "Writing code may be a solitary activity, but all the really great hacks have come from harnessing the attention and brainpower of entire communities. Developers who use their own brainpower in a closed project are going to fall behind developers who know how to create an open, evolutionary context in which hundreds or thousands of people are spotting bugs and making improvements."

"There's another lesson that's really obvious," he continues. "You cannot motivate the best people with money. Money is just a way to keep score. The best people in any field are motivated by passion. That becomes more true the higher the skill level gets. People do their best work when they are passionately engaged in what they're doing."

But don't confuse passion, he reminds business leaders, or the grass-roots spirit of open source, with a lack of toughness or a reluctance to compete. (TopCoder is certainly a vivid example of that insight.) "The open-source world is fiercely competitive," Raymond emphasizes. "People like being part of a community in which they compete for their peers' esteem. People want to believe that they're working—and competing—with the best people in their field. I routinely deal with people who are the best programmers in the world. If you're working for a company, you measure yourself against a few hundred colleagues. If you're working on a piece of open-source code, you might measure yourself against thousands of people all over the world."

What goes for free-spirited hackers, Raymond adds, applies to tough–minded entrepreneurs and company-builders as well. Ultimately, open-source innovation is more than a new way for individuals to display their talents. It's a new way for organizations to beat their rivals. "In the twenty-first century," he argues, "one of the ways that companies are going to compete—and this goes beyond software—is to compete for the attention of outside brainpower. How does the company persuade smart people, whom the CEO or the head of HR has never met, to volunteer their energy, their intelligence, and a few hours of their time to help the company perfect a product or improve an idea? Companies that successfully attract outside brainpower will absolutely eat the lunch of companies that don't."

Larry Huston, vice president of innovation at Procter & Gamble, has almost nothing in common with the fast-talking, code-writing, gun-toting Eric Raymond. Huston is a company man in the best sense of that word, a P&G lifer who exudes a fierce sense of loyalty to the world's largest manufacturer of branded consumer products, a global giant that sells a vast array of household products that are truly household names. Yet Huston is also a corporate disrupter, the sort of high-impact leader who time and again finds himself working with the company's CEO and senior executives to unleash what he calls "major discontinuities" in how P&G does business—from globalizing its product introduction strategies in the 1980s to reckoning with the "shopper revolution" at Wal-Mart and other power retailers in the 1990s. "I'm an odd duck," Huston says with obvious pride. "I've been promoted throughout my career, but nearly every job I've been promoted into is a job that I created. I have never 'replaced' anyone. I've always created new space for myself."

Huston's office in Cincinnati, adjacent to a 200-acre manufacturing complex known as Ivorydale (after Ivory soap of course), sits in the very building where P&G did some of its earliest industrial research more than 120 years ago. It looks every bit the 19th-century lab—an unpretentious building with long hallways, dim lighting, and no-nonsense offices. From inside this symbol of big business history, Huston is leading a transformation of R&D that borrows directly from the logic of open-source software. "This is a major, major change," he says. "We are trying to transform, in a really discontinuous way, our whole approach to innovation."

Huston makes his case with the fervor of a convert. "The current business model for R&D is broken," he argues. "It will not survive. In most companies, R&D budgets are rising faster than the rate of sales growth. That is not sustainable. And the explosion of technology is unbelievable. Today P&G has to look at the biosciences, we have to look at nanotechnology, we have to use cutting-edge software and computing. How can we build all of the scientific capabilities we need by ourselves?"[2]

The answer, of course, is that it can't. Not even a company as big and rich as P&G can afford a do-it-yourself approach to innovation— not in a world where thousands, tens of thousands, *hundreds* of thousands of well-trained researchers are working in labs in Russia, China, and India on all kinds of innovations that are relevant to the company's huge assortment of brands.

That's why Huston is convinced that P&G must look outside the walls of its celebrated research labs, and beyond the breakthroughs of its full-time scientists, to tap the brainpower of the whole world. Even though P&G employs many of the smartest scientists and engineers in their fields, the company's vice president of innovation understands that nobody is as smart as everybody—and not everybody can work for P&G.

"We have 7,500 R&D people who operate in 150 different areas of science," Huston explains. "But when you look around the world at these 150 areas, you see that there are one and a half *million* people outside of P&G with training that is equal to or better than our people. In other words, for every one person we have in a particular area, there are 200 people on the outside of equal minds or better. Now, it's pretty obvious that 200 can invent better than one—you don't have to be a genius to figure that out."

It's Huston's mission to figure out how Procter & Gamble can tap into that outside genius. His initiative, called Connect+Develop (that's C+D, as distinct from R&D), has a mandate to help the consumer giant import half of all new technologies and product ideas from beyond the walls of the company. It's hard for an outsider, Huston says, to appreciate the stakes of this shift: "Here you have a nearly one-hundred-seventy-year-old company with an unbelievable sense of pride in its science and marketing. And we're viewing the outside world as the other half of our R&D lab. It's an absolute sea change."

In the spirit of a sea change, Huston is unleashing a tidal wave of entrepreneurial and intrapreneurial programs. One strategy is to be more open-minded about how the company looks at and listens to the outside world. Huston handpicked 60 scientists and engineers from P&G's labs, took them away from their test tubes and microscopes, and named them "technology entrepreneurs." These technology entrepreneurs, who have been dispatched to Europe, China, Japan, India, and Latin America, are P&G's elite scouts in the battle to discover innovations beyond the walls of the company. They visit government and university labs, get to know important scientists and professors, walk trade show floors, even prowl the aisles of supermarkets, looking for innovations that P&G can bring in-house to create new products or improve existing ones.

Ed Getty, a PhD scientist and 17-year P&G veteran, was one of the company's first technology entrepreneurs. Now his job is to make sure that all 60 of his peripatetic colleagues swap ideas with one another as well as with the outside world. "We are internal champions for external ideas," he says. "Our job is to look outside, find disruptive technologies and products, and bring them back to the company. We're innovating on how we innovate. This is a real game-changer for us."

A second strategy is to become a magnet for outside ideas—to create and dominate a "deal flow" for innovation in the same way that venture capitalists cultivate a deal flow of worthwhile business plans. So Huston is creating and championing third-party "innovation networks" that reach around the world—idea pipelines that keep P&G in the global flow of creativity. For example, P&G teamed with pharmaceutical giant

Eli Lilly to help structure Your Encore, an Indianapolis-based company that matches retired scientists and engineers—talented people still brimming with energy and ideas—with idea-hungry companies that could benefit from a jolt of outside expertise, skills, and experience. Huston is also a tireless champion of NineSigma, a fast-growing outfit in Cleveland that has built what it calls a "Managed Exchange"—an Internet-based global network through which companies can issue a call for help to researchers around the world, any one of whom may be hired to deliver a solution. Forget sending a run-of-the-mill RFP (request for proposal) to the same old suppliers. NineSigma uses the Web to identify the best minds in a wide variety of fields and sends targeted RFPs to every corner of the world. The basic premise: it's extremely likely that some bright researcher, somewhere in the world, has already solved the problem on which your bright researchers are working. The trick is finding those outside researchers and persuading them to work with you.

"Innovation is all about networks," Huston says. "It's about making connections, combining things, moving things from one domain to another. P&G has always been masterful at making connections internally. I can show you diagrams of how our early work in soaps, combined with our understanding of calcium, led to our work in dental care, which led to our work in osteoporosis, where we are on our way to establishing a billion-dollar drug. The ability to make these kinds of connections *externally* has the promise to revolutionize R&D."

NineSigma doesn't sound all that revolutionary—until, that is, you travel to Cleveland, spend some time at the company's headquarters, and begin to appreciate its breathtaking global reach. Think of NineSigma as a worldwide search engine for R&D—a human-powered Google searching out good ideas. "We think we've got a secret sauce here," says CEO Paul Stiros. "We have a self-expanding network of the world's most qualified researchers. We can find people who don't know anything about us, get a technology brief in front of them, and do so in a way that's clear, concise, and compelling. We can find, directly or indirectly, anybody in the world who has knowledge, experience, or expertise that's relevant to our clients' needs."

If you think that sounds boastful, consider the statistics. According to Charles Brez, NineSigma's top marketing executive, the National Science Foundation estimates that there are three million peer-level practitioners (people doing top-flight work) in science and technology around the world. NineSigma has already gathered and organized the names, affiliations, backgrounds, areas of interest—*and e-mail addresses*—of more than one million of these researchers, and its database will soon be pushing one and a half million e-mail addresses.

It's a virtual mother lode of scientific expertise from every corner of the globe. When P&G, or General Motors, or Avery Dennison, or one of NineSigma's 50-plus big-company clients runs into a problem it can't solve or begins exploring a new field of research, NineSigma sketches out a technical brief, puts it in front of literally thousands of scientists and engineers with relevant interests and experience, and invites them to submit proposals to work with the company. "We are a massively parallel operation," explains Shauna Brummet, a PhD molecular biologist who is vice president of operations for NineSigma. "We can contact thousands of people, present a very specific need, and say, 'Here's the opportunity, here's the company you get to work with, why don't you submit a great idea?'" (A NineSigma brief typically goes to anywhere from 5,000 to 15,000 researchers and generates anywhere from a handful of proposals to more than a hundred.)

It's the ultimate flip on the age-old not-invented-here syndrome: in this era of scientific surplus, why would any organization work to invent in its own labs something that has already been invented somewhere else? "What we try to stress to companies," says CEO Stiros, "is that anytime you start a new project, anytime you size up a new technical problem, you ought to look outside your walls before you reinvent the wheel. This should become a routine part of the innovation process:

bring in solutions that are available from the outside. It's amazing to think there are people inside big companies spending millions of dollars to rediscover knowledge that already exists!"

Stiros isn't just speaking as the boss of NineSigma—he's been a satisfied customer as well. He signed on to run the company in September 2004 after a 28-year career at Procter & Gamble. Stiros was a longtime colleague and fellow traveler of Larry Huston and the Connect+Develop crowd. Indeed, Stiros helped champion some of P&G's most notable outside-in product innovations, including the Swiffer duster, Mr. Clean AutoDry, and a room freshener called Scentsories by Febreze. He became so hooked on NineSigma's scour-the-world capabilities and so convinced of its impact on his operation that he couldn't resist the chance to run the company when he was given the opportunity. All told, as of June 2005, P&G alone had commissioned more than 100 projects with NineSigma. "This is such a cost-effective way to do business," argues Stiros. "The researchers we find have invented their solutions already, for another reason. So their costs have already been sunk."

If you want to get under Larry Huston's skin, ask him if NineSigma and Connect+Develop are just fancy names for outsourcing—clever schemes that wind up encouraging true-blue American icons like Procter & Gamble to ship work to India, China, and other countries loaded with low-cost technical talent. "That's not it at all," he objects. "We're *insourcing* other people's ideas. We're not taking what we're doing already and sending it to India. We want to be in a position where when somebody in India has a great idea, an idea that will grow our business, we bring it back to P&G and ask our researchers to figure out, how do we put this in the marketplace and create value? This is about P&G working on other people's ideas, not other people working on our ideas."*

---

*Which is not to suggest that P&G, as a corporation, doesn't do its fair share of traditional computer technology outsourcing. Back in 2003, P&G signed what was then the biggest outsourcing deal of all time, as Hewlett-Packard won a 10-year, $3 billion contract to manage P&G's IT infrastructure.

To reinforce his point, Huston likes to contrast how P&G taps into the technical riches of Bangalore, India, the unofficial outsourcing capital of the world, with how most Fortune 500 conglomerates operate in the region. Unlike senior colleagues at so many corporate giants, Huston doesn't want to relocate well-defined, internal R&D to India. Instead, he wants to get early access to newfangled research that Indian professors and companies are doing on their own. So rather than building vast laboratories that employ hundreds or thousands of full-time researchers, P&G is building a small, 60-person "listening post" in Bangalore where a Connect+Develop team will scour university labs, government institutes, and small-company research departments, looking for outside innovations that P&G can put to work inside the company.

Huston is adamant. He is searching for what he calls "cooked" products and "ready-to-go" technologies—innovations that P&G can discover, adapt, and apply to launch more new products more quickly, with an emphasis on *quickly*. In just one year, he says, his various Connect+Develop initiatives around the world sifted through 10,000 ideas from the outside, identified 2,000 that warranted a closer look, whittled those down to 500 positive technical assessments, and launched 100 new products. "We've got networks all over the world now," he says. "We're putting a turbocharger on our R&D organization."

These products are a long way from the plot of science fiction novels or the intricacies of Internet operating systems—which is what makes them so relevant and important for mainstream business. One small example is the Mr. Clean Magic Eraser, a cleaning pad for the kitchen. Huston lights up when he talks about the Magic Eraser ("my wife *loves* the product"), which has been a big hit in the U.S. market. How did P&G clean up on the Magic Eraser? One of Huston's technology entrepreneurs in Japan learned about a new kind of foam that was making its way onto supermarket shelves. Originally, the foam was used as car insulation and packaging material—until a Japanese businessman noticed that when the material got wet, it developed an abrasive quality that was great for cleaning the home. This technology entrepreneur also learned that one of P&G's major suppliers, chemical giant BASF, made the foam for the Japanese market. So P&G licensed the material, contracted with BASF, and presto—a new product was cleaning America's kitchens, with virtually no traditional R&D required from Procter & Gamble.

Another small example is Pringle's Prints. P&G's famous stacked potato chips now come printed (using edible dyes) with images of movie characters (from family films such as *Madagascar*), trivia and factoids (culled from "Trivial Pursuit Junior" and the *2006 Guinness World Records* book), tidbits about television series, and questions from board games. The idea for Pringle's Prints originated inside P&G rather than outside. One day, the story goes, an employee got so excited about her brainstorm that she ran paper-thin potato dough through an ink-jet printer to see what would happen. ("Can you imagine the reaction when she called the computer help desk?" Huston quips.) But rather than assign a team of P&G researchers to solve the technical challenges of printing images onto mass quantities of potato chips, P&G tapped one of Huston's technology networks to scour the world for a "ready-to-go" solution—someone, somewhere, who was already doing something close to what P&G wanted to do.

That search quickly led to a bakery in Bologna, Italy, which had become a master at applying ink-jet printing with edible dyes to cakes and other foods. Of course, an obscure Italian bakery was in no position to operate on the mega-scale that P&G required. So the company licensed the technology from the bakery, worked with a major supplier, and outfitted its plant in Jackson, Tennessee, with the technology to make Pringle's Prints. "We had this product on the market in less than a year," Huston says. "What blows your mind is that solutions can come so quickly from the most unobvious people."

WHAT'S IN IT FOR ME?
THE ART OF THE OPEN-SOURCE DEAL

There's something exciting, alluring, and downright inspiring about the advance of Linux, the self-organizing logic of the world's largest arts festival, even the surprising story of the creation of a new potato chip. The image is irresistible: smart, passionate, self-confident engineers and entrepreneurs, scattered around the world, collaborating and competing to write software, solve problems, and design products. But business is about more than irresistible images. It's about costs and benefits, winners and losers, terms and conditions. That's why open source is about more than a new model of innovation. It's about the art of the deal. If you want to tap the best brains in the world, you've got to create compelling reasons for smart people to work with you.

Think back to the Goldcorp Challenge. Almost instinctively, Rob McEwen understood how a Linux-inspired competition could transform the prospects for his Red Lake mine. But he also understood that for the Challenge to work, it had to be about more than helping his company discover gold. It had to be about helping his industry discover the talents of the participants—raising their visibility and transforming their prospects for the future. McEwen had to make an offer that the world's best geologists couldn't refuse.

Indeed, perhaps the most critical design principle behind the Goldcorp Challenge was McEwen's open-source approach to the outcome. A year after he unveiled the competition to a skeptical audience of industry bigwigs, he returned to the annual gathering of prospectors and developers to announce the results—*with the winners in hand*. Far from keeping their insights to himself, McEwen shared the wealth of ideas with his rivals. He sponsored a daylong symposium in which the semifinalists and finalists presented their techniques and methodologies to the gold-mining industry, which was now fascinated by the global outpouring of brainpower.

For the participants, this moment in the spotlight was the real prize—and the biggest reason so many smart people were so eager to offer their best ideas to Goldcorp. Sure, the chance to win a six-figure award helped persuade geologists and scientists from 51 countries to submit drilling plans to a Canadian mining company run by a guy they'd never met. But money was a minor motivation. What mattered more was the opportunity to play on a world stage, the chance to strut their stuff before the whole industry. "It's a way to create superstars," McEwen argues, "to give people worldwide recognition they can't get in a traditional workplace. For some of our winners, it was literally a life-changing experience."

He's not exaggerating. Nick Archibald, a hard-charging geologist from West Perth, Australia, saw the Challenge as a chance to demonstrate how his proprietary graphics software could revolutionize mineral exploration. (It was his winning entry that almost knocked McEwen off his chair.) Archibald's virtual 3-D model of Goldcorp's ore body put his young outfit on the map and attracted clients from around the world. His company, Geoinformatics Exploration Inc., is publicly traded in Toronto on the TSX Venture Exchange.

For Mark O'Dea, the second-place winner, the impact of the Challenge was virtually instantaneous. On the day after the public ceremony, two longtime mining executives persuaded the Canadian geologist to join them in a new venture. Their target? Just as McEwen's colleagues had predicted, they staked out land next to Goldcorp's mine. Prior to the Challenge, O'Dea was struggling to make his mark in the mining industry and had spent six months on assignment in India for Phelps Dodge. That's a long way from his position as president and CEO of Fronteer Development Group, which, among other holdings, controls tens of thousands of acres in the Red Lake region.[3]

For third-place winner Alexander Yakubchuk, the rewards were personal as well as professional. For years the Russian geologist, a former professor at Moscow State University, had been eager to apply his talents in the West. His $75,000 in prize money gave him the means to move his family to London. He took a position with Britain's Natural History Museum and then became a London-based exploration manager for Gold Fields Limited, one of the giants in the mining industry. "I had some visibility before because of my academic work," Yakubchuk says. "But the Challenge enhanced my visibility internationally."

In other words, just below the surface of this open-minded flow of ideas were some hardheaded business calculations. Gifted geologists like Archibald, O'Dea, and Yakubchuk helped McEwen find gold. McEwen helped the geologists glitter in the eyes of their peers—and realize the next stage of their careers or entrepreneurial plans. "I'm naturally curious," the Goldcorp chairman says. "I *love* ideas. And all of us have ideas that apply beyond what we're doing right now: our current job, our current field, what part of the world we live in. That's what we wanted to unleash and attract. To do that, we had to change the status of the people who won, to help them gain fame and fortune, to create real value for them as well as us."

Darren Carroll has spent years working on the challenge of turning the promise of open-source innovation into real business value. A veteran of Eli Lilly, Carroll was the pharmaceutical giant's lead U.S. attorney for Prozac before he became CEO of InnoCentive, a "virtual R&D lab" financed by Lilly and based in suburban Boston. InnoCentive's cofounder and big-time corporate sponsor was Alph Bingham, an accomplished researcher, high-level executive, 27-year Lilly veteran, and creator of e.Lilly, an internal think tank and venture capital operation that helps Lilly conduct experiments not on future drugs but on the future of innovation itself.

Darren Carroll, Alph Bingham, and Larry Huston are friends, peers, and fellow travelers. They all backed the creation of Your Encore, they all tout the virtues of NineSigma, and they all champion the performance of InnoCentive. Yet Bingham, unlike Huston, initially positioned his future-focused operation outside the corporate mainstream. The offices of e.Lilly are about 20 miles away from Lilly headquarters, and they exude a playful style that evokes the dot-com days. Conference rooms are named after famous artists: Chagall, O'Keeffe, Pollock, Warhol. Walls are covered with business graffiti—questions and slogans meant to capture the restless spirit of innovation. "A solution is what results when you stop thinking about the problem," says one. "Only dead fish go with the flow," says another.

Still, Bingham, like Huston, is all business. He has organized, sponsored, and invested in a portfolio of initiatives designed to tap into open-source innovation as a source of hard-core competitive advantage. The goal of all these initiatives, Bingham explains, is to increase Lilly's "share of mind" in the worldwide scientific community. He doesn't use that term the way marketers do when they worry about their visibility with a target audience. He uses it more in the spirit of group intelligence. "There is a 'collective mind' out there," Bingham explains, "and the question for Lilly is, 'What fraction of it can we access?' If we limit ourselves only to the people we can recruit from the top universities and only the people we can convince to spend a lifetime with the company—well, that's a fairly small share of that collective intellect. We are talking about the democratization of science: what happens when you open your company to thousands and thousands of minds, each of them with a totally different set of life experiences?"

InnoCentive is an experiment that tries to answer that question. It is a young company, an early-stage venture investment that is years away from registering big-time sales and profits. But it has an enormous charter—to explore whether Lilly and some of the most powerful organizations in the world can turn open-source innovation into an established way of doing business. Can a set of ideas forged by computer hackers become conventional wisdom in the executive suites of the Fortune 500?[4]

The InnoCentive model is deceptively simple. It has signed up more than 30 "seeker" organizations from among the largest companies on earth. They include Lilly and P&G, of course, along with Boeing, Dow, DuPont, and NestlePurina. These are huge enterprises that together generate hundreds of billions of dollars in sales, invest billions in R&D, and employ tens of thousands of scientists and engineers. Yet they all have laboratories overflowing with unsolved problems that continue to frustrate even the best minds in their organization, either because their researchers don't have time to work on them or because the company lacks the in-house expertise to solve them.

InnoCentive has registered more than 90,000 biologists, chemists, biochemists, materials scientists, and so on—highly skilled professionals from more than 175 countries and all walks of life. These "solvers" include ambitious PhD students, retired directors of research from the world's most admired companies, nuclear engineers from Russia, and an array of specialists from China, Kazakhstan, and other faraway places. (In 2004 China passed the United States as the largest source of registered scientists. India and Russia are the third- and fourth-largest sources of scientists.)

It's up to InnoCentive to connect its seekers with its solvers. Seeker companies post highly focused, super-technical "challenges" on the InnoCentive Web site. The challenges come with a scientific description, a deadline, and an award, which can run as high as $100,000. (Postings don't reveal the name of the seeker company, and they're scrubbed clean of details that might hint at the product to which they're connected.) Solvers compete to meet the challenge in a way the seeker company deems a success, at which point the solver gets paid and the seeker owns the intellectual property.*

....

*There are small (but intriguing) differences in the business models of NineSigma and InnoCentive. NineSigma is all about forging relationships—the firm acts as a broker between a big-company client and an outside researcher, and it is up to those two parties to strike a financial arrangement. (NineSigma gets a cut of the contract.) InnoCentive is all about transactions. It is essentially a spot market for answers to thorny technical problems. Solvers never know the identity of the company that has posted the challenge. And it is decidedly bad form for a seeker company to make a direct connection with a solver, essentially going around InnoCentive.

The site itself feels like a United Nations for R&D—a digital cacophony of problems, solutions, specialized disciplines, and exotic places. A review of the award winners amounts to a virtual tour of scientific outposts across the planet, from Oxford and Moscow State to the Shriram Institute for Industrial Research in Bangalore, India, and the Institute of Bioorganic Chemistry in Belarus. As at the UN, there's even simultaneous translation: with a click of a mouse, the site shifts from English to Chinese, Russian, Japanese, Korean, German, or Spanish.

Darren Carroll can barely contain his enthusiasm about what InnoCentive bodes for the future of innovation. "This isn't even *close* to the same old way of doing business," he declares. "We're getting people to relinquish their long-held assumptions about how scientific work can be done, where work can be done, about the people who can get it done, and the terms under which they're prepared to do it."

One of Carroll's most eye-opening moments came during a visit to Chernogolovka, a once-secret city in the former Soviet Union where the regime sent scientists to work on top research priorities (many of them, of course, directed against the United States). Chernogolovka is a small place, with barely more than 22,000 residents. But these residents include more than 20 members of the Russian Academy of Sciences, more than 250 PhDs, and more than 1,000 PhD students.

"These are awfully smart people," Carroll notes, "people who had been living in total isolation until not too long ago. And there I was, talking to the head of a key department at a major research institute, about how his scientists could work with InnoCentive. I pulled up the Web site, and this guy looks at the challenges. 'You see that one? My people could solve it right now,' he tells me. 'But that other one, your seeker company is only willing to pay $75,000. I think it's worth $500,000—we'll never work on that.' And on he went. In a few short years, one of the most isolated, inaccessible places on earth is allowing me deep inside its laboratories. And my goal is to open up its research to the world and let anyone bid on it. How's that for radical change?"

Carroll has had plenty of exposure to the mind-bending changes sweeping the world of science. But his real job is to make the fantastic seem routine—to turn open-source innovation into a normal part of doing business rather than a window into the future.

So how does open-source innovation get down to business? First, by waging a nonstop battle for what Bingham calls share of mind. Forget *Field of Dreams*—just because you build a virtual R&D lab doesn't mean anyone will come. At InnoCentive the flesh-and-blood recruiting never stops. Ali Hussein, chief marketing officer and vice president of global markets, who joined the company from Amazon.com, makes an around-the-world trip every five or six weeks, personally spreading the open-innovation gospel to some of the world's most remote scientific outposts. Also, during Carroll's early years as CEO, he was on the road a jet lag–inducing 200 days a year, visiting science parks, labs, and universities to persuade potential solvers (as well as possible new seeker companies) to join the virtual R&D process. "I am out evangelizing with leading scientists, with the heads of large research organizations, with government ministers, about how they can become part of a truly global scientific community," he says.

InnoCentive doesn't just recruit scientists and hope for the best. Its Scientific Operations group (SciOps in company parlance) keeps the solvers charged up, encourages researchers with specific skills to work on certain challenges, and helps them revise not-quite-there submissions that show promise. To support a single challenge, SciOps might send e-mails to as many as 20,000 InnoCentive members. Once a solver signals interest, he or she opens a confidential "project room" where SciOps experts answer questions, read drafts, and otherwise help the submission along. (Many winning solutions go through multiple drafts before they're approved by the seeker company.)*

---

*Likewise, SciOps works with seeker companies to master the delicate balance between secrecy and openness. The more detailed the challenge, the more likely it is to be solved. At the same time, for obvious competitive reasons, seeker companies desperately want to protect their identity and the product plans connected to the specific challenge.

Russian-born Eugene Ivanov, a member of InnoCentive's SciOps team, says he has formed remarkably strong connections through his work with faraway solvers: "Our solvers want to be seen as real human beings, not just names on a screen. And they want to feel like they have an advocate, someone who is on their side. I am on a first-name basis with many of our solvers. We have never seen one another, and maybe we never will, but personal contact is crucial."

Carroll's second lesson: companies won't get the most from outside brainpower unless the best minds inside the organization rethink *their* approach to work. "Scientists and engineers have to change their job descriptions," he insists. "I tell them, 'Stop thinking of yourselves as problem-solvers. You have to become *solution-finders.*' That's not a semantic distinction. It's one of the most fundamental distinctions we make. A problem-solver is someone who gets handed a challenge, goes into the lab, and doesn't come out until he or she has an answer. A solution-finder looks around the world and is agnostic as to where the answer comes from, so long as it's the best answer at the lowest cost in the shortest time."

Like P&G's Larry Huston, Carroll insists that "solution-finding" is not a euphemism for outsourcing. He sees the world as a vast laboratory teeming with ideas, experiments, and innovations just waiting to be applied. The goal—and he, like Huston, is adamant about this—is not to ship routine work to low-cost nations but to find untapped solutions that *already* exist in labs all over the world and apply them to problems that have defied solution at home.

Indeed, the best solutions, Carroll argues, require the least amount of work from the solvers. "Our model is designed to provide windfalls for people who are uniquely prepared," he explains. "We're looking for scientists who, the moment we post a challenge on the site, say, 'I can't believe they haven't figured this out yet.' We're not looking for people to run the race from the starting blocks. We're looking for people who can start the race ten yards from the finish line—people with the right answer to the right problem at the right time."

Carroll calls it the needle-in-a-haystack moment: "You're in the lab, you're stuck, you don't know where to go next, and you say, 'Let's throw it open to the world.' And you manage to tap into a researcher thousands of miles away who's been working on just this problem for five years, who has the solution in his or her head, and who says, 'Piece of cake, I've already done that!'"

It sounds fanciful, except that it happens all the time. Carroll and his colleagues can recite chapter and verse of such needle-in-a-haystack moments—solutions that arrive from unexpected places and unexpected fields, with surprising speed. David Bradin, a patent attorney in North Carolina, read about InnoCentive in a trade journal and decided to size up its implications for intellectual property law. As he trolled through the site, Bradin, who has a graduate degree in organic chemistry, saw a challenge that had stumped a seeker company—and solved it himself.

One of Carroll's personal favorites involves a company that had been struggling for 18 months with a problem on a new drug. This "showstopper" issue had stumped its best toxicologists and pathologists, so it turned to InnoCentive as a what-do-we-have-to-lose option. A protein crystallographer saw the challenge and sensed immediately how to apply tools from her field to solve it. "When she won the award," he says, "we asked a top researcher from the seeker company, 'Would you ever have used a protein crystallographer to help with this? He told us, 'We have a lab full of them right down the hallway, and it never occurred to us.'"

Which is why, even as Darren Carroll works to make open-source innovation a routine part of the business landscape, it may never lose its power to amaze or inspire. "When we launched this thing," he chuckles, "I had no fewer than six senior executives at Lilly pull me aside and tell me that I was throwing away a perfectly good career. Now I find myself at the center of a worldwide scientific conversation. Today we operate the world's largest virtual laboratory. Tomorrow our goal is to change the very nature of work: what it means to be employed, what it means to do something productive."*

"WALK IN STUPID EVERY DAY"—WHAT IT MEANS TO BE AN OPEN-SOURCE LEADER

Recognizing the power of open-source innovation doesn't just challenge old ideas about how and where people can work. It redefines the work of leadership itself. Whether we were visiting a senior R&D official in Cincinnati or interviewing an artistic director based in Edinburgh, we were struck by what happens when senior executives invite lots of smart people—customers, engineers, rank-and-file enthusiasts—into their organizations. It doesn't just unleash more bottom-up innovation, it inspires less top-down arrogance. That's the real mind-shift for business—not reckoning with the new-wave impact of the Internet, but recognizing the limits of old-style organizations. A commitment to open-source innovation requires a commitment to a more open style of leadership.

The leaders we've met in the last two chapters demonstrate an unmistakable sense of personal transparency. Rob McEwen invited the entire mining industry to learn from the gifted geologists unearthed by the Goldcorp Challenge. Paul Gudgin makes it a point of pride not to exert behind-the-scenes influence on the content of the Edinburgh Fringe Festival, even though his title is artistic director. Darren Carroll, who made his early mark at Eli Lilly in the secrecy-obsessed world of intellectual property law, transformed his leadership style by virtue of his experience with open-source innovation. "I've become much more democratic in my approach to leadership," he says. "Seeing up close, on a very per-

---

*Far from costing Carroll his career, his InnoCentive experience shaped it. In mid-2005 Darren Carroll and Alph Bingham did a sort of job switch. Bingham, InnoCentive's corporate sponsor at Eli Lilly, became CEO of the company, while Carroll became chairman. And Carroll returned to Indianapolis, based at Lilly headquarters, to oversee the company's array of venture capital investments and its experiments with new business models.

sonal basis, how a democratic approach to innovation brings out the most incredible ideas from some of the least likely places, makes it very difficult for me to look in the mirror if I act differently in my own business."

One small but instructive case in point: during Carroll's tenure as CEO, Tuesdays at InnoCentive were known as "Truth Tuesday." That was the day when the company's most important operational meetings—from account management to SciOps—took place. "It doesn't mean people didn't tell the truth the other six days," Carroll jokes. "But we had a rule that on Tuesdays people could say absolutely anything they wanted, including about the performance of me or any other senior manager, without any fear of recrimination."

There's another defining trait among the executives we've met in the last two chapters, a hard-to-achieve (but easy-to-recognize) blend of personal confidence and intellectual humility. These open-minded leaders don't hide their aggressive goals or competitive fire. But they don't confuse ambition with omniscience. As a leader, enhancing the architecture of participation means imposing limits on your ego—overcoming the know-it-all style of leadership that seems to be the default mode in most companies. You can think big without having to think of everything yourself.

Advertising legend Dan Wieden, cofounder of the powerhouse agency Wieden+Kennedy, could be forgiven if he exudes the know-it-all air that comes so naturally to his business. He remains president and chief creative officer of the firm he launched in 1982 with David Kennedy, and W+K remains one of the world's most distinguished independent agencies. Wieden himself wrote the groundbreaking "Just Do It" tag for longtime client Nike. The agency's many other arresting ads for the sneaker giant, along with memorable campaigns for high-profile clients such as ESPN, Miller Brewing Company, and Electronic Arts, add up to a greatest-hits collection of pop-culture landmarks. More recently, W+K has been breaking new creative ground in a world less impressed by TV ads, no matter how riveting, by experimenting with documentaries, Web communities, and even a full-fledged Broadway musical.

Talk about creative genius: Wieden runs a 600-person organization, with annual billings of more than $1 billion, that has produced strong and indelible work. But when you visit W + K headquarters in Portland, Oregon, and spend time with its cofounder and his colleagues, what you detect is anything but a sense of intellectual arrogance. Wieden argues that his job is to "walk in stupid every day"—to keep challenging the organization, and himself, to seek out unexpected ideas, outside influences, and new perspectives on old problems.[5]

"It's the hardest thing to do as a leader," he concedes, "but it's the most important thing. Whatever day it is, something in the world changed overnight, and you better figure out what it is and what it means. You have to forget what you just did and what you just learned. You have to walk in stupid every day."

It's hard to find an executive who doesn't appreciate the power of the experience curve—the idea that the more you do something (make computer chips, build airplanes, write TV spots), the more productive you become. Dan Wieden and his colleagues also appreciate the power of the *inexperience* curve—the idea that the more you do something, the more important it is to challenge the assumptions and habits that built your success so as to generate a wave of innovations to build the future. At Wieden + Kennedy, seeking out fresh ideas means infusing the organization with new voices—not through the Internet but through an architecture of participation that opens the agency to outside thinking.

One crucial piece of this architecture of participation is the architecture of W + K's headquarters. Several years ago, Wieden imagined a bold new building for his fast-growing agency. (The building opened in early 2000.) He chose a 90-year-old former cold-storage facility in Portland's Pearl District, a neighborhood full of warehouses, industrial tradespeople, and artists. He commissioned a huge open space centered on a four-story amphitheater and crisscrossed with sky bridges, concrete pathways, and staircases. The building reveals a rich minimalism with its lustrous but humble materials: beams of reclaimed wood, concrete floors, stainless-steel mesh railings, steps doubling as bleacher-style seating. Its main ornament is the natural light flooding through windows that offer a full circle of stunning views of Mount Hood, Mount St. Helens, the Willamette River, and downtown Portland.

What's most distinctive about the headquarters, though, is that it was built with outsiders in mind—specifically, an open-door policy that fills its hallways, meeting rooms, and public spaces with interesting visitors and unexpected guests. Before the headquarters opened, Wieden invited the Portland Institute for Contemporary Art (PICA) to set up shop inside the building, with an eye toward infusing it with the energy and insights of under-the-radar artists and their work. In 2004 he opened a "quad" (each major account at W + K is set up in a quad with its own offices, lounge, and kitchen) for four nonprofit organizations and expanded PICA's footprint to include a street-level box office. An artist-in-residence program supplies studios and practice space to performers of all stripes, and a citywide lecture series convenes in the 400-seat amphitheater.[6]

The result is a building rich with character and color—and brimming with outside voices and fresh perspectives. "Innovation is such a subtle and inexplicable thing," Wieden argues. "Who can say where insights and ideas come from? But if we create a place that has an energy not just generated from ourselves but from the people who visit, who perform, who do other kinds of work here, we create a magnetic place of learning. It expands your view of the world in ways that don't happen when you just hang around with your own kind."* It's a make-or-break insight for an open-source world: the most effective leaders are

----

*One small example given to us by Kristy Edmunds, founder and artistic adviser to PICA, illustrates the broader point about intellectual diversity. When she invited choreographer and hip-hop historian Rennie Harris to present his work to Wieden + Kennedy, the agency got a loud wake-up call. Harris gave a tough lecture on how advertising has misrepresented the history and significance of the hip-hop form. "It was a great complacency disrupter," Edmunds says. "It also set off an explosion of energy. One team wound up using one of the sound designers from Harris's show on an advertising project."

the ones who are the most insatiable learners, and experienced leaders learn the most by interacting with people whose interests, backgrounds, and experiences are the least like theirs.

Wieden's perspective on leadership and learning explains another open-minded departure by his agency—an advertising school designed not just to immerse newcomers in how the business works but to inject the business with the energy, vitality, and insights of talented newcomers. W + K launched the school, called "12," in April 2004. Instead of delivering a formal curriculum or employing a traditional faculty, it offers a dozen students at a time the chance to do 13 months of real work for actual clients. Students pay $13,000 in tuition; clients, who contract directly with "12" as opposed to Wieden + Kennedy, pay sharply reduced rates for purposefully rough-around-the-edges campaigns.

The school's design reflects the free spirit and restless mind of its founder, Jelly Helm, a fortysomething creative director who was a rising star when he left W + K in 1997 for a career in teaching. (He was responsible for the iconic "Good Versus Evil" Nike soccer ad, and one of his spots resides in the Museum of Modern Art's permanent collection.) Helm returned six years later, not to revisit past successes but to invent a new future for advertising—to blend the agency's unrivaled experience with the *inexperience* of a dozen self-styled subversives and contrarians. The school, says Helm, is "an experiment disguised as an ad agency disguised as a school. Mostly it's an experiment in how people can create together, an experiment in inviting naïveté into the organization."

The first class of students, culled from more than 2,500 applicants, included a former stand-up comedian, a sculptor, an ex-welder, and one experienced account executive. The group was assigned four clients, including the City of Portland, a national get-out-the-vote drive, and a software company with a new product for searching the Web. But the real assignment was to devise new ways of working—a model of collaboration that remixes the ad industry's writer–art director–account executive formula, which has turned the business into what Helm considers "a horrible wasteland."

There is almost no conventional teaching at "12." In fact, the only regular class is a monthly improv session designed to focus the students on openness, teamwork, and experimentation. "We're exploring whether improv-style collaboration can influence advertising creativity," Helm explains. "The agency model has always been about the lone genius with a breakthrough idea. Then you surround and pamper that person with a team that executes the campaign and affirms the brilliance of the 'idea person.' The improv model is exactly the opposite. There's not one genius, there's a group. And it's each person's job to make everyone's ideas better."

If "12" is light on formal structures, it is built on a solid foundation at the agency. The "12" council is a group of "rock stars and oddballs" inside Wieden+Kennedy who serve as guardians of the program. Beyond making themselves available for informal mentoring, members of the council offer lectures and presentations and even lend a hand with projects. Helm also created an alumni council of twelve former W+K superstars, including writer Janet Champ, creator of award-winning women's campaigns for Nike, and director Stacy Wall, whose TV ads for ESPN's *SportsCenter* are instantly recognizable. Each member of the alumni council serves as a yearlong mentor to one of the students.

After just a few years of operation, "12" is challenging some long-held ideas inside the agency. Helm himself says that he is getting schooled by his students and their "consistently counterintuitive" approaches, sometimes against his explicit instructions. One example was a branding campaign for the City of Portland. Helm pushed the "12" team to come up with one "big idea" that summed up the city—Portland's answer to "I Love New York" or "Don't Mess with Texas." The group struggled for months to generate a killer idea, with no success and much frustration.

Finally, during an improv class, the students hit upon a mind-flip that produced a fresher and more effective campaign. Forget one big idea to define the essence of Portland. What about lots of small ideas that residents could mix and match to create their own definitions—a grassroots approach to urban branding? The team created one hundred buttons, each with a word representing something distinctive about the city: Powell's (the famous Portland bookstore), rain, Mount Hood, and so on. Helm was impressed—and reminded once again how much industry veterans can learn from outsiders and newcomers.

"It was completely counterintuitive, completely against the rules of advertising," he says. "Instead of one defining idea that we pushed out to people, this allowed people to make their own campaigns for Portland. You get to make a little poem to the city by picking up two or three different buttons. And you get very subtle but very powerful grassroots recognition on the street. It's a super-cool idea that is exactly *not* what I would have preached."

Which is, of course, precisely the idea behind "12"—and the reason why a blend of personal confidence and intellectual humility is such an important trait for leaders, whether their business is developing a new medicine, discovering gold, or creating a memorable ad campaign. "Most leaders want to 'master' their fields," Helm says. "But it's when you think you have all the answers that you become closed off. We're trying to stay open to new thinking."

What does Wieden + Kennedy think it has learned from "12"? That's an easy question to answer, since Helm and his students compiled a lavish 288-page book on the experiment called, well, *What We Learned*. The book is a full-throttle ride into the chaotic world being created at "12." It reproduces e-mails, partially censored memos, sketches, and rough drafts of marketing campaigns. It also offers 388 lessons that add up to a set of mantras—profound and profane, sweeping and silly—for doing great creative work. Lesson number 1: simple is difficult. Lesson number 381: humility is not overrated.[7]

As for Dan Wieden, he too has learned important lessons, and *What We Learned* gives plenty of space to the agency's cofounder and other leaders to discuss what this school of outsiders has taught them. "We must begin all things in ignorance," Wieden concludes. "Otherwise we never start at the beginning. We all carry so damn much baggage, so many assumptions, habits, prejudices born from experience, that it is very, very difficult to see the world for what it is. And to find our role in it, our true role, not necessarily the one we have been raised and educated to assume. '12' is an attempt, somewhat naive I suppose, to put the past on hold. To see if it is possible finally to learn how to learn. And how to unlearn."

Those aren't the words of a know-it-all boss. Those are the words of an open-minded leader who knows how dramatically the character of leadership is changing.

Chapter Six

Maverick Messages (II): Open-Minding Your Business

Open-source innovation is reshaping the logic of creativity in countless fields, from software and the Internet to pharmaceuticals and the arts. But applying the outside-in mind-set of open source means abandoning familiar assumptions about where great ideas come from, who gets to be part of your company, and how to inspire the best contributions from them.

That's why so many organizations and leaders find it hard to make the transition to this new model of innovation. We were struck by Rob McEwen's generosity of spirit when he invited his rivals in the gold-mining business to meet, interact with, and learn from the best brains unearthed in the Goldcorp Challenge. We were also struck by the fact that not a single one of his competitors chose to copy Goldcorp's innovation or launch its own version of McEwen's global brainstorming—despite the killer strategies and the wave of upbeat public attention it unleashed. How could so many smart CEOs fail to learn from such a winning idea?

InnoCentive, for all its noteworthy achievements, also underscores the limits of the traditional leadership mind-set when it comes to opening organizations to outside brainpower. Although InnoCentive has attracted vast numbers of talented solvers and enrolled scores of idea-hungry corporate seekers, its biggest piece of unfinished business is persuading in-the-trenches leaders at its seeker companies to post more problems for the InnoCentive community to work on. In the go-it-alone culture of science, R&D managers need lots of persuading before they are willing, let alone eager, to invite outside researchers to solve problems that they have been unable to solve themselves. How could so many desperate-for-results managers choose not to tap a model that has delivered such powerful scientific results?

The answers speak to what happens (or doesn't happen) when old-style leadership meets open-source innovation: just because a new model of creativity works doesn't mean that tradition-bound executives are willing to work in the new ways the model requires. But if you're prepared to break with tradition, if you're eager to experiment with the ideas you've encountered in these last two chapters, then be sure to put these design principles on your leadership agenda. They can put the logic of open-source innovation to work for you and your company.

1. Keep the focus narrow and tightly defined.

There's a big difference between tapping outside brainpower and engaging in the kind of free-form "brainstorming" that often feels vague and unproductive. Whether it's Rob McEwen during his tenure at Goldcorp or Jack Hughes at TopCoder, the most effective open-source leaders understand that collaboration works best when the focus of the collaboration is narrow and tightly defined: find 6 million ounces of gold on a specific mine site; write the best component for a particular software application. In other words, don't confuse being open-minded with being poorly organized. Define a problem crisply, and you're halfway to a solution.

That's a key insight behind the increasing effectiveness of the World Banks Development Marketplace, one of the least likely—but most inspiring—open-source initiatives we've encountered. The World Bank is one of the world's most top-down organizations, a place where impeccably credentialed PhDs make financial decisions that affect billions of impoverished people. Back in 1998, with the support of then-president James Wohlfenson, the World Bank began an experiment to turn its famously elitist culture on its head, creating a global competition for new ideas to promote economic development—innovations the bank would fund. Put simply, the Marketplace is to fighting poverty what the Goldcorp Challenge was to finding gold—a worldwide competition, complete with judges, rounds of evaluation, and prize money (millions of dollars of grants) for the winners.[1]

The Marketplace gets bigger, better, more exciting, and more effective every year, largely because it gets more *focused* ever year. Early on, the Marketplace evaluated thousands of proposals around as many as ten organizing challenges, from energy to public health to education. In 2005 the organizers limited the event to one challenge—innovations that blend economic growth and sustainable development—and attracted more than 2,600 applications from 136 countries. Because all the proposals responded to a single theme, the competition was more intense—and the impact more profound. To achieve even greater focus, the bank has organized similar open-source competitions, called Country Marketplaces, everywhere from Argentina to Zambia. By evaluating grassroots ideas in one country around one challenge (different for each country), the focus becomes even more narrow, and the results even more dramatic.

By its very nature, open-source innovation is messy, chaotic, and slightly jarring to buttoned-down business sensibilities. That's a significant part of its power. It's a big part of the job of a leader to design grassroots experiments around principles that give them the best chance to succeed—and that means keeping them focused.

2. Keep broadening the range of participants.

The real magic of open-source innovation is not just that lots of people will offer ideas but also that lots of *different kinds of people* will offer ideas. Don't limit the circle of participants to specialists in your home country, your industry, or your product categories. As P&G's Larry Huston and InnoCentive's Darren Carroll love to emphasize, the most amazing ideas often come from the most surprising places. Be sure to maximize the chances that you'll be surprised by maximizing the range of people who participate.

You don't always need to tap the Internet or aspire to reach the farthest corners of the globe. You can start by recognizing what happens when people who don't normally have a voice in your business are invited to offer their point of view. That's what makes Tom Brown's "Branch Hunts" so illuminating. They're a chance for everyone at Second Curve Capital, regardless of specialty, seniority, pay grade, or level of expertise, to size up the same situation in the marketplace— but to draw on their unique backgrounds, training, interests, and life experiences. What you see in the marketplace reflects where you're coming from as a person.

IDEO, the influential product design firm in Silicon Valley, has made a business discipline out of this different-is-better approach to creativity. One of its signature innovations is what it cheekily calls "unfocus groups"—idea sessions that bring together "extreme and exceptional people" from all walks of life who share an interest in and passion for a well-defined product category. (Unfocus groups are IDEO's maverick alternative to cookie-cutter focus groups, where panels of like-minded people with the same income, demographics, or tastes evaluate products and ideas.) Tom Kelley, IDEO's general manager, describes one unfocus group about the prosaic world of shoes. Dorinda von Stronheim, the firm's "casting director" for the groups, convened a group that included a lounge singer, an artist who worked as a limo driver, and a firewalker, along with all sorts of other people with strong (but very different) feelings about the shoes they wore for work or pleasure. This iconoclastic group then divided into small teams and collaborated with designers to create actual prototypes for new shoes based on their unique interests and strange obsessions.[2]

It was precisely because these people were so passionate about their interests, so invested in the product category, *and so different from one another,* that the unfocus group generated so much useful intelligence. That's the lesson for open-minded leaders. Lots of different kinds of people, all looking at the same thing, tend to generate the most penetrating insights. Your job is to bring those different kinds of people together.

3. Keep it fun.

Innovation is serious business, but if you're working to tap the brainpower of grassroots volunteers and outside-the-mainstream contributors, then you have to work to keep your open-source project colorful, dramatic, and energetic. That sense of drama comes naturally to the open-minded organizers of the Edinburgh Fringe Festival. The Fringe was born in the spirit of artistic collaboration, but it has won worldwide renown based on the intensity of its artistic competition—specifically, its knack for adding to the long list of prizes, awards, and accolades for which its performers compete. The 2005 festival granted no fewer than 72 awards and even tallied votes for an award . . . for the best award!

It may be a touch excessive, but there's a method to the Fringe's madness for awards. It's the same reason that TopCoder's tournaments are organized as explicit competitions, with judges, qualifying rounds, and high-stakes finals. Creativity is as much about *emotion* as invention. Human beings revel in the thrill of victory and the agony of defeat. Keep the participants charged up, and they're more likely to charge ahead with great ideas.

That principle applies inside your company as well as outside. At

Wieden + Kennedy, for example, agency employees can apply for the Slime Mold Award—a program created by Dan Wieden along with Bill Davenport, founder and CEO of Wieden + Kennedy Entertainment. Slime Mold is a grants program in which agency staffers submit their dream projects to a committee and compete to win funding for them. Why encourage people to pursue their extracurricular passions rather than keep their nose to the client grindstone? "Because creativity is basically subversive in nature," says Wieden. "You have to have subversive elements in the organization to keep yourself awake and evolving." Why the name? "Because slime mold is Dan Wieden's favorite organism," says Davenport. "It's a cell-like thing that can't move on its own but when the cells come together transforms into a fully functioning creature that can do things it couldn't do before. That's our view of people and creativity."

The rules are simple: anyone can submit a proposal, as long as it has nothing to do with advertising. The Slime Mold "council" has received proposals for everything from short films to fine arts projects to furniture building. One notable Slime Mold success belongs to W+K producer Jeff Selis, who's helped make ads for Nike and ESPN but whose off-duty passion is dogs. He proposed a book called *Cat Spelled Backward Doesn't Spell God*. According to Davenport, "it was a great proposal. The only problem was he said it was going to be more like $30,000 than $3,000 to do it. I said, 'I don't think so,' but then he proposed a deal where he thought we could break even and we gave him the go-ahead. He took the pictures, he and a friend wrote the copy, and a woman in the studio laid it out. We self-published it, and he put 6,000 books in the trunk of his car and went to all the city bookstores."

In Portland the book ended up outselling Tom Brokaw's just-published phenomenon, *The Greatest Generation*. Chronicle Books discovered it, bought it, and translated it into four languages. Selis has written popular sequels, including *Dog Bless America* and *Dog*

Save the Queen. It's great fun—and great for Wieden + Kennedy's business. "By giving people an opportunity to do something beyond ads," says Davenport, "we give them a shot in the arm creatively and we enhance our creative reputation."[3]

4. Don't keep all the benefits to yourself.

If you expect strangers (or even employees and colleagues) to share their best ideas with you, then don't be surprised when they expect something in return. It can be money, it can be recognition, but more often than not what draws people into open-source projects is the chance to push themselves, to develop their skills, to interact with the best people in their field. Whether it's the artists at the Edinburgh Fringe Festival or the geeks behind Linux, Apache, and other open-source computer code, grassroots innovators want to learn from the best of their fellow innovators—and for the world to see the best of their innovations. You've got to create an organization and a leadership style that make you as comfortable sharing ideas with the outside world as you are accepting ideas from the outside world.

What We Learned, the book produced by Jelly Helm and his colleagues at "12," the Wieden + Kennedy ad school, is a small but powerful example of this share-what-you-know approach to leadership. *What We Learned* is part monograph of the first year of "12," part creative recruiting mechanism for future students, and part cultural history of Wieden + Kennedy. The design of the book is wildly energetic, packed with photographs, original artwork, and stunning spreads—all bound in burgundy leather with gold type.

Most importantly—and most revealingly—the book shares the unvarnished results of an experiment in progress, complete with brilliant successes and messy failures. And it doesn't hesitate to share the internal skepticism about "12" before the school proved itself to the agency. Dave Luhr, the agency's COO, was open about his reservations: "My initial gut reaction was, 'Just what we need around here, twelve young people with no experience, a start-up school that would cost us time and money, and yet another agency experiment that would take our thinking away from our client's business.' Instead, '12' helped to reenergize the agency, and we had one of our strongest twelve-month periods in agency history. First reactions aren't always the right reaction. Lesson learned."

That lesson applies well beyond the corridors of "12." The opportunity to learn is the most valuable form of currency in the art of the open-source deal. Smart people will share their best ideas with companies and leaders who will share what they know—and make them smarter in the process.

5. Keep challenging yourself to be more open to new ideas and new ways of leading.

Our final design principle may be the most important: the rise of open-source innovation does not diminish the importance of executive leadership. Far from it. Even the most radical experiments in group collaboration have at their core a well-known individual leader, whether it's Linus Torvalds with Linux or Jimmy Wales, the founder of Wikipedia, the Internet-based encyclopedia that's written and edited by the people who use it.

But leaders who embrace an open-source mind-set ask different questions of themselves than other leaders. Am I the kind of person with whom other smart people want to work and contribute ideas? Can I conduct myself as openly and transparently as the participants in my project? Can I demonstrate personal strength, even charisma, along with intellectual humility? Find the right answers to those questions, and you're likely to find yourself at the center of exciting open-source innovations.

Darren Carroll, who loves to make connections between the decentralizing impact of technology and the changing logic of leadership, described the dilemma he faced as CEO of InnoCentive and how he solved it. His insights capture the problem faced by leaders everywhere who want to persuade smart people to work *with* them.

"You no longer have the classic carrot-and-stick approach to leadership," Carroll says. "We have 90,000 people who work with us, and I as a leader can't do a performance appraisal on them, can't offer them a bonus, can't demote them, can't fire them. So how do you induce them to do things they might not do otherwise? By being more open than you've ever been. In this new world, the most transparent leader is the most attractive leader. The leader who figures out a way for everybody to win is going to be the leader who wins. The leader who comes with a zero-sum mentality gets zero."

PART THREE

Reconnecting with Customers

Chapter Seven

From Selling Value to Sharing Values: Overcoming the Age of Overload

We've shown that you can decommoditize a commodity business. Nobody needs another me-too bank. We've created an unusual, unduplicatable experience for our customers. I've had more people tell me that their kids used to want to go to Starbucks with them on Saturday morning. Now they want to come to the bank!

—VERNON HILL, CHAIRMAN AND CEO, COMMERCE BANCORP

I t's Saturday night in Manhattan, and Radio City Music Hall is buzzing. The theater is filled to capacity with an audience that can barely contain its enthusiasm. There are howls of delight and raucous applause among the 6,000 people in the crowd, most of whom have packed the place for an hour before curtain time. Many of the women wear red dresses or red scarves. Many of the men wear red shirts or red ties. Men and women alike wear funny red hats.

When the show starts, it is nonstop energy. The Rockettes, decked out in bright red costumes, high-step their way through one of their trademark routines. The stage goes black, and spotlights focus on a new group of performers, dressed as hip city-dwellers, street toughs, and nightstick-wielding cops, who break into a musical number that feels like *West Side Story* updated for the *Rent* generation. The crowd sounds air horns, waves pom-poms, and literally dances in the aisles. At several points, hundreds of New Yorkers in the audience give voice to their hometown pride with a chant of "NYC! NYC! NYC!" Members of the bridge-and-tunnel crowd, who have traveled to the city to attend the show, holler back with cheers and jeers of their own.

Is this some crazed rendition of the Radio City "Christmas Spectacular"? An audience-friendly musical at risk of spiraling into chaos? Actually, it is an awards ceremony organized by a bank—a one-of-a-kind annual show staged by and for the employees of a company that has built its business by putting on a memorable show for its customers. Commerce Bank, headquartered outside Philadelphia in Cherry Hill, New Jersey, has stood out from its bigger (and less colorful) rivals by turning an industry that has become famous—infamous really—for making customers miserable into a stage for making customers laugh . . . all the way to the bank.

Commerce has been performing for more than 30 years. It was founded in 1973 with a handful of employees, $1.5 million in capital, and one location in New Jersey. It now has more than 13,000 employees, more than $35 billion worth of deposits, more than 375 locations stretching from New York City to Florida, and plans to expand to 700 locations by 2009. An investor who put $100,000 in Commerce stock in January 1985 owned shares worth $3.5 *million* 20 years later. The company's total stock market value, which was $400 million at the end of 1996, was nearly $6 *billion* at the end of 2005.[1]

No wonder Commerce has so many of its rivals seeing red. But that's not why so much of the crowd at Radio City is dressed in red. Red, it turns out, is Commerce Bank's official color. In fact, every Friday at every Commerce location—headquarters, branches, even the 1-800 call center—is "Red Friday." Employees come to work wearing at least a splash of red—sometimes just a red handkerchief, sometimes an outrageous red getup meant to attract the attention of company volunteers who record the zaniness inspired by the day. Once a month customers even get in on the act, wearing red to the bank to qualify for prizes.

The annual Wow! Awards show (a corporate Oscar ceremony crossed with a college pep rally) celebrates employees who go above and beyond the bank's sky-high expectations for service and fun. We had the thoroughly entertaining experience of attending the 2005 ceremony at Radio City Music Hall.* The investment in time, money, and energy was astounding. The bank hired professional songwriters and choreographers to create the music and dance routines for the show. More than 250 Commerce employees spent four hours a week for two months rehearsing in groups and working with individual instructors to be part of the cast. The streets around Radio City were lined with an armada of buses that had shuttled thousands of employees to be members of the audience—from new part-time tellers to bank officers with decades of experience, from teenagers in jeans and T-shirts to grandparents in their theater best.

Inside the theater, nearly 50 award-winning employees (selected from 500 red sash–wearing nominees) had their moment in the spotlight. *Best Retail Support by an Officer! Best Assistant Branch Manager! Best Loan Support! Best Credit Analyst!* One senior executive, onstage to present an award, actually flipped a pretty decent cartwheel. One special honoree drove off in a Porsche Boxster (red, of course), to the delight of her colleagues.

"Banking is a dead business," declares Dennis DiFlorio, Commerce's president of retail banking and a nearly 20-year veteran of the company. "It's a utility, like the gas company. We're creating an emotional attachment with our customers. The world didn't need another bank on the corner—and then we came along. We created a phenomenon, a buzz, around convenience, service, and the culture of our people. We're wacky. The majority of people in leadership roles in this bank are on the lunatic fringe. We have to be. We've created a cult brand in a dead business."

---

*Almost as entertaining as the Wow! Awards themselves are the commemorative DVDs, which do a good job of capturing the manic energy of the evening. Commerce has even published a CD of the unabashedly corny music composed for the shows, featuring the hit single, "It's Time to Wow!" Among the other cuts: "Commerce Beat" and "Lovin' That Bank."

COOL PRODUCTS! LOW PRICES! UNHAPPY CUSTOMERS?
WHY "GOOD DEALS" AREN'T GOOD ENOUGH

There is a tension at the heart of the relationship between most companies and their customers. Companies are offering better deals than ever, literally the best bargains in history. It has never been cheaper to fly from Dallas to Los Angeles, to make a phone call from Boston to Brussels, to buy a laptop computer or a DVD player. Yet the more companies raise quality and lower prices—and the more they spend on flashy ads and frantic promotions—the less they seem to impress their customers.

This situation would be hard to fathom if the evidence weren't so clear. The American Customer Satisfaction Index (ACSI), the definitive benchmark of how buyers feel about what business is selling them, marked its ten-year anniversary in the fall of 2004. It was hardly a cause for celebration. The index measures satisfaction in 40 industries and for 200 companies. Although some scores have moved up slowly in the last few years, many industries and companies actually rate *lower* than they did a decade ago. At the end of 1994, on a scale of 0 to 100, the overall index was 74.2. Ten years later, the score was 73.6. In 1994 the airline industry was at 72; ten years later, its score was 66. Telecommunications was at 81; ten years later, its score was 71. Personal computers were at 78; ten years later, its score was 72.[2]

What's also striking about the first decade of the ACSI is that many of the best-performing companies are in the most traditional parts of the economy. The company with the highest-ever ACSI grade, a 90, is H. J. Heinz—no one's idea of a cutting-edge enterprise. Meanwhile, the 2004 score for Hewlett-Packard, Silicon Valley's fabled innovator and a source of soap opera–like fascination among investors and the media, was 71—down from 78 in 1994. Other companies with lower ACSI scores in 2004 than in 1994 include AT&T, Whirlpool, and Wells Fargo. (Incredibly, even as these and other well-known names suffered, customer satisfaction with the Internal Revenue Service improved by 25 percent between 1999 and 2004, as measured by the ACSI.

How would you like to run a company that was less popular with its customers than the IRS?)

In other words, despite a decade of spectacular price-performance advances in computer hardware of all sorts, despite an explosion of innovation in consumer electronics, mobile phones, and Internet access, despite some of the most entertaining and arresting ad campaigns in history, customers remain unmoved and downright unappreciative. The harder executives work to make things cheaper, more reliable, and more *desirable,* the more unhappy they seem to make their customers.

If, as we argued earlier in the book, companies compete on the originality of their ideas and the power of their point of view, then what's wrong with how they're thinking about customers? One unfortunate answer is that too many companies *aren't* thinking about customers. So many companies are so busy acquiring, consolidating, downsizing, and outsourcing that meeting the expectations of their customers runs a distant second to meeting the cost-cutting demands of Wall Street. To spin the African proverb, when two business elephants merge, it's the customers who suffer.

Claes Fornell, a highly regarded professor at the University of Michigan's Ross School of Business and the creator of the ACSI, wrote an in-depth analysis of the index on the occasion of its tenth anniversary. In decidedly understated prose, he examined why so many companies had fared so poorly on this all-important indicator of long-term competitive health: "The culprits appear to have been cost cutting through labor reductions, heavy investment in technology to the detriment of customer service, mergers and acquisitions, limited consumer choice or some combination thereof."

To put it more bluntly, customer satisfaction suffered because companies made their customers suffer as executives pursued other priorities. A classic case in point: 1-800 customer service. Popular angst over outsourcing has become a staple of political debate and the business press: why should an unhappy customer in Bloomington, Indiana, have to talk to someone in Bangalore, India, about a glitch with his laptop? But the relentless *automation* of service—the near-total elimination of any human contact between companies and customers—speaks to even more misguided priorities. According to the *Wall Street Journal,* U.S. companies spent more than $7.4 billion in a single year to enhance their automated call centers—with the result that "it's harder than ever for you to reach a real person." Forget pressing zero to talk to an agent. Now, the *Journal* reports, "you have to crack the secret code or say the magic word." To reach an agent, you have to press star/zero, or zero/pound, or zero/zero/zero. But here's the rub: *companies don't tell customers which keys to press.* And when enough customers crack the codes on their own, companies change them.[3]

It would be funny if it weren't so depressing—and so transparently counterproductive.* We've lost count of how many executives have regaled us with plans to improve their company's products and services by "listening to the voice of the customer." Memo to the boss: *answer the phone!* Your customers are trying to talk to you.

The bigger problem, though, is that too many companies, even those committed to treating customers right, mistake selling good products at a competitive price with making a lasting impression on the people who are buying them. It's one of the defining perils of 21st-century capitalism: when almost everything gets cheaper every year, offering customers a "good deal" won't win them over or keep them happy— because someone invariably comes along with an even better deal. It was Clare Boothe Luce who wrote, "No good deed goes unpunished." The business world has its own version of that ubiquitous aphorism: "No good deal goes unchallenged."

---

*The *Journal* article recounted one story that was funny *and* depressing. Robert Barzelay spent 11 months trying to resolve a $110 billing dispute with his Internet provider. Despite spending an estimated 600 minutes on hold, he never reached a live operator. "I eventually concluded that there are no human beings working at the company," he told the *Journal.*

Three thankless realities define the state of competition in industries from automobiles to airlines, movies to mutual funds: oversupply, over-capacity, and utter sensory overload. Companies are selling too much of everything; they have the wherewithal to make more of what they're already selling too much of; and they are unleashing too many market-ing messages on customers who can't begin to process all that they're seeing and hearing.

A few years back, two Swedish business school professors wrote an en-ergetic (if a tad eccentric) book called *Funky Business: Talent Makes Capital Dance*. Talk about overload: Jonas Ridderstråle and Kjell Nordström of the Stockholm School of Economics tackle topics from computing to Chris-tianity, from business strategy to sex. But they are crisply elegant on what they call the "surplus society"—a phenomenon that describes virtually every market for every product and service in the developed world. In Norway, they report, a country with just 4.5 million people, readers choose from 200 different newspapers and 100 weekly magazines. In Swe-den, with just 9 million people, drinkers choose from more than 350 brands of beer, up from 50 or so just 10 years earlier. In one year alone, they marvel, Seiko sold 5,000 models of watches. "This is the age of more," the professors declare. "More choice. More consumption. More fun. More fear. More uncertainty. More competition. More opportuni-ties. We have entered a world of excess: a world of abundance."

In 2004 Barry Schwartz, a professor at Swarthmore College, offered an intriguing twist on the surplus society in his book *The Paradox of Choice: Why More Is Less*. What is most notable about the new world of endless choice, he argues, is not that it leaves store shelves more crowded, or business less profitable, but that it leaves consumers dazed, confused—even depressed.* "At this point, choice no longer liberates, but debilitates,"

---

* One eye-opening exercise for Schwartz, who doesn't seem to get out much (at least not to the mall), was to walk the aisles of a consumer electronics store and record the makes, models, and brands vy-ing for his attention. In just one visit, he found 45 car stereo systems, 42 computers, 27 printers for those computers, 100 televisions, 30 VCRs, and 50 DVD players.

he writes. "It might even be said to tyrannize. . . . Modern Americans are feeling less and less satisfied even as their freedom of choice expands." It's an unsettling conclusion—but one that hardworking executives at companies with declining ACSI scores might endorse.[4]

So the challenges are clear: How do you make a compelling offer to customers who already have more than enough of what you're selling? How do you break from the pack when the pack keeps getting bigger and louder (and better) every year? How do you forge a relationship with customers that can withstand the competition's barrage of lower prices, loftier claims, and snazzier features—a relationship that leaves customers confident that they've made the *right* choice and eager to keep making the *same* choice?

It's tempting to answer all of these questions with just one word: Starbucks. Seattle's espresso empire is one of the true entrepreneurial miracles of the last two decades—more than an iconic brand, more than a growth company, it's a destination and an institution that has become a recognizable piece of the American landscape, a so-called third place between home and work where people meet, think, relax, listen to music, check e-mail, and, by the way, happily spend $3.50 for a latte. By conceiving of his core product not as a caffeine delivery system but as a rich, consistent, and distinctive experience that embraces how the stores look, what they sell, who works there, even the exotic language customers speak to place an order, chairman Howard Schultz (who paid $3.8 million for Starbucks in 1987, when it had 17 stores and 100 employees) created an empire with more than 10,000 shops, sales of nearly $6 billion, and a stock market value of more than $25 billion. Starbucks is serving something that connects with customers, not just something to drink, and 25 million of us visit each week to buy whatever it is that the company is selling.[5]

The question, of course, is whether Starbucks is a one-of-a-kind blend of business and culture or whether its lessons can brew up successful brands in other fields. Howard Schultz and Dan Levitan, the onetime investment banker who honchoed the Starbucks IPO in 1992, have no doubt about the answer. They are the founding partners of Maveron, a venture capital firm that was launched in 1998 and has raised close to $700 million to invest in companies that aim to win big by making a big impression on their customers. Most venture capitalists search for "killer-app" technologies that will lead to a killer IPO. Maveron (whose name is a blend of the words "maverick" and "vision") searches for companies with a killer connection with customers—what Levitan calls a "psychological contract" that redefines expectations and reinvents a category.*

"A lot of people think about brand in terms of marketing or packaging, like it's a wrapper," Levitan says. "For us, the foundation of a brand is the psychological contract—the contract between a company and its employees and between those employees and their customers. Great consumer companies are built on genuine passion, plus a day-to-day commitment to great execution. Employees won't feel the passion, and can't maintain the operating discipline, unless they feel good about what the company sells and the values it stands for."

It's no surprise that Seattle-based Maveron is a major investor in Seattle-based Cranium, the high-profile board game company that, as we saw in chapter 2, has changed the game in its tired, crowded industry. (As we'll explore in the next chapter, Cranium is more explicit than almost any company we've met about developing products that strike an emotional chord with customers.) Maveron is also a major investor in a small (estimated 2005 revenues: $100 million), fast-growing, Chicago-based restaurant chain called Potbelly Sandwich Works. Nobody associated with Potbelly is prepared to say out loud what any visitor senses immediately—that the company aims to reinvent the market

---

*That said, Maveron is no stranger to technology investments. It was an early investor in eBay, and its portfolio includes a number of technology-based operations, including Capella Education Company, a fast-growing online university. Maveron is also a charter investor in eos, a premium-class-only transatlantic airline that raised $85 million in start-up funding.

for one American staple (sandwiches) in much the same way Starbucks reinvented the market for another American staple (coffee). But listen to Dan Levitan talk about the company (he's on its high-powered board of directors, as is Howard Schultz, Bob Kagle of Benchmark Capital, the first venture capital firm to back eBay, and Walter Robb, copresident of upscale grocery juggernaut Whole Foods Market), and the echoes are obvious.

"It's a very colorful environment," Levitan says of the company. "The employees are upbeat and happy. There's a certain energy that makes it fun. There's what I call a 'cauldron of consumer passion' around Potbelly. Most people will tell you that a sandwich shop is a sandwich shop is a sandwich shop. I first encountered that attitude in 1991, when I heard that a cup of coffee was a cup of coffee was a cup of coffee. Now, twenty-five billion dollars in market cap later, the rest is history."

The parallels between Starbucks and Potbelly are uncanny. Like Starbucks, which started in Seattle 16 years before Howard Schultz bought it, Potbelly was a cult brand in its hometown long before it went national. Like Howard Schultz, Potbelly's chairman and CEO, Bryant Keil, didn't start the company himself. He was a devoted customer who bought the operation from its founders in 1996. (Since then, he has raised $60 million from Maveron and other highly regarded firms. The company has grown from a handful of stores in 2001 to 100 stores and nearly 3,000 staffers at the end of 2005. The long-term plan is for thousands of stores across the country.) Also like Starbucks, Potbelly has refused to franchise, relying instead on company-owned stores. It's a more demanding, more capital-intensive strategy, but it maintains the quality, consistency, and personality of the brand—and it upholds the company's psychological contract with employees and customers.[6]

We traveled to Chicago to sample the "Potbelly experience" first-hand. Talk about a meal that doesn't just stick to your ribs but tickles your senses. The shop on the ground floor of Chicago's Merchandise Mart will never be confused with Subway, Quiznos, or some other cookie-cutter sandwich chain. It's bright, quirky, brimming with color. There are street signs, vintage posters and photographs, shelves lined with books. Unlike Starbucks, Potbelly has strikingly reasonable prices— every sandwich costs $3.79, every shake, malt, or smoothie costs $2.69. The food is served with delightful touches that customers can't help but notice. (Our Oreo milk shake, for example, was served with mini-Oreos scattered on top of the lid and a tiny sugar cookie on the straw.) There's a loft above the main row of booths where performers play live music most afternoons. And there is, of course, a potbelly stove, one of which adorns almost every outlet as a tribute to the original store.*

Bryant Keil, whose office is 23 floors above Potbelly's Merchandise Mart shop, doesn't exude the smooth air of a lifestyle marketer. He's modest, methodical, almost shy. But as he explains Potbelly's formula for growth, it becomes clear that he has huge ambitions for his company— all of which depend on maintaining a uniquely personal connection with his customers. "It's pretty easy to run a mediocre business," Keil says. "It's exponentially more difficult to do things well. That's why I don't like the word 'chain.' We're the *anti*-chain. We could build our stores faster and cheaper if everything was precut, preplanned, perfectly regimented. I like to be perfect, but I want the elements of our stores to be *imperfect*. That's part of the charm."

Indeed, Potbelly makes big investments in the pursuit of productive imperfection. The company has a full-time design czar whose job it is to be sure that all the stores, whether they're in Dallas, Indianapolis, or Washington, D.C., have the right mix of signs, books, artwork, and artifacts to give them a personal touch and a local feel. Potbelly operates its own workshop on the West Side of Chicago where carpenters,

---

*The Potbelly story is well known in Chicago. Back in 1977, a husband-and-wife team started selling heated sandwiches and hand-dipped shakes to drum up business for their antiques store on Lincoln Avenue on the city's North Side. Over time, the food business dwarfed the antiques business, so the store became a sandwich shop decorated with antiques, including a working potbelly stove.

painters, and other artisans make the booths, tables, and frames that furnish each store. Even the menu isn't perfect. Potbelly's official menu is limited to 11 core sandwiches. But over time, repeat customers learn that the shop makes lots of off-the-menu items—something known inside the company as Potbelly Underground. Maveron's Levitan argues that Potbelly Underground is a small innovation that sends a big message: "The challenge is, how does a company get big but continue to feel small? Potbelly Underground helps a loyal customer tell the person on the other side of the counter, 'I'm an insider, I'm part of the club.'"

Over time, veteran customers teach new customers how to become part of the club. "It's so funny," Bryant Keil chuckles. "Someone in line will say, 'I'll have a cheeseburger.' Other people will look around and you can see the expression on their face: they don't have cheeseburgers here! Actually, we do. It's a meatball sub without the sauce, with all the trimmings you'd expect on a cheeseburger. Then other people hear it, they catch on, and they order it too. Old customers teach new customers 'how to Potbelly.' It's one of the things I love about our stores, the sense of discovery."

Like Potbelly, the companies featured in the next two chapters have all discovered intriguing and instructive strategies to overcome the age of overload. These companies operate in vastly different industries and project radically different personalities to the outside world. But one way or another, each of them has figured out how to stop interacting with customers purely (or even primarily) on the basis of dollars-and-cents economic value. Instead, they have encouraged customers to buy into their values and forge bonds of loyalty and shared identity that help both sides cut through the clutter of the marketplace. To stand out from the crowd, these companies have come to stand for something special in the eyes of their customers. The goal of the next two chapters is to show you how they did it—and what their innovations mean for you.

TO MAKE YOUR COMPANY SPECIAL,
MAKE YOUR PERFORMANCE MEMORABLE

"Every great company has redefined the business that it's in," declares Vernon W. Hill II, sitting behind a huge desk in his spacious office at Commerce Bank headquarters. Hill, the company's founder, president, and chairman, looks like central casting's version of an establishment banker. He's dressed in a double-breasted suit, with a crisply pressed shirt, a glimmering collar clip, and, of course, a red tie. As a desktop computer lists incoming e-mails and a Bloomberg terminal flashes stock quotes, he belts out questions and instructions to an unflappable assistant.

But appearances can be deceiving. Hill is running late this afternoon because he and three of his highest-ranking executives have been poring over prototypes of a new Commerce product—a debit card that customers can load up with money and give as a gift to friends and family. Hill and his lieutenants are sweating over the card's typeface, over its design, over the size of the Commerce logo.

"How many CEOs of major banks worry about what their gift cards look like and how their stores execute the program?" Hill asks. "We *have* to worry about it. We believe in fanatical execution: how do we take this gift card and make it a 'wow' experience for our customers? Right now, most of the banks that issue these cards charge for them. We're not going to nickel-and-dime our customers; we're going to issue the cards for free."

This is the maverick mind-set that drives Vernon Hill. What separates his company from the competition in an overcrowded, uninspired segment of the economy has been his capacity to reimagine a bank as a state-of-the-art retail operation, a bank that doesn't act like a bank. "Even though I was trained as a banker, I'm *not* a banker," Hill insists. "We are growth retailers."

Everything about Hill's approach reinforces his we're-not-a-bank message. He doesn't evaluate his company's performance against

Citigroup, Bank of America, or Wachovia—industry giants that spend most of their time acquiring, consolidating, and cutting costs. He looks to Target, the Gap, and Home Depot. Commerce doesn't call its 375 bank outlets branches; it calls them *stores*. Like all world-class retailers, Hill and his colleagues are delighted when customers visit their stores, and they look for ways to keep them coming back. (Some Commerce stores get 100,000 customer visits per month. The average McDonald's gets 25,000 visits per month.)

Most Commerce locations are open 70 to 80 hours a week—an unheard-of innovation in the banking business before Commerce arrived. Remember banker's hours? The Commerce store at 94th and Broadway in Manhattan is open for more than twelve hours a day Monday through Friday (including until midnight on Friday), for more than ten hours on Saturday, and for five hours on Sunday. (Actually, all stores open 15 minutes before and close 15 minutes after their posted hours, another small way to exceed expectations.)

Hill can barely hide his amusement when asked why more banks don't keep their branches open for as long as his stores are open. "It's the simplest idea in the world," he says. "*Let's be open when the customers want us to be open*. But to this day, it's heretical in banking. People think we're crazy. The first question bankers ask me is, 'How do you staff on Sunday?' You know my answer? 'Wal-Mart stays open. The malls stay open. Every fast-food joint in the country stays open. How hard can it be?' We don't copy the stupid banks. We copy the great retailers."

He means this literally: practices that may be standard operating procedure in one setting can look downright startling in another. At one point in our conversation, Hill reaches into a shelf and pulls out a copy of *Built from Scratch*, the business autobiography of Bernie Marcus and Arthur Blank, founders of Home Depot. "This is the greatest business book I've ever read!" he exclaims. "We buy it by the case. Every management person who gets hired here has to read it. We learn more from these people than we do from anyone else."

A case in point: Commerce's so-called warm transfer policy. Hill explains: "Home Depot has a rule—which, by the way, everyone tells me they don't follow anymore—about how to shift a customer from one employee to another. Say you're in aisle eight and you want a screwdriver, which happens to be in aisle five. The employee in aisle eight is supposed to walk you to aisle five and either show you the screwdrivers or introduce you to the employee in that aisle. That's called a soft handoff. Here's how we translate that at Commerce. Say you call us on the phone, and we need to transfer you to another department. The agent doesn't just hit a button. He or she keeps you on the phone, gets the right person on the line with you, says, 'Joanne, I have Jim on the line, and here's what he needs help with,' and only then does the agent click off. We call that a 'warm transfer'—and it's a direct steal from Home Depot."

Hill may copy ideas from other industries, but he is adamant about the uniqueness of the Commerce model in *his* industry: the first order of business for a bank, he argues, is to gather as many deposits as it can. This sounds like common sense, but it's a real departure from how big banks have, until recently, tended to do business. For years, money-center banks have basically tolerated retail depositors as they vied to make high-priced loans, distribute credit cards, and jockey for advantage against the big Wall Street firms. But with hypercompetition in the capital markets, retail customers begin to look more attractive.

Yet Hill is equally adamant that he will not pay as high a rate of interest as the competition to gather his deposits. In fact, in most of Commerce's markets, including famously competitive New York City, Commerce's rates aren't anywhere near the best available. That's where the retailing mind-set kicks in. "We believe that customers care more about the retail experience than they do about the lowest price, which in our business is the highest interest rate," Hill explains. "So we do everything we can to strengthen our connection with customers, to make the experience fun. And we take a million little steps to reinforce our message.'"*

All those "little steps" are what make Commerce perform so memorably for customers—and look so strange to the competition. The company rarely misses an opportunity to turn conventional wisdom on its head. One classic upside-down innovation is its approach to the f-word in banking—the "float." At most banks customers wait three or four days to get access to funds they deposit by check. At a few big banks in New York City they may have to wait a week for checks to clear. At Commerce funds from all deposited checks are available *the next business day*—no questions asked. "The float is a rule that no bank can explain to its own people, let alone its customers," says Hill. "So we keep it simple: 'you make a deposit on Monday, it's good on Tuesday.' I don't want any procedures that an eighteen-year-old can't explain to customers."

That procedure comes with a cost: Commerce puts up with higher fraud charges than the competition. But what it loses on bad checks it more than makes up for in good faith. Tom Brown, the bank analyst and hedge fund manager we met in chapter 4, may be Commerce's most outspoken bull on Wall Street. Commerce is "the best bank in the country," he declares without hesitation. "When I first got to know these guys, I was the biggest skeptic. They didn't believe in treating different customers differently. They did believe in encouraging customers to come to the branches. They did everything the *opposite* of what most people in banking thought you should do."

----

*Careful readers may note that Vernon Hill and Arkadi Kuhlmann, both successful banking innovators, have radically different approaches to pricing strategies. As we explained in chapter 1, Kuhlmann has designed a bare-bones retail experience in support of the highest rates of interest in the industry. Hill surrounds low rates with a rich and entertaining customer experience. Both models have clicked with customers—and it's possible for individuals to be customers of both banks, since ING Direct doesn't offer physical branches, an ATM network, or other basics of personal banking.

Brown points to eliminating the float as a classic break-the-mold innovation. "Most banks look at check-clearing as a way to minimize losses," he explains. "But Vernon isn't about doing things that will minimize losses. He's interested in doing things that will maximize customer satisfaction. Nobody understands why check-clearing is so complicated. It's the number-one customer complaint and the number-one teller complaint. Commerce has a totally different mind-set. His customers—and his employees—love it."

Perhaps Hill's most memorable innovation, one that has become a huge point of differentiation among customers, is his bank's "Penny Arcade." Over the years, as part of their drive to cut costs and shoo customers out of branches, big banks have made it harder and more expensive for customers to show up with a glass jar or a piggy bank and get their coins counted. But where the establishment saw a cost to be cut, Commerce saw a memorable experience to be created. Today, in all 375 Commerce stores, attractive, colorful, easy-to-use Penny Arcades sit proudly in the lobby, available free of charge to anyone who stops by. Hill is amazed by how big a deal the Penny Arcades have become.

"These machines are getting used almost 500,000 times a month now," he says. (That's more than 1,300 times per month per store.) "We have stores in New York City where we've had to put two or three of them in. No one in the world in my business would spend the money we spend on these machines. Everyone wants to increase fees or reduce costs. But we're trying to tighten the bond with our customers. Most banks look at every product line and try to slice-and-dice it: 'can we save money here, can we charge more there?' Great retailers don't do that. They ask, 'How can we make it easier, simpler, more fun to do business with us?' They look at the whole experience. And that's what we do."

Creating a memorable experience doesn't always mean defying conventional wisdom. Sometimes it just means using common sense.

Another popular innovation in the spirit of Penny Arcades is the instant-card machine at every Commerce location. Customers who apply for or lose an ATM card or debit card no longer have to go to the bank, fill out a form, and wait for an unmarked envelope to arrive in the mail. Instead, they walk out of the store with a card that's been made and activated on the spot. "Why should it take a week to replace an ATM card?" Vernon Hill asks. "It's nuts. We're in the convenience business. It's about making the experience better."

Ultimately, though, what separates Hill's bank from the competition, what shapes the memorable experiences that have come to define its relationship with customers, is the simple act of walking into one of its stores. The Radio City ceremony was just one slice of life at Commerce. This is a bank that uses goofy mascots to entertain customers and employees, holds street fairs to celebrate the opening of new stores, and offers countless other (usually hokey) twists on what Vernon Hill calls "retailtainment."

For an outsider who encounters Commerce Bank for the first time, the company can feel eye-opening, exhilarating—and exhausting. The colors. The smiles. The sense of humor that pervades the place. *How can so many people be so upbeat so much of the time?* In reality, like everything else at the company, Commerce's loose, fun, unapologetically cheery store culture is the result of years of experience, fierce attention to detail, and an absolute determination to stand out from the crowd.

Dennis DiFlorio, who reports directly to Hill, is the cultural yin to the CEO's strategic yang. DiFlorio runs all of Commerce's retail operations. He's a man on a mission when it comes to rank-and-file employees. He nearly jumps out from behind his desk as he explains why the bank's business model can't work without its workplace culture. "I get as many as a dozen pieces of fan mail a day from customers," he says. "And they're never about the products, or the hours, or the Penny

Arcades. *They're always about the people.* Our secret weapon, what will always differentiate us, is our people and our culture."*

The challenge, of course, as Commerce Bank grows at such a fast clip, is to keep the culture consistent. That's why every Commerce employee carries a SMART card (DiFlorio thinks of it as a "pledge card") that lists the company's five principles of great service. Every manager or officer carries a roll of red stickers, in the shape of the bank's "C" logo, to slap on the back of an employee's card whenever, as DiFlorio puts it, "we catch somebody in the act of doing it right." As their card fills with stickers, employees redeem them for prizes. "It's too easy to catch people screwing things up," DiFlorio says. "What fuels this company are the high-fives, the wacky stuff we do to engage people in the business, to make them feel good. It's the job of every manager and officer of this bank to go out and catch people doing it right." (Commerce's managers and officers distributed an amazing 115,000 "C" stickers in 2005.)

If Dennis DiFlorio is the head coach for great service at Commerce, then Tim Killion is the captain of the cheerleading squad. His title—manager of the Wow Department—does not begin to capture the sense of purpose and raw enthusiasm this energetic twentysomething brings to his position: "This company lays the foundation for all of us to have fun at our jobs," he declares. "If we have fun and enjoy what we're doing, then the customer will enjoy the experience of doing business with us. I have the opportunity to put smiles on the faces of *my* customers—the 13,000 people who work at this bank—and I'm going to keep doing

---

*That doesn't mean Commerce people can't make serious mistakes. In May 2005, two Commerce executives were convicted on conspiracy counts in a municipal-fraud trial in Philadelphia. The executives got caught up in the so-called pay-to-play scheme that involved favors for city treasurer Corey Kemp, who was convicted as well. The goings-on at city hall also ensnared two executives from J. P. Morgan, who pled guilty to wire-fraud charges. Commerce itself was not charged in the proceedings, but the bank, famous for its Red Fridays, suffered a very public black eye.[7]

it until someone makes me stop. I've got a great job, and I wouldn't trade it for anything."

What is his job, exactly? "To keep 13,000 employees juiced about *their* jobs," he says, which he does by reminding them how unusual they and their company are. Killion can talk for hours about the best way for a Commerce employee to smile, the right way to greet a customer ("*May* I help you?" rather than "*Can* I help you?"), and why the bank enforces a dress code in its call centers. "We're on tour constantly," he explains. "Prospective clients come through. Wall Street analysts come through. We can't have people in sweats and sneakers. We refer to it as showtime. We're ready for showtime at all times."

Killion takes the notion of "showtime" literally. Among the Wow Department's most important allies inside the company are 150 volunteers known as the Wow Patrol. These volunteers have traditional, full-time jobs at the bank, but they also work with Killion to organize celebrations, run contests, and otherwise contribute to Commerce's culture and spirit. You don't make the Wow Patrol just by volunteering; you have to pass an annual audition—literally. "People come and show us that they want to have fun," Killion says. "Some write a song and sing it. Some come with a choreographed dance routine. Some do five minutes of stand-up. It's amazing what people come to the table with, and it's all wrapped around one thought: 'Hey, I want to have fun at work, can I be part of this?'"

"OUR CUSTOMER *IS* OUR CATEGORY"—
SELLING A SENSE OF IDENTITY

As entertaining as it is to experience the Wow-ified world of Commerce Bank, it's easy to misinterpret its lessons. Making your company memorable doesn't have to mean making it theatrical—turning your employees into a cast of thousands. The challenge isn't to *perform* as much as it is to *connect,* to offer something so distinctive that people can't help but notice, even in a marketplace bursting with low prices and big claims. In an era of overcapacity and oversupply, overloaded customers are eager to identify with companies that have an appealing identity.

Anthropologie, the vibrant, fast-growing women's clothing and home furnishings chain based in Philadelphia, stands out as a compelling alternative to the uniformity of style and stylish uniformity that characterizes so much of mass-market retail.* Over the past decade, it has forged a connection with customers that is every bit as powerful as what Vernon Hill and his colleagues have built at Commerce Bank. But in almost every aspect of their businesses, from the basics of strategy to the look and feel of the stores themselves, the two organizations have pursued decidedly different means to equally memorable ends. Commerce has broken the bank by creating a one-of-a-kind experience for a wide array of customers. Anthropologie has created new shelf space in a saturated market by delivering a wide array of products to a one-of-a-kind customer—a customer to whom the company devotes itself with single-minded intensity.[8]

Anthropologie's president, Glen Senk, calls the strategy "customer mastery"—and it has delivered masterful results in the company's stores and on Wall Street. "Most retailers either cater to a broad base of customers or specialize in a product category," he explains. "We're customer experts. Our focus is on always doing what's right for a specific customer we know very well. Every product we buy, every real estate decision we make, every action we take, is through the eyes of that customer. Our customer *is* our category."

Ask employees at Anthropologie who that customer is, and they can furnish a crisp demographic profile: a 30- to 45-year-old woman, with a college or postgraduate education, married with kids or in a committed

---

*And there is *so much* retail. With more than 30 square feet of retail space for every man, woman, and child in the United States (not to mention the virtual universe of catalogs and e-commerce), it is more urgent than ever for companies to stand for something special in the eyes of their customers.

relationship, professional or ex-professional, annual household income of $150,000 to $200,000. But those lifeless facts and statistics don't capture the living, breathing woman Senk and his fellow Anthropologists call "our friend." Senk prefers to describe his customer in psychographic terms: "She's well read and well traveled. She has a natural curiosity about the world. She's into cooking, gardening, and wine. She's relatively fit. She's urban-minded. She is very aware—she gets our references, whether they're to a town in Europe, to a book, or to a movie."

Wendy Brown, Anthropologie's director of stores, is just as emphatic about the single-minded relationship between the company and its core customers: "We have one customer, and we know *exactly* who she is," Brown says. "We don't sit around a table and say to one another, 'What do you think she'd like?' We're out there. We're in the marketplace. We live where the customer lives."

That may be because many of those customers seem to live in the stores. Anthropologie's customers visit more frequently, stay longer, and buy more than the customers of almost any other comparable chain. The average visit lasts 75 minutes. The average customer spends a relatively high $80 per visit. (Catalog customers spend an average of $161 per order.) The company's average sales per square foot exceed $800, among the highest in the industry.

The sum total of all these sales is one of the country's best-performing specialty retailers. Glen Senk joined Anthropologie in 1994, when the outfit had one store with annual revenue of $2 million. In 2005 Anthropologie had 77 stores and estimated sales of $500 million, up from $320 million the year before. Meanwhile, shares in its parent company, Urban Outfitters, have become as fashionable as Anthropologie's clothes and furnishings. Between September 2000 and September 2005, Urban shares (adjusted for splits) rose from less than $4.50 to more than $27.50, giving the company a market value of more than $4 billion.

Why are so many women willing to spend so much time (and money) at Anthropologie? Because Senk and his team aren't just selling clothes and furnishings. They're selling a sense of *identity*. This is a company that was designed from the beginning around identity and emotion, not just price points and SKUs. "Coming to our store isn't just about buying something," says Senk. "It's about connecting with people, it's about having fun. Customers come to us to learn, not just to shop."

Richard Hayne, cofounder and CEO of Urban Outfitters, first demonstrated his ability to capture the lifestyle of a core customer group more than 30 years ago.* He nailed the shopping, sleeping, and furnishing habits of the upper-middle-class college kid with his original chain. Today Urban Outfitters is an emporium for "upscale homeless"—men and women, age 18 to 30, whose purchasing behavior is still driven by their social lives.

More than 20 years after opening his first store, Hayne enlisted architect Ron Pompei, who has led the creative direction of nearly every Urban and Anthropologie space, to help envision a compelling destination for the post-Urban generation. Hayne's training as an anthropologist informed the process. The pair spent nearly two years on a "cultural odyssey"—traveling, reading, visiting museums and exhibitions, attending cultural events, and scouring outdoor markets. What surfaced in the course of this amateur anthropological dig, says Pompei, "was a return to an earthier sensibility. We saw things that were tactile and visceral. Things that engaged the whole body. Texture was very important. Storytelling was central."

These clues translated into a retail concept that was as much about human behavior as about purchasing behavior. Pompei offers this explanation: "The way people evaluate themselves and others boils down to three things: what they have, what they do, or who they are. The

---

*Thanks to the success of the Urban Outfitters and Anthropologie brands, Richard Hayne can afford a pretty comfortable lifestyle himself. He owns more than 40 million shares of the company he founded. In late 2005, with shares selling for more than $30, Hayne was officially a billionaire.

mainstream culture focuses on what you have. Recently, what you do has become more important. We wanted to respond to the shift toward who you are." Moreover, Pompei says, "we wanted to create an experience that would set up the possibility of change and transformation. People would start to connect the dots in their own way and tell themselves a personal story."

The day-to-day challenge in the stores, adds creative director Kristin Norris, who is responsible for every aspect of their look and feel, "is to capture a customer's attention so that she'll explore every corner and let her imagination go. We mix up the stock in a way that gives the customer ideas. We always try to strike a balance between making the stores easy to shop and making them intensely interesting."

Interesting is an understatement. Walk through the massive wooden doors of the Anthropologie store on West Broadway in New York City and even the best laid plans for a quick visit go awry. You can't help but pause to take in the scene. Look straight ahead, and a vintage sun umbrella tilts at a rakish angle over a wrought iron garden table covered with whimsical flower candlesticks, ceramic pots, and glossy gardening books. Make a half turn to the right, and you seem to have stumbled into an artist's studio. Vases creep up a rickety spiral staircase to the ceiling, a half-finished still life rests on an easel, and a weathered cabinet houses scented candles, glass vases, and velvety throw pillows.

As you begin to wander through the cavernous, high ceiling structure, you encounter what looks like a Tuscan country kitchen. A jumble of embroidered dishcloths, brightly patterned teacups, and (a flash of the Far East) batik dinner plates are crowded into a couple of rough-hewn breakfronts. Nearby, a pair of eighteenth century French balusters define an elegant dinner tableau—complete with cut-glass chandelier, champagne flutes, sliver and horn flatware, and lace-printed serving plates. Tucked into the back of the sprawling space, a cozy bed piled high with crisp pillows sits opposite a painted armoire filled with books, blank journals, and a tiny television playing *Roman Holiday*.

Along the way, you pass small collections of clothing arranged in artful vignettes. Strapless summer dresses and eyelet blouses hang over a table containing fifties-era sunglasses, wide brimmed straw hats, and a stack of books (called *Essential Manners for Men*). Tailored trousers with quirky detailing, shrunken jackets, and ethnic tunics share space on hand-crafted wood and metal racks; sporty slacks and crisp T-shirts are piled on marble tables set in steel frames. The eclectic mix of runway-inspired pieces, preppy staples, and exotic accents is just what you might imagine for an itinerant adventurer making a home in the city.

It's a dazzling array of goods. What makes Anthropologie even more compelling is the fact that each of its stores is designed to reflect its local customers and environment. "Our philosophy is to make each store feel as if it's a one-off," says Norris. The Greenwich, Connecticut, store was built from an old barn and features fireplaces and rolling landscaping for a country feel; the Seattle store reflects an Asian influence with river stones and bamboo flooring; the Dallas store is smaller, more intimate, more feminine. Each store has its own staff of artists and craftspeople who interpret display and window visions in their own way.

The end result is that Anthropologie maintains a boutique appeal even as it adds nearly 20 stores a year. In fact, says Senk, "we never call ourselves a chain. Many of our customers don't know that there are more than a couple of stores, and that's exactly how we like it. People shop us because we're special."

Being "special" doesn't just mean being quirky or surprising. It also means rethinking some of the most familiar conventions of retail. For example, the company doesn't advertise—ever.* Where most specialty retailers invest money and creativity into expensive, splashy, celebrity-studded

---

*So how does the word get out? Beyond the word-of-mouth connection, Anthropologie's thriving catalog business (19 million distributed in 2004) is a powerful tool in raising awareness and generating sales. Anthropologie is also a favorite of the fashion press and Hollywood wardrobe departments—not to mention devoted celebrity shoppers like Madonna, Sharon Stone, Susan Sarandon, and Julia Roberts.

ad campaigns, Anthropologie pours its creative resources into building a vibrant store experience. "One of our core philosophies," explains Senk, "is that we spend the money that other companies spend on marketing to create a store experience that exceeds people's expectations. We don't spend money on messages—we invest in execution."

The company's execution relies on a range of sensory cues to engage the customer's imagination. Kristin Norris's creative team adds a layer of visual artistry to the already rich store experience. A recent series of holiday windows in the West Broadway store featured a Victorian-style dollhouse with a roof made out of books and dress forms clad in jackets fashioned out of book pages. The next spring, a stunning sculpture of slices of whitewashed terracotta pots hung from the ceiling on thin pieces of yarn like a giant wind chime. Each store adjusts its musical playlist to align with shifts in season and mood. Even a store's *scent* is coordinated to collection and season. "Through the use of sound, sight, touch, and smell, we form a powerful bond with our customers," says Senk.

What the company doesn't use to strengthen its bond is arm's-length market research such as surveys and focus groups. To be sure, Senk and his colleagues are number-crunching fanatics when it comes to analyzing operations. ("I can tell you how things are selling based on neckline, colors, novelty feature, price point, fabric—anything, at any moment," he says. "This business is all about investing in what's selling and divesting in what's not selling.") But when it comes to understanding customers, they replace science with art, preferring to spend hours in person rather than spend days at their desks poring over spreadsheets.

Senk himself spends at least four hours a week in the stores, as do his top lieutenants. (Every six weeks he also does a "mall crawl" to size up the competition as well as his own stores.) During Senk's in-store visits, you'll often find him outside the fitting rooms, rolling up his sleeves with customers to select just the right outfit. "You have to get down on your hands and knees, wherever you are in the organization, and really connect. Once you fit a woman into pants," he smiles, "you've got a customer for life."

A few years back, Wendy Wurtzburger, Anthropologie's general merchandise manager, launched a major effort to get this fit even tighter. She introduced a quarterly ritual called a "fit party," in which customers "shop" a makeshift store, try on outfits, and pour out their comments, complaints, and pain to a diverse collection of Anthropologie staffers. One outcome of these fit parties was a private-label line of pants, called Flying Room, which has flown off the shelves. Wurtzburger has extended the fit-party concept to home goods with the "home open house"—a "fit session for the home." Her team sends 20 shoppers to the stores and then documents how they incorporate what they buy into their homes. The customers take photographs, come back to the store, and review the photos and talk about their experiences in small-group settings.

If it sounds more like a gathering of friends than a bloodless commercial transaction—well, that's how Anthropologie intends it. Glen Senk is adamant. "Our customers are our friends," he insists, "and what we do is never, ever, *ever* about selling to them. It's about helping people put a wardrobe together or create an eclectic home. It's about helping someone look great and feel good about themselves. It's never about the quick sale."

And when it is about the quick sale, Senk is quick to act. To punctuate his point, he tells a story about a star employee who unfailingly sold $6,000 or $7,000 worth of merchandise in every three-hour stretch. "Every time this woman worked, her store would have an *incredible* day," he says. "I came in to watch her, and what I saw was that she really didn't care what she was selling so long as she made the sale. She let people walk out of the dressing room with things that simply didn't look good." Was that any way to treat a friend? She was fired immediately.

That's a memorable lesson in how companies that are eager to forge a strong psychological contract treat even overeager customers. If you're determined to encourage customers to buy into your values, then you have to value more than the easy sell. It's a harder way to do business, but one that leaves a more lasting impression—and creates a more enduring relationship.

Chapter Eight

Small Gestures, Big Signals: Outstanding Strategies to Stand Out from the Crowd

A sandwich shop with its own art director, a team of artisans to make tables and countertops, and an "underground" menu so that loyal customers can feel like insiders. A retail bank with employees who are such over-the-top extroverts that they perform in Broadway-style musical revues. A clothing store that uses sight, sound, even smell, to conjure up a sensory experience to captivate shoppers and capture their imaginations. Thus far, we think you'll agree, our search for companies that have devised new ways to connect with customers and prosper in the age of overload has led us to true brand extremists— organizations that operate, in the colorful words of Commerce Bank's Dennis DiFlorio, "on the lunatic fringe" of their industries.

But you don't have to stand on the fringe to stand out from the crowd. Connecting with customers is about substance, not style— creating a more compelling way to do business, whatever business you're in. In a competitive environment defined by too much choice and too many look-alike choices, it doesn't take all that much creativity to be memorable—to be different enough in your marketplace that your customers find you hard to forget.

Unlike the show-stopping staffers at Commerce Bank, for example, the tough-as-nails employees of DPR Construction don't sing, dance, or dress in funny costumes on Friday. But the ways in which they work with customers are unique enough, and delivered with such attention to detail, that interacting with this company's hard-hats is every bit as distinctive as banking with Commerce's fun-loving tellers. The little twists to how DPR's employees work make a big impression on the companies with which it works.[1]

As we saw in chapter 2, DPR has pursued a truly original strategy in the construction industry—a business model driven by a commitment to rebuilding a seriously flawed sector of the economy. And the way it does business on a workaday basis reinforces that commitment to originality. Nearly every major project at DPR starts with a distinctive opening ritual—the creation of a project mission statement. The company assembles supervisors and key members of its crew, along with representatives from the client, the architect, the engineers, subcontractors, suppliers, vendors—anyone and everyone with a role to play. This group spends days together, getting to know one another, working with a facilitator, hammering out a crisp statement of purpose, clear timetables, and detailed metrics of success. For most of the (non-DPR) participants, it's a weird way to work: why are we debating language when we could be placing concrete? But it's the unique way DPR works— and one reason its projects tend to work out so well.

DPR builds expensive, complicated, high-stakes facilities. In 2005 the company completed work on a manufacturing complex in Oceanside, California, for Biogen Idec, the pharmaceutical giant. It was a massive undertaking, with thousands of workers, direct construction costs of $340 million, and total costs (land, equipment, and so on) of more than $1 billion. But before DPR started the four-year, six-building complex, it worked with a team of representatives from Biogen to build a sense of camaraderie by—you guessed it—collaborating to write a mission statement.

"There were team-building sessions, coaching sessions, scorecards, metrics," says Peter Salvati, a senior DPR executive based in San Diego. "We were going to work with these people for more than three years. There was a lot of focus on our journey together: how would we treat one another? You can have good results, but if people aren't talking when it's over, if you haven't built lasting relationships, is the job a success?"

In addition to timetables and technical details, the mission statement urged members of the team to demonstrate "zeal and commitment every day" and to embrace an "energetic and unflagging pursuit of project success." It also reminded them that "team members do not allow others to fail" and told them not to forget about "relaxing, recharging, rejuvenating to avoid burnout."

This is hardly the sort of language you encounter on most construction sites. But it's precisely the sort of language that makes DPR such a memorable company to do business with. "You could walk through the building and *see* what the mission was," says Salvati. "There'd be poster boards that explained how it related to each part of the facility, showed target dates for completion, with actual dates right next to them. Everybody understood what was happening."*

DPR projects finish as memorably as they start—with a closing ritual that leaves a lasting impression. DPR conducts in-depth, in-person interviews before, during, and, especially, after every project. The interviews evaluate its performance against a list of "critical success factors"—from accurate cost estimates to staffing and safety. DPR is not

*In February 2005 Biogen Idec was racked by news that two patients for its promising MS drug, Tysabri, had died during treatment. As part of its recovery strategy, the company sold its crown-jewel manufacturing complex to Genentech, the blue-chip biotech firm, for $408 million. So the Oceanside facility will continue to produce pharmaceuticals—just different drugs, for a different company.

interested in how its performance stacks up against industry norms or even against what its clients expected. It wants to know how its performance compares with the best performance the client has *ever* experienced, what it calls "better than best in class."

During these lengthy sessions, interviewers encourage customers to identify their best-ever encounter with a construction company and to rate DPR against that standard. DPR has conducted thousands of these interviews over the years, and the company tracks results by project, by office, and by technical category. Its aggregate score in 2004, 1.15, meant that customers considered it 15 percent better than their best-ever experience.

It's a powerful way to keep improving—and to keep creating memorable interactions, even if the company's zeal for the interviews can wear its customers out. "Sometimes they won't let us do them," admits DPR cofounder Doug Woods. "They say, 'You guys *were* best in class, you still *are* best in class, and we're tired of going through these interviews. Go find somebody else!'"

DPR is one small example of a huge opportunity. There are so many ways to defy expectations in the marketplace, to do enough little things that you wind up making a big impression on your customers. Remember our discussion about 1–800 service? How is it that so many companies, desperate for the loyalty of customers with more options than ever before, think it makes sense to outsource, automate, and otherwise abandon direct connections with these customers? Especially when you consider the alternative—investing to *build* those connections and strengthen the ties that bind a company and its customers.

Vermont Teddy Bear is a warm-and-fuzzy business from a picture-postcard state. But its impressive turnaround under CEO Elisabeth Robert underscores the power of this alternative strategy and sends a strong message about the limits of business as usual when it comes to making a genuine connection with your customers.

Robert chuckles about how improbable it is "to use Howard Stern to sell $85 teddy bears to grown men." Yet that's precisely what the company has done. It targets its BearGrams, nearly one-third of which are sold in the two weeks before Valentine's Day, to a customer it dubs "Late Jack"—a guy who's nervous about picking the right gift for his wife or girlfriend, who waits until the last minute, and who's looking for something personal and "goof-proof."

Everything the company does is about strengthening its connection to customers. Robert reaches her customers with live spots on guy-oriented radio and TV—Stern, sports-talk shows, auto racing. Employees even appear on the programs to banter with the hosts, exchanging double entendres with shock jocks, talking hot-stove baseball with sportscasters. "We're not selling our products," the CEO explains. "We're selling our people. We have a live relationship with our customers, on the radio and on the phone."

Before Robert took over, Vermont Teddy Bear defined its business in utterly conventional terms—selling an array of teddy bear merchandise, complete with expensive retail space in Manhattan, with a "category killer" strategy. It was a recipe for disaster. Back in 1997, the company's low point, the once-thriving business actually teetered on the verge of bankruptcy.

Redefining the strategy to meet the needs of Late Jack meant reinventing virtually every aspect of how the company did business—and it meant investing in precisely those areas where most companies are cutting. Forget outsourcing or automating 1-800 call centers. Telephone operators ("bear counselors," in company parlance) are the lifeline between the company and its uptight customers. Bear counselors spent two and a half *million* minutes on the phone in 2004. They suggest different models, offer advice about ways to personalize a bear, and reassure callers that their selections will arrive on time.

Why doesn't Vermont Teddy Bear join the cost-cutting flight overseas? "This is an emotionally charged product," Robert says, "and our people have very high standards for not letting customers down. They don't want anybody else to be responsible for dealing with our customers. It just doesn't sit right."

Vermont Teddy Bear has also made big investments to help customers recover when things go wrong. For example, 40 percent of all BearGrams ordered for Valentine's Day ship overnight on February 13. Customers can order BearGrams as late as *midnight* on February 13 and be guaranteed next-day delivery. (To pull this off, Vermont Teddy Bear creates a temporary shipping facility near the FedEx campus in Memphis, Tennessee.) If that's not enough, customers can cancel or revise a BearGram even after the bear is on the delivery truck. "You have no idea how valuable it is to be able to stop an order," Robert explains. "The guy will call in a panic and say, 'I can't tell her I love her. I've got to say I *like* her.' "*

Delivering for Late Jack has produced tangible results for Vermont Teddy Bear. Annual sales, which hit a low of $17 million before Robert took charge, now exceed $66 million, and the company is solidly profitable. It has also become an icon in its home state. Its barnlike headquarters is one of Vermont's most popular tourist destinations, attracting nearly a million visitors since it opened to the public. That's what can happen when you stop cutting costs and start strengthening your bonds with customers.

EMOTION BY DESIGN—
FROM PUSHING PRODUCTS TO TELLING STORIES

More and more companies are beginning to understand how hard it is to compete on the "hard" factors in business: price, quality, and features.

---

*Every so often, a few Late Jacks need help with a more serious, albeit unintentionally hilarious, problem: they purchased BearGrams for their wife *and* their girlfriend but mixed up the addresses. Fixing that problem wins lots of customer loyalty.

That's why so many companies are thinking big and spending bigger on the "soft" side—designing products that are beautiful to look at, or marketing products with ad campaigns that appeal to the heart rather than the head, surrounding them with symbols and icons that don't just instill trust but engage the senses. To make their offerings more memorable, companies are working desperately to make them more emotional.

They are, literally, looking for a whole lotta love. Forget trademarks. In the heartfelt language of Kevin Roberts, the high-profile CEO of Saatchi & Saatchi, the new goal is *lovemarks*—brands that become a "beautiful obsession," that inspire "loyalty beyond reason" and create a "long-term love affair" with their customers by invoking the elements of "mystery, sensuality, and intimacy." Love, Roberts argues, "means more than liking a lot. We are not talking affection plus. Love is about a profound sense of attachment."[2]

Cranium, whose one-of-a-kind approach to strategy we explored in chapter 2, has become a master at creating attachments of the sort that Kevin Roberts loves. Cranium is not a company with satisfied customers; this is a company with *passionate* customers eager to share their enthusiasm with anyone who'll pay attention. (They're Craniacs, after all.) A group of free-spending New Year's revelers marked the turn of the century with a voyage to Antarctica—and a game of Cranium. ("We have pictures of Cranium at the South Pole," marvels cofounder Whit Alexander.) Couples have gotten married in Cranium-themed weddings. One Craniac proposed to his girlfriend during a game, using Cranium cards designed just for him. (He sent an e-mail with his plan to company headquarters, and Cranium agreed to help him.) "He dropped to his knees," smiles Alexander, "and handed her a Cranium fill-in-the-blank card where the question was, 'Will you marry me?' She said yes."

Why do so many customers get so emotionally invested in the company's games and experiences? In large measure because the company designs its games and experiences to elicit just this sort of reaction. The product design process at Cranium begins with what the founders call "moment engineering." Rather than create games around familiar genres (strategy games like Risk or Stratego, word games like Scrabble or Boggle), designers create games around specific situations with recognizable emotions—situations and emotions ripe for personal connection. "We study a human moment and ask, 'How can Cranium celebrate that moment in a new way?'" says cofounder Richard Tait. "'What is the "lighten-and-enlighten" approach to that particular moment?'"[3]

Different moments allow games to tap different emotions and experiences. Cariboo (the word means "welcome" in Swahili) was Cranium's first game for the preschool set. It was designed for what Tait calls the "rainy-day moment"—when a mom sits quietly with a young child and plays a game that she wants to be fun, worthwhile, and quick. Kids match cards to secret doors, find hidden balls, unlock a treasure set—while practicing letters, numbers, shapes, and colors. "We wanted to create a fifteen-minute experience," Tait says, "something that would be cherished by both the child and the mother." Hullabaloo captures the manic energy that gets unleashed when elementary school kids get together—what Tait calls the "playdate moment." The game is active, physical, high-energy—kids bounce, twist, spin, high-five, and dance. Conga, a game designed with the whole family in mind, was made for what Tait calls the "turn-off-the-TV moment"—those times in every family's rushed, stressed, overscheduled life when everyone agrees it's time to do something together. Players use acting, sculpting, and word games to guess what other players are thinking—and to reconnect as a family. "We wanted to figure out a way of uncovering stories that had been untold or forgotten," Tait explains. "You know, 'What were you really like as a kid, Mom? What was Grandpa's dream job?'"

Don't let the warm-and-fuzzy descriptions fool you. There is a genuine engineering mind-set behind moment engineering—a 40-step methodology by which developers sketch, prototype, build, launch, and revise a new game. Even the most technical elements of game development—activities, colors, time limits—unfold with emotional connections in mind. Jill Waller, the company's CHIFF Champion, can talk at great length about the reliable "touchstones" that find their way into many Cranium games.

"Corn on the cob is a touchstone," she says. "We all ate it as kids, it has a special place in people's hearts. Cupcakes are a touchstone—they remind you of birthdays, it's just a fun, happy word. These touchstones create warm feelings and a sense of 'personalization' for players." The result of this intense focus on designing for emotion has been a collection of games that have made undeniable connections with their target customers—and become an unprecedented string of hits.

David Rockwell, the influential architect and designer, has never, as far as we know, designed a board game. But he and his colleagues have developed a knack for creating public spaces that strike a chord with the people who visit them—spaces whose design principles are as emotional as they are functional. Indeed, his model for the creation of memorable buildings is consistent with (albeit far more elaborate than) Cranium's model for the design of games. Rockwell creates landmarks by aspiring to create the architectural equivalent of lovemarks—buildings whose touchstones draw people in rather than just provide somewhere for them to go.

Since its founding in 1984, the Rockwell Group has completed more than 200 projects, including some of the world's trendiest restaurants and New York's hippest hotels, along with entertainment destinations such as the Mohegan Sun casino, Cirque du Soleil's theater at Disney World, and the Kodak Academy Awards theater in Los Angeles. Rockwell and his colleagues have designed stadiums, libraries, corporate headquarters, museums—even sets for the Broadway musicals *Hairspray* and *All Shook Up* and the feature film *Team America*.

What's more impressive than the range of its assignments, though, is the visual wit and attention to detail that his firm brings to each project. Indeed, the lavish stagecraft and riotous mix of materials that characterize much of Rockwell's work has motivated some purist-minded critics to dismiss it as "entertainment architecture." (To experience-obsessed companies such as Commerce Bank, Starbucks, and Cranium, that's hardly grounds for criticism.) But Rockwell's critics miss the fact that his distinctive talent is not for making bold statements with a brash style, but for making enduring connections with compelling (and often subtle) story lines—a design philosophy that is more than skin-deep.

That philosophy may explain why so many Rockwell restaurants (50 over the last two decades) not only become hot spots but tend to demonstrate staying power in a famously fickle business. Nobu, the three-star Japanese restaurant created by chef Nobuyuki Matsuhisa and designed by Rockwell 20 years ago, has been exported to London, Milan, and Las Vegas and has spawned countless imitators around the world. Yet limos and town cars still crowd around the Tribeca original in New York City, and reservations are still nearly impossible to come by without a boldface name.

"The first and most important piece of every job," Rockwell says, "is to tell a unique and relevant story about the space, the product, or the experience. Story is the fundamental platform for organizing ideas. That's how you connect emotionally with people."

Which is why every Rockwell job begins with a deep dive into what he calls the "secret narrative" behind the building. A team spends long periods of time with potential visitors, prospective customers, and other key constituencies. It maps out a set of themes that link the backstory of the space to the lives of its users. The resulting secret narrative guides every subsequent design decision. "For us, a project begins with reimagining everything about a space," says Rockwell. "The more time we spend tilting at windmills and pushing at dreams—long before we get to form, color, and texture—the more profound the effect. The best projects start with pure ideas rather than ideas about design."

The ideas behind two vastly different spaces—one devoted to public service, the other crassly commercial—illustrate how Rockwell's secret narrative creates memorable connections for the people who encounter his buildings. Consider first the Children's Hospital at Montefiore (CHAM), a $123 million addition to the Montefiore Medical Center that serves southern Westchester County and the Bronx, whose residents include some of the most medically underserved children in the nation. CHAM's champion, crusading pediatrician Dr. Irwin Redlener, defined a unique three-part mission for the organization. First, to create not just a hospital but a comprehensive children's health system for the Bronx. Second, to get rid of all financial barriers between sick kids and world-class treatment. Finally, to incorporate "an agenda beyond healing that would be appropriate, unique, and perhaps even life-changing for this patient population."[4]

To transform that ambitious agenda into a memorable experience, Redlener turned to Rockwell. The design brief was open-ended and ambitious. "We wanted to recast the idea of what could be achieved in a children's hospital," Redlener explains. "Our mission was to provide excellent health care and a total environment that ignites the imagination of children. Hospitals are about healing. This one is about changing lives." Specifically, he wanted to ignite youthful imagination by introducing sick kids to the worldview of the late astronomer Carl Sagan, Redlener's longtime friend—a worldview that embraced the interconnectedness of the universe and the joys of learning. (Who says hospitals have to be just about X-rays, surgery, and chemotherapy?)

Rockwell and his colleagues immersed themselves in the experience of hospitalization from the perspective of children, parents, doctors, and nurses. "You get these kids at a very terrifying time of their lives," Rockwell says. "Hospitals by and large are opaque. We went way out there in the world of ideas and came up with the core theme of kids as explorers on a journey to health. It was all about substituting curiosity for fear. We identified the moments as a child in a hospital that are terrifying, dehumanizing, and lacking in information, and used those moments as interventions to provide information, insight, and a sense of wonder and delight. We created a strong enough story for people to join in."

That story is woven into the hospital's design at every level. Each of the CHAM's seven patient floors has a unique theme and design palette. Step off the elevator on the third-floor unit for ambulatory and outpatient procedures and you can see Sagan's idea that "we are star stuff" connected by our common origin in the Big Bang rendered in a colorful etched-glass mural of sea worms, snowflakes, and stars. Travel to the fifth-floor unit dedicated to illnesses of perception (facial disorders, speech, sight) and you're in an interactive playground dedicated to exploring nonvisual senses.

Patient rooms don't have numbers; they feature constellations, animals, or water creatures, depending on the floor's theme. A teenager might stay in the Big Dipper room, while an infant might stay in the Bumblebee room. Inside each room, the window shades are custom-designed murals depicting the Bronx in different time periods. Scattered about the patient floors are dozens of glass-covered niches displaying works of art by young children from around the city. The child-height exhibits encourage kids to create their own drawings, collages, and sculptures in the fully supplied lounges on each floor.

Rockwell and his colleagues understood that 70 percent of the kids in the hospital experience it only from their beds. So they designed acoustic ceiling tiles imprinted with hopeful and fun messages. They reinvented the mechanism and tweaked the sound of the privacy curtain that closes around the bed. The attention to detail is truly stunning—and the emotional impact truly memorable.

Of course, Rockwell and his colleagues are in business largely to serve for-profit business, so it's not unusual for the firm's most compelling ideas to support the most unapologetically commercial ventures. The Mohegan Sun casino and resort in Uncasville, Connecticut, is a two-hour drive—and a world away—from the Children's Hospital at Montefiore, but it ranks as one of Rockwell's most high-impact projects. It is a momentous business triumph—the second-largest casino in the world, with annual revenues of more than $1.25 billion. It is also a monument to the power of design—a 240-acre complex whose "secret narrative" shapes how visitors experience the resort (and spend their money), even if they can't begin to understand all its layers of complexity.

The casino's narrative is an ancient one, the history of Connecticut's Mohegan tribe. The importance of the four seasons in Mohegan culture became Rockwell's organizing principle for the 600,000-square-foot original casino. A "life trail"—an abstraction depicting the Mohegan migration southward to the Connecticut region centuries ago—served as the main navigational element. Life-size howling white wolves stand guard atop rock formations and mark the entrance to a performance space.

In a nearly four-million-square-foot addition (including a second casino, a convention center, and a retail complex), Rockwell incorporated the Mohegan mythology of healing crystals once found at the Uncasville site. He constructed an indoor mountain (called Wombi Rock) out of 12,000 translucent slabs of onyx and steel that glows with a caramel light—and houses a salon for high rollers, a restaurant, and a nightclub in a series of cavelike rooms. Wombi Rock sits beneath the world's biggest working planetarium dome.

The density of the detail at Mohegan Sun is outlandish, almost unfathomable. There are woven birch-bark walls, glass-encased turkey feathers and dried cornhusk tiles, a ceiling canopied with 30 million hand-strung beads. Rockwell doesn't expect hotel guests and high-rolling gamblers to fully grasp the crafts and culture of the Mohegans, but he does expect the place to communicate something distinctive.

"It wasn't about creating an environment that people would understand immediately," he says. "It was about creating an enormous public space that refutes the idea that large, public spaces have to be repetitive and machine-made. We were on a mission to imbed detail and storytelling into every single piece. People sense that they're in this amazingly outrageous space that is crafted and cared about. They don't necessarily get *why* it's that way, but they feel it and it feels special. People don't need to 'get' every reference, to understand every thread of the story, to know that they're in a place that has an underlying intelligence."

SHARED PASSIONS—WHY SOCIAL IS POWERFUL

For all their maverick innovations, Cranium's game designers and David Rockwell's building designers are in some sense devising exciting new twists on a familiar challenge—developing products, services, even physical spaces that tug on the heart as well as challenge the mind. The next frontier for making products more emotional is to turn them into something *social*—to create a sense of shared ownership and participation among customers themselves. The more people you invite to shape your company's personality, the more you enable them to share their ideas with one another, the greater their stake in what your company does—and the more invested they become in its success. In the new world of competition, generating a whole lotta love means unleashing a whole lotta participation.

Peter van Stolk remembers exactly where he was when he understood how much passion his company, Jones Soda, inspired in its most devoted customers. He was at a Taco Bell in Mesa, Arizona, ordering a bean burrito. The woman behind the counter noticed that van Stolk was wearing a small Jones Soda pin in the shape of a bottle cap. She looks at me and says, 'What's with the pin, dude?'" he chuckles. "I tell her, 'It's a Jones Soda cap.' She says, 'I know *what* it is, but why are you wearing it?'" So van Stolk quietly told her he was the company's founder and CEO—at which point the woman climbed over the counter, grabbed him by the shoulders, and threw him to the ground. "Now I'm freaked out!" van Stolk says. "She's on top of me, really going off, creating a big scene. And then she just disappears into the back office."

Moments later, the seemingly deranged Taco Bell employee reappeared—clutching bottles of Jones Soda as if they were a prized treasure. The labels on the bottle, it turns out, feature photographs of her children. This woman, like hundreds of thousands of other Jones customers, had submitted photos to van Stolk's company in the hope that they might be selected to appear on labels for one of the 20-plus flavors that Jones sells. Her photos attracted enough votes from her fellow customers, and won enough plaudits from Jones's panel of judges, that they made the cut—and had just arrived on store shelves. "She had spent that whole morning driving around Mesa buying bottles with her kids on them," van Stolk remembers. "She was so fired up."

It's not every day that the CEO of a consumer products company gets physically (if lovingly) assaulted by a rabid fan. But that's a cost of doing business when a company works to transform everyday products into emblems of self-expression and social interaction. Jones Soda customers aren't just encouraged to drink the product; they're invited, individually and collectively, to *define* the product, to shape its identity, to exercise their voice in the brand's personality and message to the marketplace. Jones doesn't preach to its customers about the virtues of its brand; it unleashes the energy and creativity of its customers to give the brand its virtues. Jones turns soda into a platform for social interaction.

"We started this company with the philosophy that the world does not need another soda," explains van Stolk, now safely ensconced in what passes for a conference room at the company's Seattle headquarters. He's surrounded by bottles of his soda, weathered display cases, and a framed letter from Nike chairman Phil Knight. (The Jones founder is a huge Nike fan, and he sent the very first case of Jones to Knight.) "That forced us to look at things differently: how could we create a connection with customers, let them play with the brand, let them take ownership of it? It's hard for marketing people to let other people play with their brand. For us, it's our whole existence. This is not *my* brand. This is not *our* soda. It belongs to our customers. Everything at this company is about sharing ownership of the brand with our customers."

For years, Jones Soda has attracted outsized media attention for its exuberant style and rebellious attitude. The company, which targets the prized (and notoriously hard-to-reach) 12- to 24-year-old demographic, sells an array of exotic flavors, including carbonated beverages like Blue Bubblegum, Fufu Berry, and Green Apple; natural juices like Berry White, D'Peach Mode, and Bohemian Raspberry; and WhoopAss, a citrus energy drink. Its underground endorsers—including a skateboard prodigy who was just four years old when he signed with Jones— appeal to the snowboarding, file-swapping, body-piercing set. Jones Soda is also a master of PR stunts. Before Thanksgiving 2005, it released a limited-edition holiday pack featuring soda flavors such as Brussels Sprout with Prosciutto, Cranberry Sauce, Turkey & Gravy, Wild Herb Stuffing, and Pumpkin Pie. What the flavors lacked in taste—they were, truth be told, close to undrinkable—they made up for in bubbly press coverage.[5]

But the "killer app" for Jones—what separates it from the uptight giants like Coke and Pepsi and what keeps the buzz going in its target audience—is its packaging and personality, its presence on store shelves. Jones Soda labels are as striking as its flavors are exotic. Utterly distinctive, the labels—works of art, really—are designed around mainly black-and-white photography. They change on a regular basis, and customers notice the debut of the new photographs. Why? Because the photos come from the customers.

Over the years, Jones has received somewhere on the order of four million photos from customers. The company's Web site displays a selection of the images that have been mailed or e-mailed to Seattle. (Older images disappear into an archive, but the site's gallery had more than 240,000 photos on display at last check.) Jones organizes the photos into categories—cats, dogs, babies, cars, landscapes, and so on—and visitors to the site vote on which photos should go on the labels. When a photo is selected, the label includes the name and hometown of the person who submitted it. Bottles with the labels are then shipped to the relevant geographic market. (In other words, the exuberant mom in Mesa, Arizona, would not find her kids on bottles in Boston or Chicago.)*

It's a truly original branding technique (which Jones has patented, a crucial weapon against copycats). But it's just one of many techniques Jones uses to invite customers into the company and encourage them to shape the fabric of the brand. Customers e-mail favorite sayings, aphorisms, and messages, which are selected to appear on the Web site and underneath the twist-off caps on every bottle. (The "under-the-cap fortunes" are another signature element of the Jones packaging.) Customers who are adamant about having their favorite photo on a bottle of Jones can visit a special site, pay $34.95, and order a personalized twelve-pack with labels featuring their image.

What does any of this have to do with selling soda? Nothing—*and everything*. Scott Bedbury is a world-renowned authority on creating lifestyle brands. He was senior vice president of marketing at Starbucks during the company's growth boom in the late 1990s; prior to that, he spent seven years as head of advertising at Nike, where he launched the legendary "Bo Knows" and "Just Do It" campaigns. Bedbury joined the Jones Soda board of directors in 2003 after his son, appropriately enough, introduced him to the brand and his passion for it. ("My kids go to the store with me and look for the labels," he marvels.)

So if the Nike brand is about competition and performance, and the Starbucks brand stands for a "third place" in American life, what is Jones Soda about? "It's about self-expression," Bedbury says. "That's what's happening on those labels. It's kids being themselves, sharing with the world what they think is cool, whether it's a picture of them, or their dog, or a sunset, or a snowdrift. To me, this is like a petrie dish

---

*As of year-end 2004, more than 4,000 photos had appeared on Jones labels, so customers have a one-in-a-thousand chance of being selected.

for the next generation of ideas about marketing. It's a peer-to-peer phenomenon that is truly unique."*

The next medium for peer-to-peer interaction is music. In August 2004 the company established a Web site, Jones Independent Music, where bands post songs, images, bios, and contact information. Jones customers download the tunes for free, rate songs and bands, and create playlists to share with one another. Every month, 20 bands or solo artists are selected to appear on labels of Jones Soda. Each band appears on 50,000 to 150,000 bottles, complete with its photo, its name, and its Web site—valuable exposure for up-and-coming musicians.

Why should a *beverage* company provide its customers with a *music* service? "We've got to stay relevant," explains van Stolk. "There's so much energy around music. On our site, kids can discover bands, talk to each other about what they've heard, make their own CDs. It's not relevant to advertise to my consumers. But helping them spread the word about music—*that's* relevant."

Again, the message is never about making soda—it's about making the brand connect with its customers. "We're not competing with other beverage companies," van Stolk says. "They think they need to advertise to connect. We're lining up a force of people. They're not just designing great artwork or advertisements or new products. They're a force for social change."

Peter van Stolk isn't content to connect customers to the brand or to each other—he also wants to connect them to the wider world. He is sketching a plan to harness the "force" to work on bigger issues than soda pop. One likely project: encouraging and equipping customers to agitate for change on water conservation and management.

....

*For years, truth be told, Jones Soda was a bubblier brand than it was a smooth-flowing business. Peter van Stolk committed many operating blunders early on (such as having to recall the first million bottles of soda shipped), and the company actually lost money in 2002. But the strength of the brand allowed van Stolk and his colleagues to overcome their initial operating weaknesses and put the business on solid footing.

"So what is Jones?" van Stolk asks rhetorically. "Are we a soda company? Are we an Internet company? Are we a social-networking company? It's irrelevant. We're good at figuring out what gets people fired up. Everything we try may not work, but the important point is, we're playing a different game than our 'competitors.' My fundamental belief is that great brands create an emotional connection. In our case, that means individual ownership: *my* photos, *my* bottle cap, *my* music. Everything we create has to enhance that connection."

Cranium and Jones Soda have lots in common. They're both young, high-profile brands in tired categories dominated by established giants. They're both based in Seattle. And they both have customers who act more like zealots—customers with deep personal connections to the companies and their products.

These two maverick brand-builders have one more thing in common—selling strategies that emphasize their uncommon values. A big reason why customers of Jones and Cranium are so invested in the brands is that most of them discovered the companies on their own. Customers are more likely to feel a sense of personal ownership for brands that they have found themselves.

Early on, Cranium founders Richard Tait and Whit Alexander made a decision not to pursue conventional marketing strategies for their flagship game. The first versions of Cranium weren't sold at Toys "R" Us, Target, and other predictable retailers. Instead, they were sold at Starbucks, Barnes & Noble, and Amazon. Cranium was the first board game ever carried by these alternative (for the toy business) retailers. The appearance of such a colorful new product in such unexpected (and high-visibility) places created tremendous buzz—and announced to people looking for games that Cranium was determined to change the game.

"We said to ourselves, 'Let's take our games to where our customers are rather than where games are sold,'" recalls Tait. "We sold a million games based on word of mouth. That had never been done before. We changed the rules."

Peter van Stolk adopted a similar approach. Not only has Jones Soda never spent a dime on traditional advertising, but when van Stolk launched the product, he sold it exclusively in what industry rivals considered bizarre, out-of-the-way places: tattoo and body-piercing parlors, skateboard and snowboard shops, music stores, and comic-book shops. "We decided to sell where our kids were, not where our competitors were, and let people discover the product for themselves," he explains. "We wanted to put our soda where no company had ever put soda before."

This alternative distribution strategy kept Jones growing more slowly than it might have done otherwise at the outset. But van Stolk was less interested in growing fast than in demonstrating authenticity—what he calls "grounding" the brand—before it played on a bigger stage. Jones is still available in these alternative spots. But now, after years of establishing its roots, it's also available at Target, Starbucks, Barnes & Noble, and Panera Bread, to name four high-profile venues. The soda has entered the mainstream without alienating its most fervent fans. It sounds like business advice from Yogi Berra, but it's true: the best way to make a first impression (and forge a lasting connection) is to sell where your customers are—and your competitors *aren't*.

SHARED MINDS—THE COMPANY WITH THE SMARTEST CUSTOMERS WINS

Peter van Stolk has built a challenger brand around a commitment to shared ownership—inviting his customers to shape the personality and performance of his company's products. Reed Hastings, founder, president, and CEO of Netflix, the online movie-rental pioneer, is betting his company on an even more high-stakes commitment to customer interaction. Call it shared minds. In an age of endless choice and unrestrained advertising, companies do better when they make their customers smarter. And the most effective way to make customers smarter is to help them

educate one another. The most intelligent way to stand out with customers is to unearth the collective intelligence of customers.

It's another vital insight for the future of marketing—and the future
of Netflix depends on it. At one level, Netflix is a smash hit. In just a
few years, an unknown Silicon Valley start-up has become a master of
logistics, a fixture on the cultural landscape, and a true passion brand.
Netflix launched its monthly membership, DVD-by-mail service in
September 1999. By the time it went public in May 2002, it had 600,000
paying customers and annual revenues of $76 million. At the end of
2005, it had 3.5 million paying customers, nearly $700 million in rev-
enues, and a stock market value of roughly $1.4 billion.[6]

At another level, Netflix's prospects seem like a horror movie. Could
Reed Hastings have picked a *more* treacherous industry in which to start
a company? For years the company faced off against Wal-Mart and its
DVD-rental business. Amazon is likely to enter the business at some
point. And the company's nemesis, Blockbuster, is a retail behemoth
with 9,000 stores, nearly 50,000 full-time employees, $6 billion in
revenues—and a strategy to copy (on the surface, at least) whatever Netflix innovations click with customers. No wonder so many Wall Street
analysts applaud what the company has built—and hide their eyes when
they look at its stock.*

But here's what's eye-opening about the Netflix strategy—and why it
may change how an entire industry looks at its future. Retail giants like
Blockbuster are focused on *distribution*—stuffing as many VHS cassettes,
DVDs, computer games, even Raisinettes and popcorn, into as many
homes as possible. Netflix is a technology innovator that enhances the
quality of *selection*—tapping the intelligence of millions of members to

---

*Netflix has played to decidedly mixed reviews on Wall Street. The company went public at a
split-adjusted $7.50 per share. Its stock sank to a low of $4.50, soared to a high of $36, and now
fluctuates wildly based on every move by its rivals.

help individual members discover movies they wouldn't find other-wise. Its ultimate value proposition is not just to be cheaper or more convenient than Blockbuster. It is to end the "blockbuster complex" itself.

"It's possible to totally misunderstand Netflix," says Hastings. "Some people think of us just as a DVD-rental service. But the real problem we're trying to solve is, how do you transform movie selection so that consumers can find a steady stream of movies they love? It's a huge matching problem. We've got 55,000 DVD titles over here. There are 300 million Americans over there. But most people can't tell you ten movies they're dying to see because they know they're going to be great. The way you solve the problem is to use the insights of other people to build a community effect. It is absolutely the key to customer satisfaction."

This is a crucial insight about connecting with customers—one that applies far beyond the movies. In the Netflix model, customers don't just influence the performance of the brand—they influence other cus-tomers, whose choices, in turn, influence them. Netflix doesn't just as-pire to build a super-efficient DVD-shipping system. It aims to create a *social* system that changes the movies that customers see, based largely on the movies that *other* customers are seeing. "What we are trying to do is open up people's tastes," Hastings says. "Starbucks went into a flat market and created a culture of appreciation around coffee. We give everyone a platform to broaden their tastes in movies."

The word "platform" is crucial. For years Netflix had a full-time movie critic, and Hastings himself has strong opinions about what he likes. (He's a documentary buff.) But what really matters is what cus-tomers think—and how good a job the site does finding customers who think alike. Netflix customers love to show what they know. The aver-age member has rated more than 200 movies. Overall, customers have contributed more than one *billion* movie ratings to the site. (It's not un-common for Netflix to receive a million new ratings in a single day.)

Proprietary software slices, dices, and analyzes these ratings to spotlight movies and make different recommendations for each customer every time he or she visits the site.

To be sure, plenty of Web sites (most notably, Amazon) offer lots of product recommendations based on customer feedback. But few product categories (and certainly few cultural activities) are as sensitive to peer-to-peer recommendations as movies, and recommendations are becoming the *essence* of the customer experience at Hastings's company. Think of it as "the Netflix Effect." Members select 60 percent of their movies based on what the site recommends. Only 30 percent of Netflix rentals are new releases, compared with roughly 70 percent at Blockbuster. Amazingly, with 55,000 available titles in more than 200 genres— from cult comedies to gay and lesbian dramas to anime horror and battle athletes—Netflix customers rent 98 percent of all the titles every quarter.

Hastings underlines the Netflix Effect with the story of *Whale Rider,* a modest picture produced in New Zealand that was a darling of the critics when it was released in 2003. *Whale Rider,* which was nobody's idea of a box-office sensation, went to DVD on the same day as *The Hulk* and *Charlie's Angels 2.* In the aisles of Wal-Mart and on the shelves of Blockbuster, the two Hollywood mega-hits left *Whale Rider* eating plankton. But among Netflix customers, *Whale Rider* outperformed both big-budget entries and has ranked among the site's 100 most-rented movies of all time.

"That's the power of recommendations," says Hastings. "*Whale Rider* does a marginal job in the theater because it's hard to advertise efficiently. But we promote it to people who liked similar movies, people with that kind of taste. Then they rate it highly, other people see the ratings, and *whoosh,* it goes through the roof. That's what we can do with [several] million subscribers. Now, if we can get to twenty million, we're an entire platform."

That is the dream scenario for Netflix. Will it get to 10 or 20 million paying members? Can it withstand an ever-more-aggressive counterattack from Blockbuster, the possible entry of Amazon, the inevitable emergence of authorized digital downloads from the Hollywood studios? Hard to say—it would make a heck of a movie.*

But no matter how the competitive drama ends, the moral of the story is clear. In a real sense, the fate of Netflix is in the hands and heads of its customers—that is, how much they value interacting with and learning from other customers as opposed to finding the lowest-possible monthly fee or renting the biggest-budget movies the first week they're released. In early 2005 Netflix unveiled new peer-to-peer features (called Netflix Friends) that allow individual customers to share ratings and reviews with up to 50 other customers rather than just feed them into the site's database. Members can even see what movies their friends are waiting to rent by peering into their online queues.

In other words, as its deep-pocketed rivals spend to broaden their operating systems, Netflix looks for ways to deepen its *social* system. "This is the second generation of Netflix," says Hastings. "Movies are so social. We want to become a more powerful experience because your friends are on it."

Creating that sort of shared experience should be on the agenda for every company looking to strike an emotional connection with those with whom they do business. Customers might learn to love companies that keep them entertained; they can't help but love companies that help them to learn.

---

*Although many pundits portray Netflix as a scrappy underdog, it has already vanquished one potent foe. In May 2005 Wal-Mart announced that it was exiting the online DVD-rental business and handing over its operation to Netflix, a sign, according to the *Wall Street Journal*, "that the world's largest retailer couldn't beat the Internet upstart at its own game."

Chapter Nine

Maverick Messages (III): Building Your Bond with Customers

The age of overload has inspired an overload of advice from branding gurus and Madison Avenue pundits. What remains in short supply—and what the last two chapters were designed to offer in abundance—are insights and lessons from real-world innovators who are making enduring connections with their customers and, in the process, creating a maverick agenda for marketing and service.

We've always believed that marketing and customer service have special roles to play inside organizations. Marketers, almost as part of their job description, enjoy a unique license among traditional business functions to think big and challenge convention. Their charter is (or at least should be) not just to position products in the marketplace but to position the company for the future—a future that other executives might not be able to see. Customer service leaders aren't just responsible for fixing problems and fielding complaints. They are, at their best, the conscience of the company—leaders whose job it is to make sure the organization delivers on its promises to customers.

The fact that so many companies overpromise and underdeliver helps to explain why so many customers are so dissatisfied—even when these companies offer great deals in terms of price and features. Paul English, an Internet entrepreneur, a former vice president of technology for Intuit, and a self-described "phone geek," became so exasperated with the state of 1-800 customer service that he created an online "cheat sheet" (www.gethuman.com) to reveal as many secret codes for reaching live operators as he could gather.[1]

Want to reach an operator at one major New York City bank? Press five, pause, then press one/four/star/zero. Want to reach an agent at a leading wireless provider? Just press zero—*five times*. Want to reach a human being at one of the world's biggest computer manufacturers? Choose option one, dial extension 7266966, choose option one, option four, and option four again. Is this any way to connect with customers, especially when customers have so many other options for their business?

That's the dark side of the customer experience. Let's look on the bright side. Every company aspires to develop brands that click with customers and stand for something special in the marketplace. But you can't build something special with the same old ideas about designing products, delivering service, and crafting messages. As you evaluate how your brands stack up, ask whether you've mastered the new building blocks of marketing.

1. There's always a demand for something distinctive.

One downside to being honest about the overcapacity, oversupply, and sensory overload that plague most industries is that it's easy to get scared off: who wants to enter a market that's already too crowded? But even in the most crowded markets, there's room for an innovator with something original to offer and something authentic to say.

Well, at least we hope there is! Think for a moment about the market conditions surrounding this book. Based purely on data about supply and demand, our devotion to *Mavericks at Work* seems misguided at best. The book publishing business, much like every other traditional media business, is characterized by growing supply, static demand, and relentless competition. In 2004 U.S. publishers released 195,000 new titles—13 percent more than the number of titles released the year before. That's 3,750 new books every week for 52 weeks. Meanwhile, in the three years between 2001 and 2004, the number of books sold actually declined by 3 percent—and more than one-third of all the books shipped by publishers were returned unsold from retailers.[2]

It's a challenging market—and a deadly market for publishing companies that are content to sell run-of-the-mill products with more-of-the-same strategies. But is it all that different a market from, say, network television, or automobiles, or personal computers, or just about any other product you can name? That's why we've argued that companies in almost every industry face the same defining challenge: how do you make a compelling offer to customers who already have more than enough of what you're selling?

There are plenty of compelling answers to that challenge. Bryant Keil, CEO of Potbelly Sandwich Works, has watched with delight as his quirky, one-of-a-kind operation has grown from a single store in Chicago to a hundred stores across the country. Of course, by any objective measure, it's hard to argue that the world desperately needs another source of sandwiches. Subway, the 800-pound gorilla in the business, already has nearly 25,000 (mainly franchised) locations in more than 80 countries.

How does Keil think about competing against such a mammoth enterprise in such a crowded market? He doesn't: "I'm not looking at what those guys are doing, I'm looking at what *we're* doing. We have to keep doing more than our customers expect us to; we can't worry about what other companies might do." Thus far, Keil's competitive blinders are helping his company deliver eye-opening results. The average Potbelly shop generates annual sales of $1 million—three times the annual sales of a typical Subway outlet.

2. Not all customers are created equal.

If your goal is to establish a psychological contract with customers, then almost by definition you won't appeal to *all* customers. Sure, lots of different people start their day at Starbucks, and Commerce Bank depositors come from all walks of life. But most of the maverick companies we've come to know focus on a narrowly drawn set of customers. Anthropologie inspires a sense of cultural discovery among clued-in women with a particular mind-set; Vermont Teddy Bear is a lifeline for clueless men who lose their minds when it comes to giving gifts.

Indeed, when Elisabeth Robert and her colleagues embarked on a plan to grow beyond their namesake product, they went to great lengths to keep the new business separate and distinctive—in order to stay focused on the distinctive needs of their customers. Vermont Teddy Bear's second major product line, PajamaGrams, operates a lot like BearGrams. But 70 percent of the customers for PajamaGrams are women, while nearly 70 percent of the customers for BearGrams are men. The attitudes and expectations of women who buy gifts for women (sisters, mothers, daughters) differ sharply from the attitudes and expectations of men who buy gifts for women. So Robert's company uses highly tailored strategies to meet the needs of "Early Jill" as opposed to "Late Jack." The difference that matters to Vermont Teddy Bear is not the products it is selling (teddies versus teddy bears) or how it delivers the goods (pretty much the same logistics). The difference lies in the profoundly different needs, worries, and overall mind-set that men and women bring to the marketplace—and in how the company can strengthen its connections with each set of customers.

One test of how committed a company is to its most important customers is how fearless it is about ignoring (even offending) customers who aren't central to its mission. Peter van Stolk, founder and CEO of Jones Soda, has met tons of soda drinkers (and more than a few retailers) who can't relate to the flavors, the labels, or the underground endorsers around which Jones is built. His response? Jones must be doing something right. "If you believe that a brand has to have a set of convictions, then you have to be prepared to piss people off," he says. "We don't have to appeal to everyone. My attitude is, if you don't like Jones, that's cool. Don't buy it, and have a nice day."

3. Brand is culture, culture is brand.

It's a point we'll make in detail in the next few chapters, but it's worth highlighting here: there is a direct connection between a company's identity in the marketplace (how it relates to customers) and its performance in the workplace (how it relates to employees). Indeed, for all of its monumental success as a brand, Starbucks' most important contribution to the marketing agenda may be its recognition that its workforce is what makes the brand come to life. It takes a highly engaged barista to brew an engaging cup of coffee.[3]

What applies to Starbucks applies to family-friendly Cranium, service-centric Vermont Teddy Bear, even fashion-minded Anthropologie. The retailer goes out of its way to hire staffers who are "customer-appropriate," says director of stores Wendy Brown, meaning they share many of the attitudes, experiences, even educational backgrounds of the women who shop there. "The people who work in our stores are well traveled, well read, and have outside interests. We get artists, literary people, even a few doctors. They can have a real conversation with our customers."

That principle certainly applies to performance-oriented Commerce Bank, which has banked on its distinctive culture for more than 30 years. "The funny thing about culture," says Commerce president Dennis DiFlorio, "is that you can't acquire it, you can't merge it, and you can't convert it. Our culture is something that the competition can never copy."

4. Advertising to customers is not the same as connecting with customers.

With the notable exceptions of Netflix, which blankets the airwaves and the Internet with ads for its service, and Vermont Teddy Bear, which has mastered the art of direct-response radio spots, few of our maverick brand-builders rely on big-bucks advertising to send messages to the marketplace. Cranium, which does some advertising, has become a master at public relations, special events (often staged in partnership with Starbucks), and playful stunts. Jones Soda relies on an arsenal of guerrilla-marketing tactics—from introducing far-out flavors over the holidays to sponsoring extreme-sports athletes and surfer dudes.

Anthropologie, despite its presence in the ad-happy world of fashion retailing, spends literally no money on advertising. The logic: if you want customers to invest in and talk about your brand, then invest time and money in developing products worth talking about in the first place. So forget spending time on Madison Avenue designing yet another ad campaign. The company's buyers and designers spend as much as half the year searching for product ideas that they believe will connect with customers.

Keith Johnson, head antiques buyer and de facto chief product anthropologist, blazes the trail for his colleagues. For more than a decade, his job has been literally to shop the world, and he has the passport (reinforced with 72 extra pages crowded with stamps and visas) to prove it. Johnson and his colleagues scour antique fairs, flea markets, obscure emporiums, vintage shops, museums, and factories from Europe to North Africa to the Far East.

For Johnson, the ultimate find is not only a one-of-a-kind object that Anthropologie can sell in the store (found objects, such as antique botanical prints or a French armoire, make up a small percentage of home sales, which amount to 30 percent of total sales), but one that can inspire a new in-house design. "My job is to provide the store with some backbone to create wonderful displays and ambiance," he says. "We sell antiques, but the focus is to create an evocative environment. At the same time, I'm always looking for products that we can reproduce and turn into our own collection. There's a high premium on proprietary product. It reinforces the unique experience of Anthropologie, and the margins are great." One hit: a $4 ceramic latte bowl in an array of festive colors that sells by the thousands each week, while the small collection of antique originals that inspired it sold for $45 each.

Exploring the world is not limited to the leadership team at Anthropologie. CEO Glen Senk recently instituted a "five-year service award," which gives people from all over the company (from the store floor to catalog design) an opportunity to accompany Johnson on one of his four- to eight-week treks across multiple continents. Johnson has plenty of pointers to offer these greenhorn anthropologists. But more often than not, he says, "they teach me more than I teach them. Their fresh eyes and excitement always lead me to new places." Which is precisely what retailers like Anthropologie are supposed to do for their customers.

5. When it comes to creating brand value, dollars-and-cents thinking doesn't always make sense.

Vernon Hill of Commerce Bank happily spends money to install Penny Arcades in all locations, even though the contraptions don't generate a dime of direct revenue. Elisabeth Robert refuses to hire "bear counselors" based in India or Ireland rather than in Vermont, even though offshoring could mean big savings for her small outfit. DPR Construction invests countless hours creating mission statements for the factories and offices it builds, even though time is

money, especially in construction. Why are these maverick companies prepared to incur costs that traditional companies would elimi-
nate in a heartbeat? Because the goal is to maximize the value of
their connections with customers, not to minimize expenses.

One strategy for making an impression with customers, especially
when rivals insist on nickel-and-diming them, is to give away something that other companies charge for—or wouldn't think of offering in the first place. The investment can be small; the returns can be
priceless. A little generosity can go a long way.

The "Genius Bars" inside Apple Computer's 100-plus retail stores
are one high-profile example of this phenomenon. Back in 2001,
when the first Apple stores opened for business, they made a big impression on customers with their sleek design and whiter-than-white
color scheme. But the most memorable element of the stores turned
out to be their offer of free, in-person tech support. Customers who
were willing to wait in line, without an appointment, could bring in
their ailing laptop (or now their iPod) and an in-store "genius" would
try to fix the device on the spot.

Ron Johnson, Apple's senior vice president for retailing, summed
up the impact of the Genius Bars this way: "It's the part of the store
that people connect to emotionally more than any other," he told
the *New York Times*. Does free service (delivered with a sense of style)
cost Apple extra money? Of course. But how do you put a value on
the goodwill it creates?[4]

What works for iPods and software works for sandwiches too. "So
many companies try to outsmart their customers, to figure out angles
to get more out of them," says Potbelly's Bryant Keil. "We try to figure out how to give more *to* our customers. That sugar cookie on
your straw? We could cut that out, but those cookies mean the world
to our customers. We could build our stores for half of what we
spend, but that would be a mistake. Even if our customers didn't

notice, our employees would notice. And that would create a culture of cutting corners.

"That's just not our philosophy," Keil continues. "In every Potbelly store, we have a little cutout of a pig. And we handwrite on the pig, when the store opens, a 'P' and an 'H.' It reminds us that 'pigs get fat and hogs get slaughtered.' If you try to grab every last dime out of everything you do, it comes back to haunt you."

PART FOUR

Redesigning Work

Chapter Ten

· ·

The Company You Keep:
Business as If People Mattered

This is not about finding the most phenomenal programmer or the business student who's won all the awards. This is about finding people who could run the company someday. What we offer is cool projects, small teams, and dynamic places to work. We look for virtuoso skills, unique life experience, and genuine passion. Our people groove on this work. They love it. And you can't fake that.

—JANE HARPER, DIRECTOR OF UNIVERSITY RELATIONS AND INNOVATION

PROGRAMS, IBM, AND FOUNDER OF EXTREME BLUE

K en Aponte is ready for his moment in the spotlight. No, he's not at Radio City Music Hall, and there's not a Rockette in sight. He's on an auditorium stage in Armonk, New York, face-to-face with IBM chairman and CEO Sam Palmisano, chief technology strategist Nicholas Donofrio, Irving Wladawsky-Berger, vice president of technology strategy and innovation, and a couple of hundred other IBM executives and research wizards. Talk about the fast track: less than three months earlier, Aponte was pinning on his ID badge for the first time in a lab at IBM's Austin, Texas, campus. Now he and three teammates have exactly four minutes to present their "biz-tech" strategy for the so-called Cell chip, a superfast, ultrasophisticated microprocessor that is the brain inside the Sony PlayStation 3 and has huge potential in avionics, medical imaging, and other graphics-intensive fields.

The group presents its plan without missing a beat. One reason they're so confident is that they know the material cold. They refined their ideas during marathon days of writing code, soldering parts for prototypes, and wrangling for resources. What's more, they've been presenting and revising nearly every day for the last several weeks. They presented to scores of fellow IBMers. They presented to Toshiba's president and CEO, Tadashi Okamura, when he visited the Austin lab from Japan. (The Cell chip is part of a four-year, $400 million joint venture among IBM, Sony, and Toshiba.) In a sense, the Armonk session is just one more remarkable moment in a three-month whirlwind of researching, brainstorming, and arguing.

What's most remarkable, though, is that Aponte and his colleagues aren't award-winning scientists or gray-haired executives—lifetime achievers who might merit such a high-powered audience. They're *summer interns,* part of an elite cadre of engineering, computer science, and MBA students chosen for IBM's Extreme Blue program. IBM describes Extreme Blue as an incubator for talent, technology, and business innovation. To the participants, it's a sink-or-swim immersion experience that divides highly accomplished students into small teams, assigns them to work on major problems, supplies them with barely-out-of-the-lab technology, and gives them three months to, in the words of the Extreme Blue manifesto, "start something big."

Think MTV's *Real World* meets the Manhattan Project—groups of smart, ambitious, high-strung young people, living and working in close quarters, under intense pressure, focused on technologies and business opportunities with huge potential. "This is not for the faint of heart," declares Jane Harper, a 25-year IBM veteran who created Extreme Blue in 1999 and has presided over its expansion from a few teams working in a lab in Cambridge, Massachusetts, to a year-round program with hundreds of students working in twelve labs across the world, including Amsterdam, Beijing, Dublin, San Jose, and Toronto. "The teams are all aiming to hit the ball out of the park, to do something that will knock us off our feet. Do all of them get there? No. But some of them do. We all overestimate what can get done in a year. But we *underestimate* what can get done in twelve weeks."

Still, the real aim of Extreme Blue isn't to launch new businesses or conquer new markets. In the short term, the aim is to make IBM more compelling to new sorts of people—a generation of talented, impatient programmers, engineers, and entrepreneurs whose first instinct is to write their own business plan or head to Silicon Valley rather than become a foot soldier in IBM's 320,000-member global army. The company's most senior leaders understand that life at Big Blue can be a tough sell to hotshots mesmerized by the geek chic of Google, the cultural influence of Apple, or the wide-open spirit of open-source code. They also understand that any company determined to increase its market share (even a company as powerful as IBM) has to claim more than its fair share of the best young talent in its business.

Back in the late 1990s, when Jane Harper was a leader of the company's nascent Internet strategy, a sign outside her lab's door read: "This is not your father's IBM." That's a core message of Extreme Blue. In 2004 more than 4,500 students applied for just 200 spots in the program. Over the years, nearly 80 percent of the participants in Extreme Blue have accepted full-time positions at IBM. Spend any time with these Extreme-Bluers-turned-Big-Bluers and you hear the same refrain: "I thought I'd sworn off corporate America," or, "I'm a start-up junkie, I never saw myself at IBM." Those are the sounds of an old, established, once-out-of-favor company sowing the seeds of its future.[1]

In the long term, the aim of Extreme Blue is to demonstrate new ways for IBM itself to work—to accelerate the turnaround strategy unleashed by the now-legendary Lou Gerstner and advanced by his successor, CEO Sam Palmisano. IBM's leaders seem determined to pull off a deep-seated cultural transformation of the sort that has eluded so many giant organizations, from General Motors to Kodak. And the most enduring way for the company to work differently, Big Blue's brass understands, is to fill the company with individuals who bring different styles to their work.*

A case in point: Extreme Blue alumnus Jason Kelley, who got his trial by fire in a computer security project back in 2002. Now a rising star in IBM's software-industry group, he reflects on the experience: "You may make mistakes, but the mistakes should be because you're doing things too fast or going after things that are too hard. When I was doing my project, I needed input from a very senior executive, who wound up leaving IBM to become CEO of a major software company. I called his office *every day*. I talked to his assistant *every day*. After a while she said, 'You're driving me crazy.' I said, 'You can stop it by letting me talk to him.' So she did. We hounded these top people because we *had* to if we wanted to complete our projects. It was reinforced fearlessness."

Extreme Blue is reinforcing that kind of behavior throughout IBM. The program has generated so much impact over the last few years that Jane Harper and her colleagues have unveiled "Shades of Extreme Blue"—different versions of the model tailored for different constituencies. Extreme Blue "Speed Teams" offer an internship program similar to the original, but they allow even more young people to participate. (There were 50 Speed Team projects in 16 locations in 2005.) Extreme Blue "BizTech" teams allow early-career executives and technologists to have an intense project experience similar to what students get. BizTech teams work together one day a week and get a taste of the more immersive program. There's even a version of Extreme Blue that includes customers.

So what is the ultimate product of Extreme Blue and its offshoots? According to Harper, it is a new perspective on the future of IBM

---

*There's a widely shared perception that IBM is stuffed with Big Blue lifers. In fact, the reality is more complex. Fully half of IBM's 320,000 employees have been with the company for less than five years. Even in a slow year, the company adds more than 20,000 new employees.

itself—one that elevates the human side of enterprise to the same level of urgency as the company's research labs or its long tradition of customer service. "Sure, Extreme Blue is about unleashing innovation," she says. "But it's really about unleashing *people*. This virus is infecting the rest of the company. And what it's spreading is vitality."[2]

BEYOND CREDENTIALS—
THE CHARACTER OF COMPETITION

It is the most ubiquitous platitude of corporate life: "People are our most important asset." The undeniable reality, of course, is that the human side of enterprise remains the ultimate backwater. It's the last item on most CEOs' list of strategic priorities. It's where mediocre executives go when they can't cut it in the "real" parts of the organization. Be honest: how many companies do you know that are as creative, as disciplined, as *businesslike* about the people factor in business as they are about finance, engineering, and marketing?

Over the years, as we've traveled the world to evaluate the changing state of business leadership, we've searched for those companies. We haven't found many. In fact, we haven't met all that many CEOs who could provide a compelling response to a simple question we like to ask when we visit an organization for the first time: *why would great people want to work here?* (The answer, we add, can't be about salaries, bonuses, or stock options.) What is it about the ideas your company stands for, its point of view in the marketplace, the ways in which employees interact with customers or collaborate with one another, that becomes irresistible to the best people in your industry? How does your company's standing in the talent market enhance its position in the product market?

These are not trick questions. They are the building blocks of long-term prosperity. For one thing, you cannot have happy, satisfied customers if your organization is filled with unhappy, dissatisfied people. Maverick competitors such as Commerce Bank and Anthropologie, as we explored in chapter 7, understand the direct connection between delivering a one-of-a-kind performance and recruiting the right collection of performers. Moreover, if you believe that companies compete on the power of their ideas, then you also have to believe that they compete on the brainpower of their people. Because (to spin that old slogan from the NRA), companies don't have ideas, people do. The most direct way to fill a company with great ideas—in addition to opening its walls to outside brains—is to fill it with great people.

This is not, we hasten to add, a plea to return to the bad old days of the Internet boom—that brief shining moment when the "war for talent" became an excuse to lavish big signing bonuses, fat stock option packages, and design-it-yourself job descriptions on every self-absorbed MBA or self-impressed Java programmer. Building an organization filled with stars doesn't mean succumbing to a me-first star system.

On the heels of the dot-com meltdown, in a long *New Yorker* essay called "The Talent Myth," best-selling author Malcolm Gladwell launched a withering attack on just this sort of star system. He took aim at a high-profile target, a book by three McKinsey & Company consultants called—you guessed it—*The War for Talent*. Unfortunately for the authors, one of the star companies in their starstruck book was Enron, whose top brass boasted about the ambitious, aggressive, sharp-elbowed individualists who populated its ranks. The fact that the book appeared just two months before the scandal-plagued company filed for bankruptcy did not exactly endear its main arguments to the skeptical Gladwell. "What if Enron failed not in spite of its talent mind-set but because of it?" he asked. "What if smart people are overrated?"

In his signature style, Gladwell drew on social science research that documents the importance of practical skills ("tacit knowledge") over raw brainpower; the tendency of individuals who think they're smarter than others (and get treated that way) to worry more about acting smart than learning new things; and the dangers of what three psychologists have called "the dark side of charisma." In making his case, one of the

New Yorker's star writers offered a cutting-edge version of an argument against stars that's been advanced in business for years, nowhere more poignantly than in a now-forgotten essay in a long-gone journal whose founding writers included social critics Lincoln Steffens and Ida Tarbell.

In the February 1924 issue of the *American* magazine, an anonymous business leader wrote an essay called "Why I Never Hire Brilliant Men." The still-gripping article is a school-of-hard-knocks account of an executive who has to fire yet another fast-talking, big-promising, high-IQ colleague who served up plenty of ideas but delivered few tangible results, who started lots of projects but quickly lost interest in them. "Business and life are built on successful mediocrity," the world-weary author concludes, "and victory comes to companies, not through the employment of brilliant men, but through knowing how to get the most out of *ordinary* folks."

That was then—and this is Gladwell, almost 80 years later. "The broader failing of McKinsey and its acolytes at Enron," he argues, "is their assumption that an organization's intelligence is simply a function of the intelligence of its employees. They believe in stars, because they don't believe in systems. In a way, that's understandable, because our lives are so obviously enriched by individual brilliance. Groups don't write great novels, and a committee didn't come up with the theory of relativity. But companies work by different rules. They don't just create; they execute and compete and coordinate the efforts of many different people, and the organizations that are most successful at that task are the ones where the system *is* the star."[3]

We believe that's a false distinction—a phony war on the war for talent. The maverick companies you'll meet in the next two chapters invest in stars *and* systems. They are determined to secure more than their fair share of the great people in their business. But they understand that what it means to be great is as much about values as virtuosity, as much about what makes people tick as how much they know. Call it the character of competition—the relationship between a company's identity in the marketplace and the sense of identity that talented people bring to the workplace. Not every great performer is a great fit with the ideas that animate an organization. But organizations that are content to fill their ranks with unremarkable performers aren't likely to achieve remarkable performance.

John Sullivan is a colorful character who has devoted his career to explaining the connection between how organizations compete for talent and how they compete for customers. He runs the human resources management program at San Francisco State University, advises some of the world's best-known companies (including Nike, Starbucks, Microsoft, and MGM Grand) on HR strategies, and issues a stream of books and polemics that challenge the conventional wisdom of his all-too-conventional colleagues.*

"I'm a capitalist, not a social worker," Sullivan thunders. "Too many companies spend too much time trying to 'fix' their mediocre performers. They should spend more time recruiting and retaining great performers. It's like in sports. If your basketball team has Shaquille O'Neal, you've got a good shot at the title every year. But two six-foot-tall guards will never equal one seven-foot Shaq. It's HR's job to go out and find lots of Shaqs—and then to create a system that allows them to shine. Of course you need a 'system.' But a system without stars is not going to win."[4]

Extreme Blue speaks to this "both-and" (rather than either-or) mindset. At first blush, IBM's talent offensive looks like Gladwell's worst nightmare—one of the world's top companies offering plum assignments to child prodigies. "Eighty percent of Extreme Bluers would not come unless they knew what their project was," says Jane Harper. "They want to know, What am *I* going to be working on? Is it going to see the light of day? Am I going to make a difference?"

....

*Sullivan's Web site (www.drjohnsullivan.com) is one of the smartest, funniest, most useful collections of resources we've seen when it comes to understanding the role of talent in business. Spend time on this site and you'll never again think that HR is boring.

But from the moment they report for duty, Extreme Bluers get immersed in a system that emphasizes group cohesion over me-first individual achievement. Indeed, Harper and her colleagues have produced a manual called "Staying Extreme" for all participants in and alumni of Extreme Blue. "Staying Extreme" is the most instructive document we've read about how talented individuals can make a difference inside a big, complex organization like IBM. The watchword of the document is *humbition*—the subtle blend of humility and ambition that, the authors of "Staying Extreme" believe, drives the most influential innovators in business.[5]

"To be clear," the manual warns, "when you leave Extreme Blue and join another group at IBM (or any other company for that matter), we will be watching. And if we find out that you are making the program look like we are producing a bunch of arrogant wannabes, we will forget we ever knew you. Be ambitious. Be a leader. But do not belittle others in your pursuit of your ambitions."

Even the land of stock options and sports cars is developing a healthier respect for the character of competition. Think back to the start-up stories of Marc Andreessen and Mike McCue, the chastened mavericks who made history at Netscape and are applying the lessons they learned in the roaring nineties to their 21st-century business ambitions. In chapter 2, the Silicon Valley hotshots explained how the Netscape saga forever changed their approach to strategy. But it also taught them a lesson about the human side of entrepreneurship. The difference between success and failure, Andreessen and McCue now understand, is not just a function of the markets a company enters or the products it launches. Just as important are *the people it lets in the door*—who it hires, who it turns away, and the criteria for making those decisions.

"The gap between what a highly productive person can do and what an average person can do is getting bigger and bigger," Andreessen argues. "Five great programmers can completely outperform a thousand mediocre programmers, especially since those five great programmers can use the Internet to reach 800 million people. There's just no question about it."

There's also no question that it's easier to recognize the power of great people than it is to fill your company with them—especially when the lure of fast growth can lull you into complacency about maintaining high standards. "It's easy to weed out the bad people," Andreessen says. "The tough part is passing on the *good* people. We all know the scenario: at the end of the interviews, executives who are desperate to fill an opening sit around and say, 'This candidate is good. Let's make an offer.' It's at that point that you as the leader have to say, 'No, we *can't* make an offer. Good is not good enough.' You've got to hold the line on the quality of your people."

Fail to hold the line, Andreessen argues, and you inevitably succumb to what he calls the Rule of Crappy People: "There are good people and there are great people. Great people tend to hire other great people, because that's who they want to work with. But good people tend to hire people who aren't so good. They don't want to manage people who are smarter than they are. So over time, unless you're tough and disciplined, the talent level in the company declines to the lowest common denominator, and you wind up with lots of crappy people. It's a disaster. But it takes tremendous willpower not to compromise."[6]

That's a lesson Mike McCue has learned as well, one that he has been determined to put into practice at fast-growing Tellme Networks. "What I learned so viscerally at Netscape, and what has influenced everything we do at Tellme, is that you have to be willing to slow down in order to build the company properly. If you grow too fast, if you go public too soon, if you hire too many people too quickly—it backfires. It doesn't take a lot of mediocre people to spoil it for everybody. You have to be willing to sacrifice growth in order to hire the right people."

But hiring the right people, McCue is quick to add, doesn't always mean choosing the most talented people in the raw technical sense— the fastest programmers, the hippest marketers, the cleverest financial wizards. There's a difference between having great credentials and being a great contributor. McCue isn't just searching for the sharpest minds. He's probing for the closest fit.

How does Tellme find that fit? One test is a set of deceptively simple questions that probe for what makes candidates tick and whether their values click with the company's strategy to create value. McCue is on the lookout for people "who want to work with other great people." There's more than enough ego to go around in high-tech, he says. As is the case at IBM (where McCue was a young star), people who thrive at Tellme "have a certain humility. They know they can get better; they want to learn from the best. We look for people who light up when they are around other talented people."

McCue and his colleagues in start-up-crazed Silicon Valley also look for people who aspire to build an enduring company—and understand the headaches that accompany such an aspiration. "We don't want people who just want to be part of an outfit that's fun and cool," he says. "We don't want people who are going to complain about processes or the pressures of scale. We want people who want to build something big and have an impact on the world."

ATTITUDE AND APTITUDE—WHY "WHO YOU ARE" BEATS "WHAT YOU KNOW"

Of course, it's one thing to be highly selective about who you admit to a fast-track program like Extreme Blue or who you recruit to a start-up that's generating buzz in all the right circles. But what happens when you're adding people to the middle ranks of an established organization, a company that's been around for decades, one that can't maintain the excitement and allure that attracts hotshots to start-ups? Over time, doesn't every company, one way or another, succumb to the Rule of Crappy People?

Don't make that argument to Sherry Phelps, who spent 33 years ("my entire adult life") at Southwest Airlines and, as a top executive in the People Department, helped design many of its hiring practices. Phelps is adamant about the unwavering character of competition at Southwest—the direct connection between the company's disruptive purpose and the offbeat characters who keep the planes in the air. As we explored in chapter 1, Southwest now ranks as the most prosperous airline in the United States. But rank-and-file employees still exude the air of scrappy underdogs in a fight for their existence. How does a giant organization, with more than 30,000 people, maintain the fighting attitude of a maverick start-up? By restricting admission to those who demonstrate that attitude—and devising clever ways to identify the right hires among a vast pool of candidates.*

"The first thing we look for is what we call the 'warrior spirit,'" Phelps says. "So much of our history was born out of battles—fighting for the right to be an airline, fighting off the big guys who wanted to squash us, now fighting off the low-cost airlines trying to emulate us. We are battle-born, battle-tried people. Anyone we add has to have some of that warrior spirit."

That's one reason Southwest, much like ING Direct, another disruptive competitor we visited in chapter 1, is reluctant to fill its ranks with industry veterans—people with the right skills but the wrong attitude to contribute to the cause. When it comes to flight attendants or baggage handlers, Phelps and her colleagues prefer to recruit, say, teachers or waiters or police officers over grizzled airline veterans (and often do). "We would rather take an eager, hungry, customer-oriented mind and mold it to what works well at Southwest than try to change the habits of someone who's come up through an organization that views life differently," she says. That's not to say Southwest never hires

---

*One of the virtues of success is that Southwest can be choosy about whom it hires. In 2005, according to company data, it received 260,109 résumés and hired 2,766 employees—an average of 94 candidates for each open slot.

refugees from the legacy airlines. But, notes Phelps, "it doesn't happen as often as you might think."

In other words, the company evaluates talent based on the proposition that who you are as a person counts for as much as what you know at any point in time. It puts as high a premium on character as credentials—and subjects prospective employees to a barrage of character tests before they join the organization. Over the years, Southwest has elevated to something of a science the practice of identifying its star performers, understanding what makes them tick, and devising interviews, group exercises, and other techniques to probe for those same attributes in new employees.

One of our favorites is called "Fallout Shelter." (Southwest has designed many variations of this exercise, but the logic is the same.) Imagine you've applied to be a flight attendant. You show up for an interview and learn that it's a group session rather than a one-on-one discussion. Seated in a semicircle, facing three representatives from Southwest's People Department, you and 15 or 20 other candidates are greeted with a scenario: The bad news is that the world is on the verge of nuclear apocalypse. The good news is that you're in a fallout shelter. But the shelter is nearing capacity—and it's your job, as a group, to reach a consensus about who else gets in. Then comes a list of possible occupants: a biochemist, a farmer, a teacher, an adventure-racing champion, a famous musician. Keep in mind, the officials add, that your choices will seed civilization for generations to come. Now get to work!

The candidates leap into action: some people speak out fast and forcefully, others hang back and listen, someone steps in as a diplomat when tempers flare, someone else cracks under the strain. What's the point of the exercise? To simulate the challenge of keeping cool while flying at 30,000 feet in an aluminum tube filled with grumpy passengers and fidgety kids. The time compression, snap judgments, and group dynamics of Fallout Shelter are meant to reproduce the cabin pressure that all flight attendants confront (and have to master) on a daily basis.

As the group becomes absorbed in its task, the Southwest judges watch intently. They're not looking for the right answer. They're looking for the right *attitude*. "It doesn't matter what solution the group comes up with," Phelps says. "What matters is how they're interacting with one another. Who's emerging as a leader? Who's soliciting other people's help? Who's pushing to be the star? It's not a fail-safe test. But you really see who's bringing what to the table. We're not interested in specific answers or a particular style. We're looking for what makes you who you are."[7]

In other words, the company is looking to maintain a distinctive character of competition that allows it to outperform its rivals, even as it gets bigger and more successful. "At Southwest, we had such a clear idea of what a great employee looked like," confirms Libby Sartain, the 13-year airline veteran who is now "Chief People Yahoo" at the Internet media company. "We had certain cultural attributes that we looked for in all employees, and we screened exhaustively to find those attributes. We didn't hire anyone—flight attendants, reservation agents, computer programmers—unless we were certain they were Southwest kind of people. It was non-negotiable. That's why the customer experience has been so seamless, even as the company has grown so much."

Sartain is instilling that same non-negotiable discipline at Yahoo, which has been growing like gangbusters over the last few years. She joined the company in August 2001, when Yahoo's stock market performance had crashed to an all-time low, along with the morale of the company's wannabe Internet millionaires. But in Silicon Valley, what comes down must go up. In terms of employment, from early 2003 through 2005, the company more than tripled in size, from 3,000 people to more than 10,000.*

To be sure, the character of competition at 10-year-old Yahoo will never be confused with what makes 35-year-old Southwest Airlines tick.

---

*Yahoo, like Southwest, has plenty of candidates from whom to choose. The company receives more than 10,000 résumés per month—or 45 résumés for every open job.

Yahoo's purple-and-yellow-splashed campus looks like a relic from the dot-com boom. Low-slung glass-and-metal buildings surround grassy quads punctuated by beach volleyball courts and barbecue pits. The cubicle-packed offices overflow with vintage geek perks—including a full-service free espresso bar in the main lobby, a state-of-the-art gym, free car washes, ubiquitous foosball tables, and a sun-soaked cafeteria called "URLs."[8]

Talk about culture shock: Libby, we're not in Texas anymore. And that's precisely the point. Any company with a disruptive business model has to be clear about the distinctive work experience it creates to support that model—and how that work experience shapes the customer experience. Sartain labels the phenomenon "branding from the inside out." There is, she argues, a direct connection between the values that motivate a great Yahoo employee and the values that animate Yahoo's best, most loyal, most satisfied customers.[9]

Sartain calls those attributes the "Y Gene"—and as she squares off against Google, IBM, and Microsoft to attract the most talented programmers and the most gifted researchers, she is determined to evaluate their character as well as their credentials, to hunt for the Y Gene in every candidate. Y-Gene people (whether employees or customers) "marvel at life and milk it for all it's worth," Sartain explains. "They're curious and energetic. They value openness and want to live unbridled and unrestricted. They appreciate that life is huge. They don't settle for the status quo—they want to grow. That's the kind of person we look for. That's also what our best customers look for when they use Yahoo."

CASTING THE COMPANY—"YOU FIND US" VERSUS "WE FIND YOU"

You may find Libby Sartain's description of the Y Gene intriguing. You may find it unappealing. No matter. The real challenge is to find your own answers to the urgent questions raised by Southwest, Yahoo, and other organizations devoted to enhancing the character of competition. Ask yourself: Why would great people want to be part of my company? How do I know a great person when I see one? Have I established a great fit between the customer experience and the work experience?

Then ask one more question: *do I know where and how to find great people in the first place?* Leaders who are determined to claim more than their fair share of the best talent understand that great people almost always have great jobs. So if you want to fill your organization with knockout contributors, you can't wait for them to knock on your door. You've got to knock on their door and persuade them to walk into your office. HR guru John Sullivan calls it the "we find you" versus "you find us" principle of recruiting—and it's one more principle that separates organizations that are serious about competing on talent from those that aren't.

It's a point that Sullivan drives home to whomever will listen. "The first rule of recruiting is that the best people already have jobs they like," he argues. "So *you* have to find them; they're not going to find you. It's amazing that so many companies still use job fairs to recruit talent. Who goes to job fairs? People without jobs! All you get are worthless résumés and lots of germs. Recruiting has to be a clever, fast-moving business discipline, not a passive, paper-pushing bureaucracy."

Consider the serious-minded approach to discovering and evaluating talented contributors perfected by Cirque du Soleil, the world-renowned entertainment company headquartered in Montreal, Canada. Founded as a band of street performers in 1984, Cirque has grown into a $600 million-a-year global entertainment brand and a darling of the business strategy set. Cirque's rise to prosperity has been celebrated in countless business magazine profiles, in a long *Harvard Business Review* essay, even in MBA case studies by professors on both sides of the Atlantic.[10]

The attention is easy to understand. Founder Guy Laliberté invented a fabulously successful business (he's on the *Forbes* list of billionaires) by reinventing the circus itself. Laliberté and his troupe of stilt-walkers, trapeze artists, tumblers, and knife-jugglers reimagined the standard formula of acrobats, animal acts, and clown antics as a sweeping spectacle in which artistry and storytelling guide jaw-dropping athleticism. Daniel Lamarre, Cirque's president since 2001, calls the formula "creation without compromise." The company's first rule of strategy, he says, "is that we only do things that are exciting to us. If it's boring, we walk away."

Walk into Cirque headquarters and it's hard to imagine that life could be boring even for a moment. The place bubbles with energy and color. It's the creation and production center for all of Cirque's shows—home to an ever-changing cast of directors, artists, and coaches, along with a permanent population (1,300 strong) of marketers, IT staffers, costume designers, and prop makers. A gaggle of gymnasts in leotards sashay by, executives gather on concrete steps for a meeting in the agora, a magnificent, three-story open space, while a performer perfects his rock-climbing skills on the indoor rock wall. Meanwhile, clerks in the payroll department sit in their cubicles on the fourth floor and look through a glass wall at an acrobat whizzing by on a trapeze in one of the building's cavernous, 75-foot-high training gyms.

Like the company's headquarters, Cirque's productions are singular works of imagination—surreal dreamscapes roiled by broad human dramas and populated by intricately costumed creatures. In *Alegría,* the age-old clash between wisdom and youth plays out as a gang of young toughs bound and soar through the air on a series of connected trampolines embedded in the stage. The jubilant journey culminates in a blinding snowstorm that envelops the audience. *Varekai* launches a meditation on the myth of Icarus with a solo free fall into a forest where exotic amphibian creatures slide, twirl, and intertwine as if on ice. *O* explores the concept of infinity on a liquid stage that swells and shrinks from a 25-foot-deep pool to a mere puddle as synchronized swimmers cavort beneath a massive boat carrying a team of acrobats high above the water.

The result of all this high-powered creativity is a high-performing business—an entertainment experience with wide and enduring appeal. Seven million people bought tickets to Cirque shows in 2004, and more than 42 million people in nearly 100 cities have seen one of its ten original productions over the last two decades. (An eleventh show, called *Corteo,* debuted in April 2005, and a twelfth, based on a partnership with Apple Records and built around the repertoire of the Beatles, debuted in 2006.) The company's custom-built big tops (the "Grand Chapiteau," in Cirque-speak) are raised on as many as four continents at any one time. Cirque has even changed the face of the Las Vegas Strip. Together, its four shows in Sin City attract some 10,000 people a night.* All told, the company is on track to generate $1 billion in revenues by 2007, and it continues to experiment with new ventures such as a TV series, publishing, restaurants, and clubs.

There's no question that Cirque has pioneered a truly original business strategy. But you can't understand the company's business performance unless you understand its approach to the performers themselves. Cirque's shows have become masterful works of art in large part because Cirque has mastered the art and science of scouting, evaluating, and recruiting the most compelling talent available. It makes an explicit connection between the people it attracts and the product it delivers, between how it does business and who it invites to become part of the business.

"Our mission is to invoke the imagination, provoke the senses, and evoke emotions," explains Lyn Heward, who joined Cirque in 1992 from her post as head of Quebec's gymnastics federation and spent nearly 15 years in senior leadership positions. "But that's not just a goal for our customers on the outside. It's also what we want our people on

---

*Cirque's longest-running Vegas show, *Mystère*, still generates more than $500,000 a week in profits after 14 years. Its most expensive show, *KÀ*, debuted at the MGM Grand in early 2005. The $170 million production plays in a theater that seats fewer than 2,000 people.

the inside to feel. Cirque never wants to repeat itself. That's why we never stop casting. In and of itself, casting is a creative act. The first mandate of the casting department is to feed the show creators with ideas—*human* ideas."

That job falls to Line Giasson, Cirque's casting director, and her team of 40 scouts, audition coordinators, and contract negotiators. To be sure, Giasson and her colleagues take on some traditional assignments— filling openings in current shows and assembling the cast for about-to-be-launched shows. But it's impossible to mistake them for HR traditionalists. Their most important job is to identify exciting talent long before any vacancies arise, while a new show is still a glimmer in the eye of its creators. "Our job isn't to 'hire' people," explains Giasson. "It is to find and present people we believe in."

Giasson and her casting colleagues are so enthusiastic about the talent they unearth that they instituted an annual event called "Coup de Coeur" (or "Heartthrob"). Everyone at Cirque's Montreal headquarters gathers in the soaring agora to watch a presentation of each scout's five favorite finds of the year. The scouts show videos and play music to showcase talents as varied as African jig performers, pot-and-pan percussionists, period musicians, and extreme-sports champions. The idea isn't to hire these people (though that's often a happy result) so much as to inspire, stimulate, and celebrate the individual talents at the heart of Cirque's creativity—talents that Cirque's scouts have discovered, independent of any well-defined need.

That's an acid test of whether an organization is serious about discovering and attracting the best talent available: Is it searching for talent independent of current openings or immediate plans? Does it scout for talent ahead of the need for talent? At Cirque, scouting ahead of need involves casting a wide net. Members of the casting department scour the world nonstop for exciting and unusual performers. They make between 20 and 40 trips a year to destinations as far-flung as the gymnasiums of eastern Europe, the barrios of Brazil, and the yurts of

Mongolia. They also make the rounds of a staggering variety of sports competitions, performing arts festivals, circus schools, and cultural events.

"Talent is everywhere," says Giasson. "That's why we look everywhere. If we want to reinvent ourselves—which is what everybody at Cirque is trying to do—then we have to constantly bring in new things. We never close off any avenue where we might discover new talent. Our responsibility is to have our eyes open."*

Cirque's scouts see talent everywhere because they keep their minds open to almost anything. After twenty years of casting acrobats, athletes, contortionists, actors, and musicians, they have developed strong networks in all of the associated communities. They've crisscrossed every continent. But they know that covering familiar ground is just a first step in the hunt for talent.

"The world is small," says Giasson. "We understand the disciplines. We know the best choreographers, coaches, and festivals. We have to keep pushing down new paths."

Indeed, Giasson's team has made a determined effort to get off the beaten path. That's how Cirque discovered a new discipline called "urban bounding." One of the scouts saw a movie by French filmmaker Luc Besson called *Yamakasi*, which is also the name of group of Paris teens who bill themselves as "modern samurai" dedicated to fighting the gravity of ghetto life with a patented form of acrobatic trespassing. The kids leap and flip through the cityscape—jumping from roof to roof, climbing tall buildings, and bounding between structures. The sheer skill and swagger, along with the group's street appeal, intrigued the casting department. A few years after meeting with the group, an

---

*That openness explains how a scout discovered the acrobat locked inside a woman named Teuda Bara, a sixtysomething Brazilian actress who looks more like an opera singer than a trapeze artist. The energy of her street-theater adaptation of *Romeo and Juliet* sold the scout on her potential. After a four-month training session, Bara is now climbing up to dizzying heights for a free fall in Cirque's show at the MGM Grand in Las Vegas.

adapted form of the art debuted in *KÀ*, a show packed with aggressive martial arts.

Sometimes the show itself pushes the scouts into entirely new realms of talent. That was the case with *O*, which opened up the world of water sports to Cirque. It certainly was the case with *Zumanity*, a bold experiment in an entirely new genre, the "erotic cabaret." The lusty celebration of human sexuality in all of its guises, which is a nightly sellout in its custom-designed Las Vegas theater, added a whole new layer to the organization's scouting vocabulary. The scouts made their way (not altogether unhappily) through the world's strip joints, S&M clubs, the Imperial Orgy (an erotic-arts festival in New York City), and venues like the Lido and Moulin Rouge in Paris in order to populate the "human zoo" with dominatrices, burlesque dancers, transvestites, and a Tantric handbalancing duet.

Cirque's approach to talent is about science as well as art. There is real discipline woven into the process of translating scouting discoveries into ideas and inspiration for new shows. The primary tool is a massive database in which Giasson's team records the details of every encounter with potential Cirque talent. Her department screens all incoming résumés, videotapes, and scouting reports and opens a file for each performer who participates in an audition. (Nearly every applicant participates in at least one of the 100 or so auditions held every year.) The database contains 30,000 active artist files, each of which is continuously updated with audition evaluations, added skills, new contact information, and so on. For the most promising performers, the department digitizes audition and performance tapes into easily accessible clips. Talk about video on demand: the database houses some 5,500 clips of performers exhibiting their skills.

This talent bank serves as the "collective memory of casting," says Line Giasson. It can produce a match for even the most bizarre request: a giant violinist, say, or a beanpole clown with a background in classical dance, or a contortionist who can sing. The talent bank doesn't just match performers to well-defined requests from a show's creator. It supports casting as a member of the creation team. Directors often create roles based on the candidates that casting presents, a process that Giasson calls "presentation as inspiration."

For example, Giasson sat down with the creation team for Cirque's most recent touring show, *Corteo,* two years before the April 2005 premiere, eager to share a collection of new performers. Among them was a young man named Sean Lomax, who had impressed her at a singing audition. "He walked in and just started to whistle," Giasson recalls. "He sounded like a musical instrument, not a person. And he had this character, this face, this presence. We said, 'Wow! What could we do with this?' So we put him in the database. Later, when we were presenting for the director of the 2005 show, we brought him up. He immediately said, 'He's perfect. I want him. I don't know what he'll be, but I'll find a way to get him in the show.'" Sure enough, Lomax was given a wonderfully oddball act in *Corteo,* created just for him.

Of course, there's a difference between discovering a talented performer and figuring out whether that performer has what it takes to thrive at Cirque. Heward and Giasson are emphatic about the character of competition. At Cirque, who you are as a colleague counts for as much as what you can do onstage. Filling a company with stars doesn't mean creating a star system in which the needs of gifted individuals overshadow what's best for everyone.

"There are no stars here," insists Lyn Heward. "The show is the star. That's why our evaluation goes deeper than a talent evaluation. We need to learn about the person behind the artist. How many somersaults you can do is not as important as an open-mindedness to our process, the tough-mindedness to get through the job, and what we call a 'fire to perform.' That's what we're looking for."

Like Southwest's Fallout Shelter, Cirque has designed its own audition process to test for that "fire"—a process that encourages performers to express what makes them tick as well as what they can do. Most

auditions begin with presentations of an individual act or a specific talent. Experts from a variety of fields (music, dance, acrobatics) issue
grades on a range of criteria, from physical categories like flexibility to
mental categories like attitude and passion. Those grades go directly
into the talent database.

Then the audition team pushes candidates beyond their prepared act
by asking them to sing, dance, stretch, and clown around. They mix up
the pure displays of talent with a variety of group and individual
exercises—from setting up improvisational scenarios to asking a candidate to describe a relationship with a beloved family member to putting
people on the spot by prompting them to "show us what you do when
you're alone in the bathroom."

The idea is not to trip people up. Rather, says Giasson, "we try to
create the conditions for people to be themselves. If we have someone
who is technically great but not our kind of person, and someone with
less skill but great charisma and generosity, that's who will interest us.
It's a joint venture between skill and character."

It's also a blend of enthusiasm and patience. Giasson and her team
understand that just because they've found a great person doesn't mean
it's a great time for that person to drop everything and join Cirque. Her
scouts often discover prospects who are under contract with another
production, uninterested in the vagabond life of a touring show, or simply too green for the demands of performing more than 400 shows a
year. That doesn't mean Cirque can't hire them. It just means it can't
hire them the moment it discovers them.

"A lot of this is about timing," Giasson explains. "So we stay in
touch as personally as possible. Even though we have thousands of people in the database, we're always picking up the phone or sending out
e-mails. We're the first person the artists meet and often the only person
they talk to at Cirque for years before we find a place for them. We're
not just scouts. We're ambassadors."

Over the last two decades, this creative approach to discovering creative talent has produced an extraordinary high-performance mix of skills and personalities that no "diversity program" could ever generate. The halls of Cirque headquarters bubble over with different languages (25 all told) and a startling variety of people (ranging in ages from 5 to 69). Even the building's internal signage features four languages (English, French, Russian, and Chinese), more than most international airports. And yet, insists Line Giasson, the challenge of discovering new performers, tapping their ideas, and recruiting them into the organization is a challenge that never ends—and never stops expanding Cirque's performance repertoire and business strategy.

"We have to keep pushing down new paths," she declares. "Anything we've never seen before, we explore. We want to know where it started and who's associated with it. It could be a new kind of dancing on a street corner in Rio or Mongolian throat singing. We don't care. We just keep digging."

HIRE CALLING: RECRUITING AS A WAY OF LIFE

You don't have to unleash scores of talent scouts, conduct hundreds of auditions, or invest in massive databases to be serious about the people factor in business. Sometimes all it takes is a handful of determined innovators—a senior executive or a team of in-the-trenches recruiters who are prepared to use creativity and guile, along with a little common sense, to run circles around flat-footed competitors. When it comes to landing more than your fair share of the best people in your industry, a little innovation goes a long way—especially if those innovations reflect a genuine commitment to winning the battle for talent.

"The best-performing companies I know don't just have a strong corporate culture, they have a deep-seated *recruiting* culture," argues John Sullivan, the HR maverick. "They understand that recruiting is not some obscure function buried in the human-resources bureaucracy. It is a prime driver of business success. There aren't many of those companies, but when you see them in action, it makes a powerful impact on you."

Sullivan identifies Google, the search-engine giant, as an organization that is on the verge of becoming what he calls a "recruiting machine." The company, which has made headlines with its pitched (and often acrimonious) battles with Microsoft and Yahoo for top talent, is equally aggressive in its search for talent at lower levels. For example, when people do Google searches on technical terms that are relevant to open jobs at the company, they are likely to see recruitment ads placed by the company itself. (Google, not surprisingly, is skilled at using its AdWords program to place the right jobs in front of the right people.)[11]

Likewise, Sullivan reports, Google places job ads beside searches that involve the names of its top scientists and engineers. If people are interested in the company's high-profile employees, the logic goes, perhaps they are interested in becoming employees of the company.

The "Friends of Google" program is another important cog in the recruiting machine. Google is associated with all kinds of products, services, and technologies—from payment systems to satellite maps to news-gathering operations—in which all kinds of people are interested. By creating e-mail networks that keep thousands of people informed about developments at the company, Google keeps developing its pool of potential talent: Who knows when someone's interest in a technology becomes interest in a job?

But you don't have to be an Internet giant to make the right recruiting connections. Consider Starbucks, whose one-of-a-kind psychological contract with customers we discussed in chapter 7. The senior leadership of Starbucks understands that it can't deliver on its ambitious plans for top-line growth unless it delivers an ever-growing cast of rank-and-file employees whose personal ambitions are consistent with the company's brand. There is a direct connection between the identity of Starbucks in the marketplace and the distinctive character of its workplace.

It's up to Jason Warner, director of North American recruiting for the coffee giant, to make that connection. He is positioned in the middle of a hiring boom spurred by one of the most far-reaching growth stories in retail. Starbucks, with more than 10,000 stores and roughly 120,000 employees worldwide, reported plans to open 1,800 stores in 2006, after opening 1,500 in 2005. The long-term goal, according to the company, is 30,000 stores around the world, including 15,000 in the United States alone.

By definition, adding thousands of new stores means adding tens of thousands of new employees. (In 2006 the company was hiring people at the rate of 200 *per day*.) Mr. Warner and his colleagues in the recruiting department are determined that these head-spinning numbers will not lead to the creation of a paint-by-numbers hiring bureaucracy, or to a weakening in the quality of the company's front-line staff.

So the company has devised all sorts of ways to add personal touches to how it hires. Whenever possible, job interviews include coffee-tasting sessions, in which Starbucks veterans discuss the virtues of different blends with applicants. A "candidate bill of rights" emphasizes the use of phone calls and handwritten notes over form letters, sets goals for how quickly applicants should hear back from recruiters, and encourages them to send out preloaded Starbucks cards as a goodwill gesture, whether or not applicants get an offer at the end of the process.

"Our aim is to treat our candidates as well as we treat our customers, to do something memorable for them," says Warner. "You can't treat people shabbily, especially in a world where there are far more open jobs than there is available talent to fill them. We try to put the humanity back into the recruiting experience."

Few companies seem to share that goal. Be honest: When's the last time that you, or anyone you knew, had an interaction with the HR department of a prospective employer that could be described as memorable (unless it was for all the wrong reasons)?

Starbucks, on the other hand, keeps looking for ways to make its recruiting more memorable than it is already. "People covet these jobs," concedes John Sullivan, who has researched and written case studies on the company. "It's not like working at the mall or at McDonald's. But that doesn't make it any less urgent for Starbucks to devise recruiting strategies and practices that make it special. This is a company that can't grow if it ever stops adding enough of the right people."[12]

For example, when we talked to Warner in mid-2006, the company was considering a plan to issue small-denomination Starbucks cards to all of its current employees. The employees would hand out the cards to people they encountered during the course of their day—a shop clerk, a bank teller, a flight attendant—who had done something special or impressive. (The cards would be good for a cup of coffee, and would include a message inviting the recipient to consider a career at Starbucks.) In essence, it's a strategy to turn every employee into a potential recruiter.

"I'd like to distribute these cards like water," Warner explains. "We have tens of thousands of people who work for this company. But folks who aren't recruiters often have a hard time approaching other people. This makes it easy. If you have a remarkable encounter in a grocery store, or if you hear that a neighbor's kid is taking six months off from college, you just reach into your pocket and hand them a Starbucks card. It's just another way to be more purposeful around creating a recruiting culture."

It's also a small innovation in service of a much larger point: Companies that are serious about talent understand that the most promising source of new employees who can make a difference in the organization are people who are *already* making a difference or have made a difference in the past—that is, current and former employees. The first building block of a recruiting culture is a *referral* culture—a collection of committed employees who are eager to refer their most talented friends, colleagues, and professional associates to consider joining or rejoining the organization.

Booz Allen Hamilton, the worldwide strategy and technology-consulting firm (and hardly anyone's idea of a maverick organization) has made tremendous strides with just such a strategy. Nearly half of its new recruits, the company reports, begin as referrals from current employees. And nearly 10 percent of the people who join the firm each year worked for the firm before. In fact, former employees have proven to be such a powerful source of new employees that the Booz Allen recruiting team launched a program, called Comeback Kids, to encourage more of this "boomerang" effect.

All of which, notes Jason Warner of Starbucks, puts even more pressure on the quality of the candidate experience. "You're not going to refer someone you know and like unless you're certain they're going to be treated well," he says. "But if you exceed everyone's expectations, you create an incredible competitive advantage."

That's a fitting note on which to end this chapter. The human dimension in business is both more energizing and more demanding than it's ever been: Smaller and smaller groups of smart, passionate people can do bigger and bigger things. The companies with the most star performers, deepest in the ranks, create the most value.

But workplace stars don't just fall from the skies. They fall to companies with the best answers to some basic questions. Are you articulate and persuasive about why talented people are more likely to thrive at your company than with your rivals? Have you identified untapped sources of talent—sources that the competition tends to ignore? Do you invest the time to stay in touch with these potential stars, to act as an ambassador as well as a scout, so that when they're ready to consider a move, you're ready to move them into a high-impact position? Are the best people inside your company committed to recruiting and referring the best people they know outside the company? If not, why do you expect to win more than your fair share of the best talent in your business?

Chapter Eleven

People and Performance:
Stars, Systems, and Workplaces That Work

The logic is so simple, and the results so compelling, that it amazes us how few organizations embrace the idea with any degree of conviction: there is an ironclad connection between an organization's standing in the talent market and its success in the product market. The best-performing companies we've encountered recognize that their most important decisions include not just what new segments to enter or what new offerings to launch but which new people to invite to become part of the enterprise. These companies are as unconventional and uncompromising about the people factor in business as they are about every other factor.

That's why a change-minded giant like IBM thinks so creatively about how to attract talented young technologists who might have big reservations about working with Big Blue. That's why Southwest Airlines designs exercises like Fallout Shelter to probe for the "warrior spirit" that distinguishes it from its dispirited rivals. That's why talent scouts from Cirque du Soleil span the globe searching for gifted performers, and why Cirque builds shows around their unique talents rather than slotting them into fixed roles.

So why are these organizations the exception rather than the rule? Why do so many companies still seem to take their cues from that long-ago essay in the *American* magazine and make a virtue out of "successful mediocrity" and "ordinary" employees? The answer, we suspect, is that star performers do require star treatment—not the self-aggrandizing, me-first treatment that rightly troubled Malcolm Gladwell about the dot-com-era war for talent, but treatment that reflects the high expectations that high performers bring to their work. HR guru John Sullivan, as is his style, makes the point bluntly. "Remember," he warns, "stars don't work for idiots. So as you raise the quality of your talent, you've also got to raise the quality of your management." Think of this as the flip side to Marc Andreessen's Rule of Crappy People: the better you are at attracting great people, the more you have to do to design the conditions under which they can do great work.

For many of the maverick competitors we've encountered, that design takes shape as soon as a new recruit signs on, with a *redesign* of one of the most awkward moments of life at most organizations: day-one orientation. Most companies understand the power (for good or ill) of first impressions in the marketplace. What goes for customers goes for employees. At service-crazed Commerce Bank, for example, orientation is not a day to fill out forms, sign up for benefits, and watch a dry welcome-to-the-company video. It is a meticulously choreographed day that sends a powerful (and, true to form, intensely colorful) message about how Commerce works and why it works so differently from the competition—a day in which new employees experience for themselves the one-of-a-kind customer experience that Commerce delivers.

The program is called "Traditions," and it is the official starting point for every job at Commerce: part-time tellers, store managers, even vice presidents and senior executives. New recruits gather in 30-person classes (held twice a week nearly every week of the year) at Commerce

University in Cherry Hill, New Jersey, or at one of many satellite site locations. A greeter is positioned outside the building to welcome each newcomer and escort him or her into a room where *another* greeter— the bank's mascot "Mr. C," outfitted in a shiny red outfit and white gloves—hands out high-fives. Music is blaring, the energy is high, and before the recruits can find a seat, they're greeted by two more bank officials. The first, from human resources, captures relevant personal information, while the second, from the training department, takes coats and serves coffee.

High-fiving what looks like a giant, lopsided M&M may seem like a strange way to begin a career in the banking business, but it is just one of many immediate demonstrations of the loose, open, over-the-top enthusiasm that defines how the best people at Commerce work. "We do these things because you would never expect them from an orientation program," says Tim Killion, the bank's irrepressible manager of the Wow Department. "When you're driving to work on your first day, you probably expect to have coffee. You don't expect somebody from the company to serve it to you." (Killion has personally taught more than 4,000 new employees in Traditions courses.)

Of course, delivering service that goes beyond what's expected is how Commerce connects with customers in the marketplace. So it's vital that Commerce project that same expectations-busting attitude in the workplace. On the day that employee number 10,000 showed up for Traditions, Killion stormed the room with 75 company officials, including the director of human resources and the head of training. Armed with dozens of roses, nonalcoholic champagne, and champagne glasses, Commerce executives offered a toast to celebrate the milestone. After the toast, everyone cleared the room with the exception of two Commerce officials dressed like waiters at a four-star restaurant. They set up a table with fancy china and served the startled newcomer a gourmet lunch of her favorite food (which she had revealed in an ice-breaking exercise that morning).

"It was just a phenomenal day," says Killion. "And the experience wasn't just memorable for her. *Everybody* remembers that day. It got to the heart of the message we're trying to send to our new employees: this is a bank that loves to perform for its customers, and you are the main characters in the show."*

What Commerce means metaphorically, Cirque du Soleil means literally—its employees do perform for customers, and they are characters in the one-of-a-kind shows that define the company's presence in the marketplace. Which is why Cirque's introductory program is far more intensive than what even Commerce's intense culture requires. The Cirque program has a forgettable name, "General Training," but it is an unforgettable (and downright grueling) experience. General Training lasts 12 to 16 weeks (longer than the 9 weeks of basic training for the U.S. Army). It is targeted at the 60 percent of Cirque performers who join the company from the world of competitive sports (gymnasts, trampolinists, divers, and synchronized swimmers, for example) as opposed to the world of entertainment.

Line Giasson, Cirque's casting director, describes General Training as "the transformation process of an athlete into an artist." So, along with intense, physically challenging work in everything from flying trapeze to Chinese poles to synchronized swimming, General Training provides a menu of mentally draining, limit-testing exercises in artistic self-expression. In any given session during a typical 10-hour day, directives might include: "Be Monday," "Jump with happiness," or "Stand for three hours in a single pose."

One participant, Natasha Hallett, described General Training's impact on her: "It was like discovering things about myself I had no idea were there. That transition . . . you learn so much about yourself and

*Not every character who signs up with Commerce is ready to perform. Traditions is so intense, packed with so much personality, that it serves as a wake-up call for newcomers who've been miscast. "We've had people who come up to us at the end of the day and say, 'Thank you very much, but this is not for me,'" Killion reports. "That's a good outcome."

your talents in other areas. You go, 'Yeah, I can be funny, I can express myself.' The hardest part of the training process was 'the Door.' There was a door, with all the members of the cast on the other side, and you had to come out and show them who you were. If you didn't know who you were, you had a problem. That was really what [the exercise] was trying to get at. What is it inside you that makes you special? I think that's what Cirque brought to an extreme."[1]

Hallett joined Cirque in the house troupe of *Mystère* and mastered a role that she played for years. Eventually, though, the self-described "loner" and "troublemaker" requested a transfer not just to a different role but to a role designed for a different gender. Hallett became the Firebird, originally a male character; the role was rewritten (complete with new costume, of course) for her. That's the sort of freewheeling creativity that Cirque is looking to unleash in its athletes-turned-artists and what keeps even the longest-running shows fresh for the audience. And that's why General Training is such an important part of how Cirque works. The goal is not just to enhance people's skills but to change how they think—to immerse them in the creative point of view that defines the organization.

Whether it's a day of culture in New Jersey or weeks of mind-expanding exercises in Montreal, the message to employees is clear: you're not showing up for a job, you've signed up for a cause. The broader message for business is clear as well: organizations that aspire to create a disruptive presence in the marketplace have to devise a distinctive approach to the workplace. Companies that *compete* differently tend to *work* differently from the competition.

That's the central message of this chapter. Think of it as a guided tour of companies where talented individuals have learned how to work together—companies that have mastered the interaction between stars and systems we discussed in chapter 10. A word of warning: like the extreme brands we met earlier in the book, the companies we're about to visit have done what can only be described as extreme makeovers of the workplace. We don't expect anyone to copy them. But everyone can learn from them. Spend time inside these organizations, watch how they work, and think about your organization: what kind of workplace have you designed, and how does it reflect your designs on the marketplace?

FROM FREE AGENTS TO TEAM PLAYERS—TEACHING SMART PEOPLE HOW TO WORK TOGETHER

If you want to learn from a disruptive competitor that has built an utterly distinctive workplace, then visit Pixar Animation Studio in Emeryville, California. An imposing iron fence separates the sweetly rolling, 16-acre campus from its gritty urban surrounds and leads to a massive steel gate. Pass through the gate and you sense that you've been granted access to a secret world. Your visitor's badge sets the tone: A STRANGER FROM THE OUTSIDE! it shouts. Inside the vast steel-and-glass atrium of the head-quarters complex, busy "Pixarians" roll across the expanse of wood flooring on scooters and skateboards. A nonstop stream of people flows in and out of the mailroom, which looks like the lobby of a ski lodge with big wooden beams and cubbyholes. To a "stranger from the out-side," it feels like a meticulously designed movie set, as opposed to the setting for the creation of a collection of hit movies.

Pixar, of course, is the creative and commercial juggernaut responsible for *Toy Story* (*I* and *II*), *A Bug's Life, Monsters, Inc., Finding Nemo,* and *The Incredibles*—films that have reinvented the art of animation, captured the imagination of audiences around the world, and grossed more than $3 billion at the box office. The studio produced the first fully computer-generated animated feature film (*Toy Story*) in 1995. It has won 20 Oscars for its films and pioneering technology, and it has generated dozens of patents. *Finding Nemo* is one of the highest-grossing animated films of all, with a worldwide box office of $865 million. *The Incredibles* won the Oscar for Best Animated Feature and pulled in $630 million worldwide in the six months after its November 2004 release.

The company's breakthrough performance has attracted lavish attention in Silicon Valley, on Wall Street, in Hollywood, even in the halls of high culture. (The Museum of Modern Art in New York presented a massive exhibit of the studio's 20 years of film art.) Indeed, Pixar itself has become a kind of movie star—with a price tag to match. In January 2006 Walt Disney Company announced that it would acquire Pixar in a deal valued at $7.4 billion. (This for a company Steve Jobs bought in 1986 for $10 million.) No wonder so many movie moguls are obsessed with replicating Pixar's storytelling prowess and technology chops in the hopes of generating their own computer-generated hits.[2]

Ultimately, though, Pixar's rise to stardom isn't just about clever strategy, powerful technology, or affecting scripts. How the company works helps to explain why its films work so well with audiences—and shows how organizations in all sorts of industries can teach talented people to work together. To be sure, the movie industry is one of the few industries that puts talent at the top of its agenda. But much of that talent—actors, directors, studio bosses—spends much of its time jockeying for advantage, scheming against rivals, demanding star treatment of the most unappetizing sort. Pixar has a different model. The company doesn't just make films that perform better than standard Hollywood fare. It makes its films differently—and in the process, defies many familiar Hollywood conventions.

"Most companies eventually come around to that idea that people are the most important thing," says Randy Nelson, who joined the company in 1997 (when its only feature film was *Toy Story*) and is the dean of Pixar University.* "It's fine to have wildly talented individuals.

---

*First Commerce University, now Pixar University. Whole Foods Market, which we discussed in chapter 3, also has its own university, and DPR's Global Learning Group, which we encountered in chapter 2, is often called DPR University. Companies that build their strategies (in the marketplace, the workplace, or both) around an original set of ideas understand the importance of teaching those ideas to executives and rank-and-file employees—and often embrace the language of a university to deliver their curriculum.

The real trick, the higher degree of difficulty, is to get a bunch of wildly talented people to make productive partnerships, to produce great work."

Nelson, an energetic, colorful, fiftysomething artist and executive, is himself a wide-ranging talent. He has juggled knives on Broadway as a founder of the Flying Karamazov Brothers, acted in feature films, and served in the leadership ranks of Apple and Next. But his real talent is coordinating how other talented people express their most creative ideas, collaborate with colleagues, and meet high-stakes deadlines—all without burning out. His challenge at Pixar is to help craft answers to one of the defining questions facing the organization, a question that's become something of a leadership mantra for him: how do you do art as a team sport?

That's not a common question in the movie business. More than one management pundit has drawn parallels between the flat, decentralized, networked "corporation of the future" and the ad-hoc collection of actors, producers, and technicians who come together around a film and disband once it's finished. In the Hollywood model, the energy and investment revolve around the big idea (the script) and the nitty-gritty of the deal. All sorts of highly talented people (from above-the-title stars to screenwriters to key grips) agree to terms, do their jobs, and move on to the next project. The model allows maximum flexibility but inspires minimum loyalty.

Turn that model on its head and you get Pixar's version of the right way to make movies—a tight-knit company of long-term collaborators who stick together, learn from one another, and struggle to get better with every production. Consider the case of Brad Bird, writer and director of *The Incredibles,* who spent the first decades of his career shuttling around Hollywood as an ever-promising, never-quite-recognized animator. From Cal Arts he eventually went to work on *The Simpsons* and then directed his first feature, the critically acclaimed but commercial dud *Iron Giant.* When Pixar recruited him, Bird went immediately to work on *The Incredibles,* which went on to win two Academy Awards plus a nomination for Best Original Screenplay. (In a nod to Hollywood lore, Bird himself provided the voice of Edna Mode, the film's costume designer to the superheroes, whose fierce demeanor conjures up memories of the late Edith Head, the real-life designer who won more Oscars than any woman in history.)

Unlike almost every other Oscar-winning director, however, the now-celebrated Bird is not a free agent with his sights set on the next big-budget negotiation. He is a salaried employee of the studio that produced his film, and he intends to remain one. In fact, he's part of a group of top directors and technical talents at Pixar, including *Finding Nemo* creators Andrew Stanton and Lee Unkrich, and *Monsters, Inc.* director Pete Docter, who have staked their long-term impact in their field on their long-term work at Pixar. Again, in contrast to standard Hollywood procedure, all of these star performers have traded contracts for salaries and contribute to all of the studio's projects rather than work just on their pet projects. According to Randy Nelson, that no-contract custom is "Pixar's specific critique of the industry's standard practice." He says, "Contracts allow you to be irresponsible as a company. You don't need to worry about keeping people happy and fulfilled. What we have created here—an incredible workspace, opportunities to learn and grow, and, most of all, great coworkers—is better than any contract."

In other words, there's a tough-minded strategy behind Pixar's we're-all-in-this-together workplace. A single animated feature takes four or five years to complete, the last 18 months of which feel like a breathless sprint to the finish line. Meanwhile, even as Pixar raises the creative bar for storytelling and animation, it's stepping up the pace of production—from one new film every 18 months to more than one new film a year by 2010. We paid our first visit to Pixar just days after *The Incredibles* had opened to rave reviews and boffo box office. But in "the Animation Pit," where Pixar's most creative people do their most taxing work, one of the most eye-catching artifacts was a wall-size clock counting down the days, hours, minutes, and seconds until the final production deadlines for *Cars,* the company's next highly anticipated release. In such a high-stakes workplace, even the most outrageously talented individuals are bound to suffer setbacks, to stumble, to buckle under the pressure.

"The problem with the Hollywood model is that it's generally the day you wrap production that you realize you've finally figured out how to work together," says Nelson. "We've made the leap from an idea-centered business to a people-centered business. Instead of developing ideas, we develop people. Instead of investing in ideas, we invest in people. We're trying to create a culture of learning, filled with lifelong learners. It's no trick for talented people to be interesting, but it's a gift to be interested. We want an organization filled with interested people."

Pixar University is where interested people go to learn new things—and learn how to work together. Indeed, it's hard to imagine Pixar working without it. Nelson began work on the institution just a few days into his tenure at the company, when Ed Catmull, Pixar's founder and president, handed him a brilliant, eight-page memo that roughed out a set of ideas about elevating the art of animated filmmaking by creating a "scientific approach" to the craft and teaching animators how to practice it. Catmull had not written the memo. Its author was the original Hollywood maverick—Walt Disney—and it was written a few days before Christmas 1935.* Catmull was betting that history would repeat itself: the creation of the Disney Art School

-----

*Randy Nelson was a little daunted by the fact that the eight-page missive was a 61-year-old memo from "Walt" to legendary drawing teacher and director of the Disney Art School Don Graham. The memo fleshed out a set of ideas around elevating the art of animated filmmaking by educating animators. It read, in part: "I think we shouldn't give up until we have found out all we can about how to teach these young [people] the business. . . . There are a number of things that could be brought up in these discussions to stir [their] imagination, so that when they get into actual animation, they're not just technicians, but they're actually creative people."

in the early 1930s had ushered in the golden era of Disney animation. Could the creation of Pixar University help to usher in a second golden era of animation?

The results speak for themselves. Today, more than 70 years after Walt Disney wrote his memo, Randy Nelson's operation offers more than 110 courses: a complete filmmaking curriculum; classes on painting, drawing, and sculpting; creative writing workshops; even belly-dancing lessons. "We offer the equivalent of an undergraduate education in fine arts and the art of filmmaking," says the dean. Every employee—animators, techies, production assistants, accountants, marketers, even security guards—is encouraged to devote up to four hours per week, every week, to their education. The logic is as simple as it is compelling: specialists from a wide range of business functions and technical disciplines are more likely to work well together if they appreciate the fundamentals of the work the company does. Star performers at Pixar generate the most value when they can see beyond their small part of the universe.*

Nelson is adamant: these classes are not just an invigorating break from office routine. "This is part of everyone's *work*," he says. "We're all filmmakers here. We all have access to the same curriculum. In class, people from every level sit right next to our directors and the president of the company."

We couldn't pass up the chance to sit in on a class and experience the curriculum firsthand. On a November evening, a pack of animated Pixarians makes its way across the back lawn of the campus toward the headquarters building. Having just finished a two-hour improv session

---

* Everything old really is new again. Walt Disney wrote the memo to his colleague Don Graham, who was widely considered the best art teacher of his generation. Graham's out-of-print book *Composing Pictures* is a classic in its field and highly prized by animators and art students alike. Pixar had hundreds of copies printed in a limited run for in-house use. The "Walt memo" and Graham's book are the first things Nelson points to when he explains the origins of Pixar University and the inner workings of Pixar itself.[3]

at Pixar University (a boxy brick building nicknamed "Big Art"), they laugh and gesture wildly, replaying bits from the class with comic exaggeration. They stop briefly to greet those of us traveling in the opposite direction, heading for a four-hour workshop on "Lighting and Motion Picture Capture."

Our group arrives at Big Art and huddles in a studio wolfing down vegetable curry and brown rice. The students represent an intriguing cross-section of Pixar staffers: a postproduction software engineer, a set dresser, a marketer, and an exhausted techie fresh off a nonstop stretch writing "shaders" (programs that apply color and texture to sets and characters) for *The Incredibles* and already hard at work on *Cars*. As we file into a small screening room packed with sofas and comfy chairs, a first-time production assistant rushes in from a "shoot," and the company chef, Luigi Passalacqua, arrives fresh from setting up dinner for some visiting executives. ("I speak the language of food—now I'm learning to speak the language of film," he says excitedly.)

It's the sixth session in a nine-week course, and the instructor, cinematographer John Aliano, dives right in. The evening's subject is highly technical (the use of dimmers in the lighting of movies), but the conversation is anything but. Aliano starts with a scene from Ingmar Bergman's *Wild Strawberries* in which a circle of light closes in on a single angst-ridden character. "Here the language of film rises and the visual becomes as important as the dialogue," he enthuses. "That assumes the audience's intelligence. It doesn't have to be real, it has to be *believable*, it has to be true." He moves on to a scene from Norman Jewison's *A Soldier's Story*. The virtuoso camera work elicits murmurs of appreciation, and someone in the back yells, "Play it again!"

The room really heats up during repeated viewings of a scene from *A Simple Plan*. (The students will split up into small crews to replicate the scene in an all-day shoot over the weekend.) The question on the table is, what does rack focus have to do with emotionally compelling storytelling? Everyone calls out: "It's about meaning." "It reveals character." "It's brutal—it tells the truth." By the end of class, students are out of their seats, setting up massive lights with the finesse of professional grips and experimenting with a tool for casting evocative shadows called a "cookie." They're also trying on their roles as first-time directors, cinematographers, and producers for the upcoming shoot, discussing the script, blocking out the shots, dreaming up makeshift props.

It was, admittedly, just a four-hour glimpse of an ongoing education, but the takeaway was obvious. From the software engineer to the marketer to chef Luigi, Pixar employees weren't just learning about lighting, they were learning to see the company's work (and their colleagues) in a new light. "The skills we develop are skills we need everywhere in the organization," Nelson says. "Why teach drawing to accountants? Because drawing class doesn't just teach people to draw. It teaches them to be more *observant*. There's no company on earth that wouldn't benefit from having people become more observant."

That's the real lesson plan behind Pixar University—not just encouraging people to learn new skills but encouraging a diverse group of people to sit in a room, try new things, mess up, get embarrassed, and learn how to bounce back—together. That helps to explain why the Pixar University crest bears the Latin inscription *Alienus Non Diutius*. Translation: *Alone No Longer*. "It's the heart of our model," Nelson says. "Giving people opportunities to fail together and to recover from mistakes together."

It's worth noting that the Pixar University crest has a second Latin inscription, *Tempus*Pecunia*Somnus*. Translation: *Time, Money, Sleep*—three precious commodities in an organization whose track record of unrivaled creativity has to confront the harsh realities of rising expectations and an unforgiving marketplace. That's the next huge challenge for Pixar (and Nelson) going forward—to moderate the pace and sustain the energy of an organization that is expected to keep producing blockbusters even as it ramps up production.

No single class can teach people how to master that challenge. But by creating an organization in which employees from different levels, backgrounds, and disciplines get the chance to learn together, experiment together, and solve problems together, Pixar University creates the conditions under which people can do their best work without embracing a destructive culture of overwork.*

We saw an intriguing artifact of these working conditions in the form of a strange-looking, felt-covered board littered with numbered Popsicle sticks and characters from *The Incredibles*. Brad Bird's film presented an avalanche of technical challenges to Pixar's computer wizards: How do you make long hair move realistically? How do you create the fabric for superhero costumers in varying states of disrepair? How do you render an underwater explosion? Solving each of these challenges without compromise would have made for an absolutely perfect movie—and an absolute disaster in terms of the release schedule.

So the production team created a low-tech answer to its high-tech dilemma. The Popsicle sticks represented the finite units of person-hours budgeted for each element of the production. If Bird called for extra time to be spent perfecting a certain character or a particular scene (say, Mr. Incredible's superhero costume), another element (Violet's hair, for example) had to lose a Popsicle stick. This ridiculously simple tool allowed a small army of world-class computer filmmakers to stay true to the movie's promise and stay focused on the clock. It was, says Nelson, classic Pixar—a clever innovation that becomes a routine part of doing business when you practice art as a team sport.

The best way to understand the nuts and bolts of how the company works, he concludes, is not to look at Popsicle sticks but to go back to

---

*Randy Nelson is a fierce critic of Pixar's neighbors in the video game business, who, he says, "are eating their young by working nonstop. They finish one project and immediately start on another. It's no surprise their products all look the same." Pixar's technical employees, in contrast, get paid for a 50-hour week with the expectation that they will work between 40 and 50 hours. What's more, workers planning to spend more than 50 hours a week on the job must get permission from their manager. Needless to say, at plenty of points along the four-year life of a movie, plenty of people ask for and receive permission to work beyond the weekly limit.

headquarters and look at, well, nuts and bolts. As he runs his hand over one of the massive steel H-beams that support the atrium, Nelson explains the message behind the metal: "We secured these beams with bolts instead of welds because you can really see the craftsmanship that went into it. We wanted to create a handmade building in which to create handmade films. Every bolt was turned by hand, every brick laid by hand. Like an animated film, this place is built from a number of simple and small elements that accrete into something better and bigger. The message is, 'Without you, my ideas are lonely.' "

FROM BUREAUCRACY TO ADHOCRACY—THE MANY VIRTUES OF A MESSY WORKPLACE

It's possible both to marvel at what Randy Nelson and his colleagues have built and to wonder how much their experiences apply to more, shall we say, mundane industries. Is it any wonder that the most gifted animators on the planet have created such a colorful place to work? But as we noted earlier, the point is not to copy how Pixar operates. The point is to recognize, as sharply as Pixar has done, that organizations that aspire to create a singular identity in the marketplace have to design a signature approach to the workplace—a blend of individual stars and operating systems that matches up with the strategy. That principle applies to company-builders from all walks of life and in all kinds of industries.

SEI Investments, based in Oaks, Pennsylvania, is a maverick presence in a decidedly unglamorous field. Basically, the company serves as a back office for the vast wealth management industry. It administers more than $312 billion in assets for mutual fund companies and other financial service firms, handles processing and administration for the trust departments at 100 of the top 200 banks, and is one of the largest manager-of-manager investment firms, with more than $130 billion in assets. It's a huge amount of money, but it's not very sexy stuff, which is why SEI's public persona will never rival that of Pixar, Cirque du Soleil, or even Southwest Airlines. But its workplace persona is just as distinctive as those in these high-profile organizations—and its marketplace performance just as dramatic.

It's hard to imagine that the offices of an asset management firm located 30 miles outside Philadelphia could be as arresting as Steve Jobs's computer animation paradise, but seeing is believing. Set on 100 acres of rolling fields and woodland, SEI's headquarters looks like a 19th-century farm reimagined by high-modern architect Robert Venturi. A long drive brings you to a cluster of metal, barnlike buildings painted in muted green, blue, and purple and connected by covered elevated walkways. A gigantic silo houses the main lobby, which is filled with avant-garde art—including an enormous sculpted mushroom outcropping on a brick wall and a miniature winter wonderland (complete with its own weather system) sealed in a Lucite box.

The tranquility of the grounds, which roll down to a burbling creek and feature the original centuries-old stone farmhouse, contrasts sharply with the intense activity inside the buildings. In the lobby, people clatter up and down the wide staircase that spirals around the silo, while SEI's in-house curator guides a group of art enthusiasts through the collection. Past the concierge's desk and up a short flight of stairs, the place turns into a high-tech hive. The open, light-filled room looks like a cross between a high-gloss sewing factory and a Wall Street trading floor. Red, yellow, and black cables ("pythons," in SEI parlance) coil down from high ceilings to each desk—umbilical cords of power, data, and telecommunications. Less obvious, but just as important, all the furniture (desks, file cabinets, conference tables) is on wheels, ready to roll across the recycled rubber floors and reconfigure the company on short notice.

The eye-opening environment is the brainchild of Al West, SEI's sixtysomething founder, chairman, and CEO, and it is meant to showcase how the company sees the world. "This place sends a daily signal about who we are," he says. "You walk in and you get it. Everybody has the same desk and works together in an open room. There isn't a visible hierarchy, and there isn't a perk hierarchy. The message is: ideas are the most important thing, and everybody's ideas are equal. You're not given power here; the only power comes from making things happen."[4]

Actually, SEI's unconventional workplace is about more than sending signals—it's about enacting strategy. The company took shape in 1968 when West built a business out of the strange new idea of using computer simulations to train bank loan officers. Ever since, his company has prospered as a classic strategic disruptor—challenging the competition and reinventing itself with a series of advanced technologies and big-bang innovations that have reshaped the money management business. Those big bangs have produced huge returns. SEI's share price has increased by a factor of 15 since 1990 and registered average annual gains of 36 percent since its IPO in 1981. In 2002 *American Banker,* the bible of the business, called Al West "the most successful financial-services chief executive over the past decade."*

This workplace-on-wheels stands in sharp contrast to how most of the financial services establishment organizes itself. The contrast seems to go with the maverick territory. Pixar makes waves in an industry notorious for self-serving free agents by designing a workplace that brings everyone together. SEI makes waves in an industry noted for starched-shirt hierarchies by dismantling formal structures in order to incubate grassroots innovation.

"We tend to walk down the unproven paths early in our industry," says Carl Guarino, a 16-year veteran of SEI. "It's not that we are smarter or more insightful than the competition; other people in the industry see some of the same things we see. But they're more inhibited by their

---

*West owns 20 percent of SEI's outstanding shares, and the company's stock market value hovers around $4 billion, making his personal fortune worth roughly $800 million—not bad for a guy whose company grew up in a barn.

business models and more worried about the market reaction than we tend to be. The view here is, it's a bigger risk for us not to innovate."

To be sure, SEI has many of the trappings of a traditional financial services company, with five formal business units and plenty of executives with lofty titles. But it's the team, not the org chart, that determines who does what, and it's the project leaders, not the official hierarchy, who shape day-to-day priorities. At any one time, the company's 2,000-plus employees are divided into as many as 400 teams. Each employee belongs to one "base" team along with three or four virtual (part-time) or ad-hoc (temporary) teams. Some teams have a few members, some as many as 100 members. Some stay together for months or years, some disband in a matter of weeks. People move their workstations so much based on team assignments that SEI developed tracking software to identify each employee's whereabouts so their colleagues can find them.

The informality, flexibility, and sheer mobility of SEI's workplace is what lets teams get organized without bringing work at the organization to a screeching halt. This is a company where rank-and-file employees vote with their feet about what they work on and where they work. Carl Guarino, for example, held several of the top spots in the SEI org chart. As an executive vice president, he ran the company's all-important investment advisers business unit. Yet Guarino never relied on the power of his position alone. When he wanted to get something done, he started a project, reached across the organization, and tried to persuade potential team members that he had got something worth working on.

"We reject the idea that because people sit at the top of the organization, power resides with them and control comes down the line," he says. "Power is much more diffuse and dispersed in this organization. Power doesn't come from position, it comes from influence and the ability to engineer consensus—not in the Japanese sense of unanimity but in terms of the participation and support required to get things done."

Guarino recalls one large-scale technology project for the investment adviser group. At the event to celebrate the completion of the project, it dawned on him that fewer than half the people on the team came from his business unit. "I'm critically dependent on large areas of the organization that do not report to me," he says. "But even I can't get people to move if a project isn't seen as innovative or leading-edge. Innovation is the big driver here. If you're not pushing things in a meaningful direction, people tend to put it on the back burner. No matter how high up you are in the organization, it's hard to marshal the resources."

Consider the fate of a leadership development project proposed by Al West himself and launched by Marcia Noa, head of SEI's digital-media unit. In late 1999, at West's urging, Noa developed a program based on SEI's particular brand of leadership, created a "personal business plan" for use throughout the organization, and started a project to roll out a series of leadership labs to bring the plan to life. The whole thing fizzled. "It didn't pass the ripeness test," Noa concedes. "Either we have to be feeling the pain or there have to be really high stakes for something to succeed, because so much is going on all the time. But that doesn't mean the work was wasted. We never throw anything away." Indeed, five years after the project withered, Noa was getting flickers of renewed interest from her rank-and-file colleagues.

In a sense, SEI's embrace of managed chaos is designed to make explicit what most everyone in a large organization knows implicitly: formal lines of authority rarely determine how things actually get done. Most creativity happens *in spite of* the organization, not because of it. That's why successful innovators don't ask for the most resources or the strictest oversight; they ask for the most room to maneuver and the fewest bureaucratic hurdles.

"Because we do all of our work in teams, working together is more important than managing up," says CEO West. "When people don't get ahead here, it's not because of their boss, it's because of their peers. People who are always making sure their boss sees them, who direct their efforts up the chain rather than to their colleagues, are the ones who don't work out. Your success here is a direct function of how well you get along with your peers."

It's a point of view about grassroots leadership that would make the authors of Big Blue's "Staying Extreme" manifesto green with envy. At SEI, the most effective leaders exude a blend of humility and ambition—*humbition*—that relies on the power of persuasion rather than formal authority. The best way to get along with your peers, especially when it comes to enlisting them in a project, is to emphasize what's in it for them and for the company, rather than what's in it for you.

"As a team leader, you're not going to have a lot of luck if you just want people in execution mode," says Guarino. "But if you involve people in the strategy, give them a chance to work with clients, and share the credit, people will be lobbying *you* for a spot on the team. And the next time you come around, people will jump at the chance to get involved."

It is, to be sure, a messier way to work, filled with false starts, crossed signals, and often-conflicting opinions and priorities. But West and his colleagues insist that there is merit to the mess, especially when compared to the alternatives. "We distrust formal programs and prescribed processes," the CEO says. "We don't have job descriptions or an org chart for a reason. The problem with hierarchies is that they require you to engineer everything in advance. There's no way we could have engineered in advance everything that's gone right for us in this business."

As a leader, West goes out of his way to engineer sharp debate, even discord, inside the organization, and there's a real art to his style. Literally. The CEO's passion for art has spawned a 2,500-piece collection that focuses on mature, innovative, but not necessarily recognizable approaches—a collection that looms large throughout the SEI campus. The art is meant to provoke discussion, not just please the senses. "We're trying to break new ground," West says. "You don't have to like it, but I'm pretty sure you'll talk about it."

Sometimes the talk gets so heated that a piece of art will be exiled to the "Hot Hall"—an exhibit space in the basement dedicated to the company's most controversial works. Striking (sometimes startling) paintings, photographs, and sculpture are surrounded by comments submitted by employees: "You have gone too far"; "Disturbed"; "Too weird"; "This is about free expression. If you look at it differently, you could have a completely opposite interpretation."

The rules of the conversation are stated clearly on the walls of the Hot Hall. First, "speak your mind." (People can e-mail comments on any piece; the art team uses those comments to determine if it should be transferred to the basement.) Second, "continue to speak and hear what others have to say." (Every comment, positive or negative, is posted next to the relevant work.) Finally, "adopt and shop." (If a team feels strongly enough about a certain piece, it can bring it out of perdition and put it on display, as did a securities-industry team with an especially controversial painting, infused with Islamic themes, called *Red Veils*.) These rules are as relevant to sizing up new ideas about markets and technology as they are to evaluating controversial art. Innovation is a messy business; problems arise when business makes the work of innovation too neat and tidy.

There's another virtue to encouraging lots of little messes: it tends to prevent huge disasters. Why do so many companies pursue dead-end projects long after they should be dead and buried? Because they load those projects up with financial resources and top-management prestige; projects become too famous to fail. At SEI, ad-hoc teams bootstrap their ideas until actual results justify more resources. Not only does that allow the company to kill weak ideas without lots of mourning, but it encourages grassroots innovators to try more things without a huge fear of failure.

"For us to start something new means a couple people and a couple of desks," says Carl Guarino. "It lowers the barriers to innovation in terms of investment capital and psychological capital. We approach everything we do as if we were incubating a little new business. When you start by allocating big money to something, you end up creating a lot of pressure to produce immediate results. It has to be a big win in order to justify the investment. We put a couple of people on it and see what happens."

That highly dispersed model of innovation and growth—try a bunch of things and see what happens—is also a good description of career development at SEI. The company is recognized as a model employer (it has landed on *Fortune*'s "100 Best Companies to Work For" list five years running), but it's hardly a mellow employer. The most successful performers are the ones who are most comfortable with extreme mobility and personal responsibility—individuals who can translate the wide-open spirit of the Hot Hall into the perpetual-motion hallways of the organization.

"You're responsible for your career," says CEO West matter-of-factly. "You need to look at it like a business. What do you want to happen? How do you want to be known? We encourage and reward people for moving around, and not just within one area. You can stay in one place and become an expert and a leader. You can have a good career that way. But a *great* career is all about movement."

Review the résumés of most SEI veterans and you see a career trajectory full of sharp corners and unexpected twists. Take Guarino: he started out as SEI's general counsel, spent six years in that role, and then lobbied to run the company's IT center (with no prior experience). After an 18-month stint in technology, the aspiring techie created a new role for himself in new-business development. After six years in that role, West tapped him to run the company's investment adviser business unit.

Marcia Noa has a similarly checkered past. She started out as something of a techie, managing the installation of large computer systems for banking-industry clients and designing tax and regulatory software. Several years into her tenure, she switched gears to work with West on organizational change, with a special focus on learning and communications. In the course of that job, she's launched a variety of projects, including a digital-media operation that runs as an internal business. "It's the opposite of the traditional career arc, where you know you've made it when you can rest on your laurels," Noa says. "Here you know you've made it if you keep getting pulled into messy situations."

It's one more example of how a messy-by-design workplace supports a disruptive strategy in the marketplace. "People here are used to getting out of their comfort zone, finding their bearings, and just dealing with it," explains Al West. "It's an enormous learning experience for the individual. Spending time in sales, recruiting, technology, and project management across different units just creates better businesspeople. And it builds a lot of flexibility, speed, and innovation into the whole organization. Winning is about being able to change as fast as, or faster than, the world is changing. That's what we're designed to do."

FROM EMPLOYEES TO OWNERS— EVERY PERSON A BUSINESSPERSON

There's at least one design principle that seems to connect all of the one-of-a-kind workplaces we've explored in the last two chapters: companies that are serious about understanding what makes their people tick equip their people with a serious understanding of what makes the company itself tick. Whether it's Southwest Airlines, Pixar, or SEI Investments, there's little room for talented employees who can't see beyond their narrow specialties. Inside the most idea-driven, talent-centered organizations we've come to know, every person is expected to think like a businessperson. Even the most glittering stars have to understand their place in the broader constellation of the business.

At Cranium, for example, Jack Lawrence, the company's CFO (aka "Professor Profit") holds all-hands meetings to review, explain, and interpret the company's operating performance. The sessions, like most things at Cranium, have a colorful name, but they are all business.* Every two months, Lawrence schools everyone in the organization in the intricate details of budgets, retail sell-through, financial ratios, cash flows—all of which translates into how the still-private company gets valued on a price-per-share basis.

It's the kind of no-holds-barred presentation that should (and does) get made to the board of directors—only in this case every person at Cranium reviews the numbers and figures out how his or her efficiency and productivity in the game business affect the great game of business in the financial markets. "At the end of these meetings, we make a list of the top ten priorities that every person in the company should be focused on," Lawrence says. "People know that if they're not focused on those priorities, they're focused on the wrong things."

Even a free-spirited outfit like Cirque du Soleil schools its creative stars in the rigors of the business and its worldwide operations. Every year, president Daniel Lamarre circles the globe to share detailed financial results with every member of the organization. He visits the cast and crew of the permanent shows in Las Vegas and Orlando and catches up with each of the touring shows somewhere in the world. The tour requires nearly a month of travel, but Lamarre believes it generates huge returns in terms of rank-and-file commitment and a willingness to keep an open mind about new assignments, new demands, and new shows.

If General Training is designed to turn athletes into artists, Lamarre's briefings are designed to infuse carefree artists with some hardheaded business savvy. "I'm very transparent about our financial performance," he says. "We're making a healthy profit, and I'm not shy about it. People know that one percent of our revenue—not profit, revenue—goes to changing the world. They also understand that we share profits with

---

*The meetings are called, for reasons too complicated to explain here, "My Aunt Peggy's Cheesecake." And yes, they do involve baked goods.

everyone. And we're investing a ton of money back into the organization to produce new shows."

These are, to be sure, informal (and largely informational) techniques for immersing rank-and-file performers in the day-to-day performance of the organization—techniques that fit offbeat cultures like Cranium and Cirque du Soleil. In more traditional settings that allow for an even more rigorous commitment to teaching every person how to think like a businessperson, the results can be even more powerful—and the lessons for business even more revealing.

It's a long way from Cranium's CHIFF-happy headquarters or Cirque's Grand Chapiteau to the "frozen tundra" of Green Bay, Wisconsin, but it's there that we encountered another truly distinctive workplace—one that underscores what can happen to a business when every person understands what makes the business tick. Dick Resch, president and CEO of KI (formerly Krueger International), took charge of the company back in the early 1980s, when it was a tiny (annual revenues: $45 million), undistinguished, virtually unknown manufacturer of run-of-the-mill office furniture. Since then, he has engineered a transformation of its presence in the marketplace—a transformation that has resulted in sustained growth in sales, profits, and shareholder value. The company is still not as big as Steelcase, Herman Miller, or Haworth—the three well-known giants of the office furniture world. But during the last 15 years alone, KI has climbed from the 25th-largest player in its industry to the 5th-largest—a remarkable trajectory in a business where slow and steady defines the competitive race.

It's hard to overstate the scale and character of KI's transformation. The first product made by the company, which began in 1941, was the lowly metal folding chair. (It still sells a million folding chairs a year.) Resch signed on as a junior executive in 1964, when the company had sales of just $4 million. The modern KI has 3,500 employees, annual revenues of $600 million, and a leadership position in several highly desirable, highly demanding markets, from outfitting university campuses (where it is the undisputed leader) to being a top supplier to cutting-edge giants such as Microsoft and Sun Microsystems. (KI provides an estimated 90 percent of Microsoft's furniture, a powerful endorsement from one of the world's most powerful competitors.)[5]

In general, the secret to KI's prosperity has been its agility. In an industry where most companies rely on third-party dealers to sell standardized products to a vast range of customers, KI directly targets end users in select markets—including health care, government, higher education, and high-tech—and provides tailored (sometimes designed-from-scratch) furniture that addresses the specific ways these organizations work. The company's product development model relies on rapid prototyping and frequent revisions to deliver highly customized products.* Resch and his colleagues call it a "market-of-one" strategy, and it has made the company a force to be reckoned with in its market.

Resch himself has become something of a folk hero in Green Bay, applying his personal wealth (and corporate resources) to help build the Resch Center, a 10,000-seat arena, and the KI Convention Center, a 45,000-square-foot meeting facility. The Resch Center is a snowball's throw from Lambeau Field, legendary home of the Green Bay Packers. Indeed, it's hard to overstate the hold of the Packers over the citizens of Green Bay—including Resch. He and another high-powered executive led the fund-raising drive to build the Bart Starr Plaza outside the Resch Center, a tribute to the quarterback and coach complete with a seven-foot-tall sculpture. For the last 15 years or so, Resch has lived in the house that was owned and occupied by Starr during his glory days as a Packer.

---

*A case in point is the so-called Wharton Lectern, developed from scratch to meet the demanding standards of the Wharton School. KI spent months working with the school to design a classroom podium that could house all the latest high-tech teaching aids but also look sleek and elegant. Wharton ordered only 50 or 60 of the gorgeous lecterns (it doesn't have all that many classrooms), but it's now a hot product at graduate schools and universities across the country.

But when you visit Green Bay and spend time inside KI, its president and CEO is less interested in reminiscing about Vince Lombardi and Jerry Kramer, or showcasing the new products developed for Silicon Valley and the Ivy League, than he is in explaining how 3,500 employees have immersed themselves in the company's strategy and operations and how this transformation of the workplace has fueled the company's advances in the marketplace. Put simply, KI couldn't engage so deeply with its elite, demanding customers if its employees weren't so deeply engaged in the intricacies of the business.

How would Resch, who turned 67 shortly before our visit, describe the legacy of what KI has built? "It's about freedom and responsibility," he says. "When I joined the company, there were three shareholders. They owned everything, and there was no information on how we were doing financially. My first boss actually read my mail! Today everyone at the company is an owner, either directly or through shares in their retirement accounts, and I have tried to teach everyone, right down to the technicians on the floor, how to think like a businessperson. Second, there are no secrets here. Everyone here has access to whatever data they need to do their job and help run the business."

Resch speaks with the reserve and humility you'd expect from someone who's made his fortune in America's heartland. But don't let the quiet demeanor fool you. He's every bit the maverick, and what he's engineered in the workplace at KI offers powerful lessons for all kinds of businesses in working more productively and more fairly. Consider the issue of ownership. Back in the 1980s, Resch pulled off a high-wire financial act that transferred ownership of KI from a small number of senior executives to the workforce as a whole. It's a complicated story, complete with jockeying against Wall Street investment banks, LBO firms, and assorted other high-risk maneuvers. But the end result is that for 15 years KI has been an employee-owned operation whose solid growth has spread real wealth across the ranks of the company. Thousands of managers and employees personally share in the value they help to create.

And everyone knows how much their shares are worth. Although KI is privately held, Credit Suisse performs an annual appraisal that values KI as if it were a publicly traded company. Back in 1981, shares in the company were worth less than a dime each. By the end of 2004, even after the disastrous office furniture downturn of the dot-com bust, shares of KI were valued at an all-time high of nearly $27. That's a 24-year compound annual rate of return of more than 30 percent—a healthy performance that would be the envy of just about any company, no matter the industry.

It's no surprise that managers and rank-and-file employees are eager to adopt an "ownership mind-set" about the business when they do, in fact, own a stake.* But this equity stake becomes even more meaningful when employee-owners are also steeped in the operating details of the business—when they get a microscopic look at how product lines and markets are stacking up against budgets, which plants are running most effectively, which customers are experiencing quality problems or delivery delays, and all the other short-term factors that drive long-term financial returns. At KI, employees get access to just this kind of information in another one of Dick Resch's maverick innovations—a monthly roll-up-the-sleeves-and-look-at-the-numbers gathering that's called a "Heath meeting." (The meeting is named after the Heath Corporation, a consulting firm in Milwaukee that gathers and organizes the data.)

We attended the June 2005 meeting. It was, Resch said with obvious pride, the 384th such monthly gathering to review the operating details of the company. "We're finally starting to get the hang of it," he joked. A handsome, thoroughly state-of-the-art conference room (no surprise

---

*There are no stock options at KI. Managers and employees own actual shares worth a total of $150 million in their retirement accounts. Once a year, employees get the chance to buy KI shares for their personal, nonretirement holdings. The minimum purchase is $10,000. Employees can sell shares back to the company at any time at the current "market" price.

at a successful office furniture company) was overflowing with executives and frontline managers from sales, marketing, product development, finance, manufacturing—every nook and cranny of KI. With little fanfare, Resch called the meeting to order and *whoosh*—thus began a three-hour blizzard of data, questions, market intelligence, wisecracks, and history lessons that was intense, entertaining, and (for a visitor at least) exhausting. For this meeting, Heath had produced 850 separate charts, and the group reviewed nearly 400 of them with blazing speed. Behind every piece of real-time information about a product line, a customer, or the price of a raw material was five years' worth of historical data that could be summoned with the click of a mouse. It felt like the office furniture equivalent of an air-traffic control tower—lots of people making sense of lots of data in very little time.

Resch himself said very little. The point of the exercise, he explained, was for KI's managers to size up the results, identify the most pressing business issues, and figure out how to resolve them.* The participants, regardless of rank or seniority, threw themselves into the fray. They were unsparing in their evaluations of a new product that wasn't meeting expectations: "It's just a regular chair, there's no buzz about it." They confirmed the popularity of a high-end product created for KI by an Italian designer: "I never thought this thing would sell. Now it's off the charts." They swapped intelligence about contracts and projects with the IRS and the Census Bureau, the Los Angeles public schools, and the Associated Press. There was worried talk about the rising price of steel and the potential delays caused when seven truckloads of substandard steel were shipped to one of the factories.

---

*At the top of the written agenda for every monthly meeting is a reminder of the two main goals. First, "to assist each participant in developing an entrepreneurial point of view." Second, "to develop each participant as a Divisional Manager and/or CEO. Each participant should develop the skills required to understand how to run a business."

The no-nonsense session was an eye-opening snapshot of how well KI was working and what parts of the business needed to be worked on most urgently. Resch emphasizes two other points about this open-book style of operation. The discipline of holding these meetings every month, for 384 months in a row, amounts to an advanced business education. ("It's a shared learning experience," he says. "It helps me, as CEO, teach everyone about the levers we can pull to be profitable over the long term.") Just as important, these monthly gatherings trigger follow-through sessions throughout the ranks. Manufacturing managers review data and war stories with the self-managed teams that operate the company's production lines; designers get together to figure out the impact of that month's Heath meeting on their product development priorities.

KI can be more agile in the marketplace because it has built such a highly engaged, highly informed workplace—one filled with employees who own a piece of the business and have developed a clear understanding of how the whole business works. "I remember when I was allowed, after two or three years, to buy a tiny piece of the company," Resch says. "I thought it was the greatest day of my life. We've tried to extend that dream to everyone here. I am a quantitative, numbers-driven manager. I like to feel good inside, but I really like results. And the power of an entrepreneurial company, owned by its employees, with total freedom of information—it's just a phenomenal competitive engine."

It may be a phenomenal way to compete, but it's really not a phenomenally complicated idea. So it's been with all of the organizations we've encountered in the last two chapters. When it comes to the human factor in business, there are few breakthrough innovations or earth-shattering insights. There are just new and exciting answers to old (and often unanswered) questions. What makes great people tick? What kinds of people tend to work out great inside an organization?

How do great people do their best work? Now it's time for you to get to work. Think about how this collection of maverick companies operates, reflect on how their design of the workplace relates to their designs on the marketplace, and ask yourself: why can't my company work this way?

Chapter Twelve

. . . .

Maverick Messages (IV): Practicing Your People Skills

I t's easy to agree that the quality of a company's performance can't exceed the quality of the performers in the company. It's not so easy to figure out how to attract more than your fair share of the stars in your industry, where to look for them (especially if they're not looking for you), and how to encourage talented individuals to work together. On the other hand, precisely because so many companies are so mediocre at the people factor in business, it doesn't require earth-shattering innovations to stand out from the crowd and outperform the competition.

We've visited literally hundreds of workplaces over the years, and it's always pretty obvious (and unfortunately, pretty rare) when companies are as creative and rigorous about the people factor in their business as they are about other business disciplines. Often the evidence is staring us right in the face—in the form of employee faces. At the visually arresting headquarters of Wieden+Kennedy, the first thing you see when you open the giant steel mesh front door is a wall of photographs. Not photographs of the star athletes and A-list celebrities who populate the agency's iconic campaigns, not snapshots of the agency's founders with high-powered clients or political luminaries, not even samples of award-winning work. Instead, the wall, which follows a wide concrete staircase up to the second-floor reception area, is paved with black-and-white portraits of rank-and-file contributors. Every single one of the agency's 300 Portland-based employees, from famed creative directors to accountants and Web producers, is captured in a uniquely individual pose—dressed up in a bizarre costume, playing air guitar, holding a flower between her teeth, just playing it straight. The message is as simple as it is meaningful: this is an organization built around the individuals who populate it.

A similar message is communicated at the Montreal headquarters of Cirque du Soleil. One of the most striking elements of this striking complex is a ghostly gallery of white plaster head casts. Talk about casting the company: as soon as an artist is selected for a Cirque show, he or she sits through a laborious (and uncomfortable) two-hour process to create a head cast. The cast is a necessity for the costume department, which often has to work up new hats or replacement masks for Cirque performers who are thousands of miles away. But the casts also make a statement about how Cirque works. A round Chinese face with a small smile, a furry-eyebrowed eastern European face with a wide grin, a child's head. The exhibit is an overt celebration of diversity and individuality. It's also, says Gabriel Pinkstone, Cirque's assistant vice president of production, "about remembering why we're here—not to create a bureaucratic machine but to create works of the imagination."

These are two small examples of a larger point: there's a difference between preaching about the human factor in business and practicing the people skills that shape the character of competition inside your company. Are you as determined to excel in the talent market as you are in the product market, or do you still treat talent as a business backwater? Being honest about the answers to five simple questions may help you practice what you preach.

1. Why should great people join your organization?

The best leaders understand that the best rank-and-file performers aren't motivated primarily by money. Great people want to work on exciting projects. Great people want to feel like impact players inside their organizations. Great people want to be surrounded with and challenged by other great people. Put simply, great people want to feel like they're part of something greater than themselves.

Early on in their company's history, long before it became synonymous with the rebirth of the Internet economy, Google's founders made it clear that they considered the talent issue a make-or-break strategic issue for the future. So they published a top ten list of why the world's best researchers, programmers, and marketers should work at the Googleplex—and never once did they mention stock options or bonuses. Reason number two: "Life is beautiful. Being part of something that matters and working on products in which you can believe is remarkably fulfilling." Reason number seven: "Good company everywhere you look. Googlers range from former neurosurgeons, CEOs, and U.S. puzzle champions to alligator wrestlers and former Marines." Reason number nine: "Boldly go where no one has gone before. There are hundreds of challenges yet to solve. Your creative ideas matter here and are worth exploring."[1]

What's your version of Google's top ten list? Have you set out—clearly, crisply, in language that reflects the spirit of your organization—the most compelling reasons for great people to work on your team, in your division, at your company? If not, it's a great project to start working on Monday morning.

2. Do you know a great person when you see one?

From Southwest Airlines to Yahoo to SEI Investments, the workplaces feel different, but the organizing principle is the same: character counts for as much as credentials. In other words, at organizations that are serious about competing on talent, who you are as a person is as important as what you know at a moment in time. There's a hardheaded business logic to this softhearted mind-set. Companies with a distinctive set of ideas about how to create value in the marketplace need people whose values are in sync with the strategy. That's why Southwest tests for the "warrior spirit" and Yahoo searches for programmers and marketers with the "Y Gene."

It's also why the creators of IBM's Extreme Blue program are so adamant that its rising-star participants immerse themselves in the "Staying Extreme" manual. Sure, Big Blue wants to attract world-class programmers and business strategists. But it only wants talented individuals who understand how to get things done inside a huge, worldwide organization. "Staying Extreme" documents in painstaking detail (and commonsense language) the character of competition that makes IBM work.

It emphasizes people who "lead from the front": "Remember," the manual advises, "no matter who you work for, they work for you, too. You aren't an order taker. You have a responsibility to develop insights and try to convince your peers, employees, and management to go that way. You won't get your way every time, but keeping in the habit of driving the agenda is crucial. Don't just wait for someone to tell you what to do. Understand their business and then tell them what you are going to do to help them win."

It also emphasizes people who embrace "disruption with purpose": "All organizations—even a one-year-old startup—maintain norms of behavior and assumptions of right and wrong that are predicated on the past," the manual explains. "At this point, you might expect us to tell you that you should start tearing apart these norms post haste. Not quite. Plenty of those experiences that created the norms are perfectly valid in today's—and even tomorrow's—environment. Yes, you have been trained to take no assumption for granted. But also don't trip over the most common assumption of all: the assumption that seemingly stupid practices or norms actually are stupid."

Do you know what values make your star performers tick—and how to find more performers who share those attributes? Could you write a plainspoken manual, your version of "Staying Extreme," that explains the most productive ways for these stars to make a difference inside your organization?

3. Can you find great people who aren't looking for you?

It's a commonsense insight that's commonly forgotten: the most talented performers tend to be in jobs they like, working with people they enjoy, on projects that keep them challenged. So leaders who are content to fill their organizations with people actively looking for new jobs risk attracting malcontents and mediocre performers. The trick (and the challenge) is to win over so-called passive job-seekers— people who won't work for you unless you work hard to persuade them to join. Starbucks recruiter Jason Warner is endlessly creative when it comes to the urgent task of discovering new sources of talent. One crucial tactic: Turn committed employees and loyal alumni into scouts for great candidates in unlikely places. Cirque du Soleil's talent scouts understand that the company can't hire every rising star the moment it discovers them. So they hire talented performers when they're open to joining, not just when Cirque has an opening to fill.

That said, connecting with great people doesn't always mean concocting extraordinary measures to win them over. Consider something as homely as help wanted ads. Over the years, even the most advanced companies we've come to know have used traditional help wanted ads to prospect for recruits. What's instructive about their ads, though, is how *untraditional* they are. They emphasize character rather than credentials and spotlight how the company works rather than where an individual might be working.

Southwest Airlines cemented its reputation for colorful (sometimes zany) service early in its history by communicating to prospective employees the spirited culture it was working to create.

Cofounder and then-CEO Herb Kelleher posed for one help wanted ad dressed in full Elvis attire. The text read: "Do you want to work in a place where Elvis has been spotted? Qualifications: Outgoing. A little off-centered. Be prepared to stay awhile. If that sounds good to you, send us your résumé. Attn: Elvis."[2]

Life at SEI Investments can also be zany, at least by the standards of financial services organizations. So when it recruits high-ranking college graduates to its prestigious associates program, it uses an ad that distinguishes the program (and the company) from conventional Wall Street firms. "Position Title: Irrelevant," it reads. "Team Name: Any," it continues. Then it offers a "job description" that refuses to describe an actual job: "As a candidate, you will not hear about a specific opening or openings which we are looking to fill. You will not meet with your future team leader, and you will not be told of your wonderfully laid-out 'career path.' . . . This may sound bizarre as you sift through all the formal job descriptions and 'programs' advertised by prospective employers. But think of it as we do: If you knew, in September, what role you would fill in August of the following year, how important could that role be?"

Can you craft an old-fashioned help wanted ad that captures the newfangled ideas around which your workplace is organized? Can you make it fun? Can you make it fresh? Can you make it compelling enough to attract the attention of talented people who aren't looking to change jobs?

4. Are you great at teaching great people how your organization works and wins?

Even the most highly focused specialists (programmers, designers, animators) are at their best when they appreciate how the whole business operates and what determines whether it wins or loses in the marketplace. That's partly a matter of sharing financial statements: can every person learn how to think like a businessperson?

But it's mainly a matter of shared understanding: can smart people work on making everyone else in the organization smarter about the business?

Pixar does a smarter job of answering that question than any company we've come to know—and not just in the halls of Pixar University. One of Randy Nelson's favorite workplace mantras, borrowed from the language of total quality management, is "measure and display." Pixar "is always marking what we're doing and where we are, visually, for everyone to see," Nelson explains. "People aren't given information here, they bump into it."

The Popsicle-stick time budget that helped keep *The Incredibles* on schedule is one example of the measure-and-display approach to learning and working. So too are the companywide "science fairs" that take place after the completion of every movie. The fairs are a weeklong series of keynotes, Q&As, and demos. Much as with Pixar University, every member of the organization is invited to attend all sessions, which focus on technical advances as well as problem-solving lessons. The week also includes fun and games, like a scavenger hunt for aquatic artifacts after the completion of *Finding Nemo*. One way to treat everyone like a filmmaker is to school everyone in what the company learned from its latest film.

In a more fundamental sense, daily life at Pixar is a sort of open-ended science fair. Story art, in the form of paintings, sculptures, sketches, and collages, covers the walls and seeps into the far corners of the Pixar complex. It is not merely "decor"—it's a form of inspiration and communication. The main arteries on the second floor serve as galleries. The East Gallery is dedicated to the inspirational art of the current release, including drawings and 3-D clay models of characters and sets. The West Gallery features revolving exhibitions of employee art—showcases for the "secret identity" and "personal passions" of Pixarians.[3]

Color scripts for each of Pixar's films hang on the walls. The alternately dainty (*A Bug's Life* in muted pastels) and larger-than-life (*The Incredibles* in 20 huge boldly colored panels) paintings map a movie's mood and pacing with color and provide a preanimation cut of the story. The upstairs lobby features "Story Corner"—a multimedia exhibit deconstructing the art of storytelling for animated film, complete with an interactive computer simulation of storyboarding, a wall-sized display of the *Finding Nemo* story reel, and several well-thumbed versions of the script dangling on twine.

These visuals communicate in a language that all Pixarians speak—the language of art. "We make puppet shows inside a computer. This art is our design language. It nails the feeling of the movie. That's critical when you have diverse artists and technicians with different visions working on a project. For us, it's about show, not tell. We maximize fidelity by keeping everything in visual form."

5. Does your organization work as distinctively as it competes?

It's a simple question with huge implications for productivity and performance. Leaders who are determined to elevate the people factor in business understand that the real work begins once talented people walk through the door. HR maverick John Sullivan says it best: "Stars don't work for idiots." As you fill your organization with stars, it's up to you to keep them aligned—to master the interaction between stars and systems that defines everyday life at the most effective organizations we've encountered.

That means redefining some of the most overlooked and underappreciated elements of organizational life. That's why SEI Investments has devised such an unorthodox model for organizing work and reorganizing teams. That's why KI invests so much time and energy in—and why CEO Dick Resch made such a risky financial bet on—teaching the company's employee-owners how to think like well-rounded businesspeople. That's why Commerce Bank has infused new energy into something as basic (and boring) as employee orientation. If you want great people to do their best work, the logic goes, then you've got to create the right working conditions from the moment they walk through the door.

"When you go through orientation at other banks, it's eight hours of policies and procedures, eight hours of how to get fired," says Dennis DiFlorio of Commerce. "Our program is eight hours of culture, culture—and when we're done, more culture. It's about smiling, shaking hands. It's about greeting customers. Our message is about head, heart, and guts. Head—you have to think it. Heart—you have to believe it. Guts—you have to act it, twenty-four hours a day, seven days a week. You have to smile in your sleep."

Maverick Material

Resources to Help You Out-Think, Out-Innovate, Out-Sell, and Out-Work the Competition

We've made the case as forcefully as we know how that you can't do big things in business if you're content with doing things a little better than your rivals. That's the central message behind the performance of every company we visited and every executive whose work we explored in this book. But to make our case even stronger—and to make the book even more useful—we've gathered material to help you think more boldly about how you compete, to think more openly about how you innovate, to think more deeply about how you stand out in a crowded marketplace, and to think more creatively about how your organization works.

In other words, this is material to help you think more ambitiously about how you lead. We've assembled the books, monographs, Web sites, case studies, and business practices in this appendix around our core themes of rethinking competition, reinventing innovation, reconnecting with customers, and redesigning work. Remember, the most effective leaders are the most insatiable learners. We hope this collection of "essential reading" and "maverick models" helps you to keep learning long after you've finished *Mavericks at Work*.

RETHINKING COMPETITION
Essential Reading: Competing on Ideas

Karaoke Capitalism: Daring to Be Different in a Copycat World by Jonas Ridderstråle and Kjell A. Nordström (Praeger Publishers, 2005)

Just as the world of business is afflicted with an overload of me-too competitive strategies, the world of business strategy books is afflicted with a surplus of me-too titles. This is not one of them. Two professors from the Stockholm School of Economics have written one of the most jarring, disorienting, downright unusual riffs on strategy we've ever read. The book's offbeat performance (indeed, parts of it read like performance art) is true to its core message—that playing it safe is no longer playing it smart. We live in a world, the authors playfully remind us, where "the best rapper is white, the best golfer is black, France accuses the U.S. of arrogance, [and] Denmark sends a mini-submarine to a desert war." In this topsy-turvy environment, is it any wonder that the companies generating the most economic value are the ones with the most original strategies? Warning: this book is intended for maverick audiences only.

Blue Ocean Strategy: How to Create Uncontested Marketspace and Make the Competition Irrelevant by W. Chan Kim and Renée Mauborgne (Harvard Business School Press, 2005)

Another eye-opening take-on strategy from Europe, in this case two professors from INSEAD, the highly regarded business school outside Paris. If *Karaoke Capitalism* revels in persuasion as performance art, this book is cloaked in pinstripes and power ties. But its message is disruptive to the core. The book draws lessons from a cast of high-performing innovators around the world, including Canada's Cirque du Soleil, Mexico's Cemex, Japan's Nissan and NTT DoCoMo, even a Hungarian bus company called NABI—breakthrough competitors that avoid shark-infested "red" oceans and instead make waves in predator-free "blue" oceans. It's easy to drown in the metaphor, but the argument is rock-solid, as are the data and case studies. If your company is reluctant to take the plunge into a more unorthodox business strategy, then persuade your colleagues to dive into this book. You'll surface with a new perspective on competition—and a new appreciation for the futility of strategy based on mimicry. As the authors put it, "The only way to beat the competition is to stop *trying* to beat the competition."

> *The New Pioneers: The Men and Women Who Are Transforming the Workplace and the Marketplace* by Thomas Petzinger Jr.
> (Simon & Schuster, 1999)

Few books on strategy written at the height of the nineties boom withstood the harsh glare of its aftermath. Too many pundits were intoxicated (and ultimately embarrassed) by their faith in world-changing technologies, change-the-world start-ups, and a business world in a state of perpetual change. But this beautifully written book is as instructive today as it was when it was first published, mainly because its author, a former columnist for the *Wall Street Journal,* devotes his attention to feet-on-the-ground entrepreneurs rather than pie-in-the-sky venture capitalists, and because he selects his characters based on the authenticity of their values rather than the grandiosity of their claims. He introduces us to pharmacists, bakers, booksellers, even a maker of musical cymbals—small-scale entrepreneurs with big ideas about the best ways to work and win. Petzinger's pioneers are first cousins to our mavericks, and their insights offer valuable lessons to entrepreneurs eager to rely on distinctive values rather than easy-to-copy economic models.

Jim Collins on the Web—www.jimcollins.com

If you're reading this book, chances are you've already read *Built to Last* and *Good to Great*—two of the best (and best-selling) business books of all time. When it comes to setting the mainstream agenda for strategy and leadership, Jim Collins is to business ideas what Bruce Springsteen is to rock 'n' roll—he's the Boss. You can't be serious about reckoning with the ever-changing logic of competition if you don't reckon with the ever-expanding set of insights championed by Collins. This site lets you do just that. From the "Lecture Hall" to the "Discussion Guides," to the long list of books in Collins's online library, this is a refreshing (and frequently refreshed) source of ideas and debates.

Leading the Revolution by Gary Hamel
(Harvard Business School Press, 2000)

In chapter 1, we raised an eyebrow at the to-the-barricades tone of this call for radical innovation in the halls of Big Business. Now we want to tip our cap to its substance. The book is filled with savvy insights about how to see beyond the conventional wisdom, and it highlights the power of an original point of view—what Hamel dubs "business concept innovation." Of particular value is his advice for becoming a thought leader at your company—an eight-step plan to persuade your colleagues of the power of your ideas and their value in the marketplace. Our advice: find the book, forgive the dot-com-era excesses, and work through the eight steps.

Maverick Models: Strategies That Make a Statement

Google's Letter from the Founders (August 18, 2004)—
http://investor.google.com

Google has proven itself to be good at many things, from searching the Web to creating billions and billions of dollars of shareholder value. Founders Sergey Brin and Larry Page have also been good at explaining to the outside world the ideas the company stands for. Google's operations may be driven by technology, but its strategy is driven by a clear sense of advocacy. A classic case in point—the 4,000-word letter from the founders that was a prominent (and controversial) feature of the company's 2004 IPO prospectus. Talk about a maverick message: the letter is an edgy, articulate, thoroughly engaging expression of what makes the company tick. Read it, share it with colleagues, then ask whether your company could write a statement of purpose that comes close to what Brin and Page produced.

"Is Grameen Bank Different?" by Muhammad Yunus (June 2005)—www.grameen-info.org

If there were a Nobel Prize for social entrepreneurship, Bangladesh's Muhammad Yunus would win in a landslide. Famous worldwide as the inventor of "micro-lending," the founder of Grameen Bank has spent nearly three decades supplying desperately needed credit to the poorest of the poor—people who want to start a small business, tend a plot of land, or build a house. Over the years, his bank has made loans totaling nearly $5 billion to nearly 5 million borrowers, done business in 54,000 villages, and hired a staff of nearly 14,000 people. Grameen is a moving human story, but it's also a story based on a maverick business model—one that Yunus sets out in great detail in this and other essays on the bank's ultra-informative Web site. Grameen's loans require no collateral, the poorest borrowers get the highest priority, 96 percent of its customers are women—and its re-payment rate is 98.95 percent. Spend time on this site and you'll be inspired to reshape the sense of what's possible in your industry. You can bank on it.

"Why Craigslist Works" by Craig Newmark
(February 8, 2005)—www.changethis.com/13.craigslist

In chapter 2, we explored the "nerd values" at the heart of the world-wide popularity of Craigslist, the online bulletin board that gets literally billions of page views per month. In this essay, founder Craig Newmark explains, in his famously mild-mannered voice, the commonsense ideas and down-to-earth practices that have powered Craigslist for more than a decade and kept it growing through the Internet's boom-and-bust cycles. Words matter: maverick leaders don't sound like traditional executives, because their companies speak a competitive language all their own.

GSD&M—www.gsdm.com

In chapter 1, adman Roy Spence argued that "what you stand for is as important as what you sell." This site is devoted to explaining what his agency stands for. There's lots of rich language about purpose-based branding. ("We have proven that when you unleash the power of purpose, it creates a sea change in the category in which [you] compete. It hits consumers like a bolt of lightning and competitors like a bolt of envy.") There's a virtual tour of Idea City, the agency's office complex, including views of the "Roytunda" with its set-in-stone vocabulary. And of course, there are plenty of ads. The real value of this site, though, lies in the values it communicates—the hard-to-miss message that this is not just another advertising agency. What kind of message is being sent by your company's site?

REINVENTING INNOVATION
Essential Reading: The Best Open-Source Thinking

Open Innovation: The New Imperative for Creating and Profiting from Technology by Henry Chesbrough
(Harvard Business School Press, 2003)

The unofficial bible for executives who evangelize the cause of open innovation at mainstream organizations such as Procter & Gamble and Eli Lilly. (We saw it on desks and bookshelves at many of the offices and research labs we visited.) Chesbrough himself, who teaches at Berkeley's Haas School of Business and runs the Center for Open Innovation, was a high-tech executive before he went into academia, so he knows how to speak to corporate managers steeped in traditional thinking. And his case studies draw from some of the most established companies around, including IBM, Lucent, and Xerox. Indeed, that points to the book's one shortcoming: its ideas are more advanced than many of its examples. Chesbrough was so early to the open-innovation party that what qualified as cutting-edge examples a few years ago now seem downright quaint. Still, this is a great book to open up a conversation at your company about open innovation.

The Success of Open Source by Steven Weber
(Harvard University Press, 2004)

No matter what business you're in, it's virtually impossible to reckon with the implications of open-source innovation without understanding its roots in the strange, freewheeling world of open-source software. This book is without peer as a primer for nongeeks as to why Linux, Apache, and other open-source software projects work so effectively and what their growth means for the rest of us. Weber is a political scientist, not a tech guru, and he does a masterful job at explaining the sources of motivation, patterns of participation, and leadership styles in the open-source world. A wonderfully accessible guide to a sometimes inaccessible field.

> "Harnessing the Hive: How Online Games Drive Networked Innovation" by J. C. Herz (release 1.0, October 2002)— www.edventure.com

It's a white paper, not a book, but J. C. Herz packs more intellectual punch in this mind-altering essay than we've seen in almost anything else we've read on the subject. If the value of Steven Weber's book is that it is a G-rated guide to the open-source world, the power of Herz's white paper is that it should be rated NC-17. This is tough-minded thinking about open-source innovation, fueled by case studies from its most advanced practitioners—hard-core computer gamers. You don't have to like the games (most are pretty violent) or relate to the gamers themselves (they're an undeniably strange breed) to appreciate that they represent the vanguard of creativity and product development. If you want to push yourself (or your colleagues) outside the comfort zone, push yourself to read and reflect on Herz's white paper.

> Everything Tim: Tim O'Reilly's Archive—http://tim.oreilly.com

The founder of O'Reilly Media is one of technology's most taken-for-granted gurus, a thinker who's been so far ahead of the curve on so many topics (including business) that he rarely gets the credit he deserves. His online archive offers essays, white papers, interviews, even PowerPoint slides that explore every facet of the open-source phenomenon. Don't count on making a quick visit. Once you realize how much is here, you'll be reluctant to leave.

The Wisdom of Crowds: Why the Many Are Smarter Than the Few and How Collective Wisdom Shapes Business, Economies, Societies, and Nations by James Surowiecki (Doubleday, 2004)

Thankfully, Surowiecki's book, which made many "recommended reading" lists in 2004, is not nearly as long as its subtitle suggests. Truth be told, it's more about sociology than strategy, more about making decisions than creating products. But it offers fascinating riffs on everything from Linux (of course) to traffic congestion and the *Columbia* space shuttle disaster. And it's one of those rare books that puts a piece of language ("the wisdom of crowds") into the popular vernacular. There are plenty of opportunities to make direct connections between the bottom-up patterns that Surowiecki showcases and new patterns of innovation in business. A no-brainer choice for the well-read, open-minded executive.

Democratizing Innovation by Eric von Hippel (MIT Press, 2005)

Professor von Hippel runs the Innovation and Entrepreneurship Group at the MIT Sloan School of Management and is the unofficial dean of a field he calls "user-centered innovation." For years, his research and writing have revolved around a basic question: who has greater motivation to contribute their best thinking to a company than the most passionate and advanced customers of that company's products? This book chronicles what happens when organizations make it easy and rewarding for so-called lead users to modify products, contribute ideas, and communicate with one another. It's rich with examples from unexpected places (extreme sports such as windsurfing) and brimming with rigorous analysis and insights. Word of warning: von Hippel is an academic guy, and his book is published by an academic press, so don't expect much entertainment value. Still, this is the definitive guide to a vital frontier in open-source innovation.

Maverick Models: Open Source in Action

Wikipedia—www.wikipedia.org

Put simply, it's both the most loved and the most loathed open-source project since Linux. Wikipedia is the brainchild of Jimmy Wales, a former options trader who launched a free-for-all encyclopedia on the Internet in 2001. But the real brains behind Wikipedia are the users themselves, a global army of volunteer participants who write and revise Wikipedia's always-expanding catalog of entries.

The quality of the open-source encyclopedia can be wildly uneven—and sometimes false and malicious—but even its toughest critics concede that overall it's pretty darn good and getting better every day. The English-language version offers more than 600,000 articles (*Encyclopedia Britannica* offers fewer than 100,000 articles), and active versions of Wikipedia exist in about 100 languages. *Britannica,* which has been around for nearly 240 years, likes to boast that it relies on "the world's very best minds" to oversee its content. Wikipedia, which has existed for barely five years, attracts as many minds as possible to create and revise its entries—and more than 5 million visitors a month who use them to expand their minds. Visit the site, enter a few topics, and judge whether globally dispersed, volunteer brainpower can power a world-class encyclopedia.

Edinburgh Fringe Festival—www.edfringe.com

We devoted plenty of space in chapter 4 to the grassroots creativity of the Fringe, but it's worth visiting the festival's remarkably robust site to see how the operation comes alive. Paul Gudgin and his colleagues have mastered the Web as a way to sell tickets, attract performers, and, perhaps most important, allow members of the audience to plan their trips, post reviews, even keep personal diaries of their experiences. It's a vital tool for how this self-organizing operation gets organized—and the next-best-thing to visiting Edinburgh in August.

TopCoder—www.topcoder.com

Here again, it's one thing to read our (hopefully instructive) account of TopCoder and its intriguing blend of head-to-head rivalry and group collaboration, but it's truly eye-opening to explore the site itself, register as a member, and experience firsthand this competitive, transparent, learning-oriented community. (Don't worry, membership is open to anyone; you don't have to be the fastest Java programmer in your city to qualify.) Visit the competition arena, hang out in a chat room, or read the member-written match analyses and you'll appreciate how tens of thousands of gifted programmers can exude both self-centered machismo and real generosity of spirit when it comes to sharing their knowledge.

Tom Brown's BankStocks.com—www.bankstocks.com

The Wall Street analyst and hedge fund manager doesn't just draw on the grassroots insights of his own staff to inform his investment decisions. Brown is a rare member of the hedge fund crowd who shares his thinking (and that of his colleagues) with the outside world. His one-of-a-kind Web site is filled with blunt opinions, hilarious rants and raves, and a collection of in-depth essays about the world of financial services, many of which rankle CEOs and even the media.

Why would a savvy investor who's always looking for an edge on the market reveal some of his best thinking to anyone who visits his site? Because, he explains, he winds up getting more knowledge than he gives away. The site "lets us build relationships with midlevel employees of the companies we write about," he writes. "Investors typically don't have access to such individuals. Yet those employees give us added insights about what's happening at the companies they work for—over and above what top management and investor relations tell us." It's a classic example of why the most transparent executives are the most successful executives.

RECONNECTING WITH CUSTOMERS
Essential Reading: Marketing Ideas That Matter

Purple Cow: Transform Your Business by Being Remarkable
by Seth Godin (Portfolio, 2003)

Seth Godin has become the most provocative and prolific voice in marketing. Over the past few years, in a flurry of books and manifestos, he has challenged companies to pursue outstanding results by figuring out how to stand out from the crowd. This book remains the standout among everything else Godin has written. It's surprising, fun, and filled with bright ideas, intriguing case studies—and genuine passion. "How can you market yourself as 'more bland than the leading brand'?" he asks his readers. "The real growth comes from products that annoy, offend, don't appeal, are too expensive, too cheap, too heavy, too complicated, too simple—too something." This book is too smart to pass up.

The Experience Economy: Work Is Theatre & Every Business a Stage
by B. Joseph Pine and James H. Gilmore
(Harvard Business School Press, 1999)

This book forced business leaders to confront the showstopping idea that how you perform for customers can be as powerful as what you deliver. Truth be told, *The Experience Economy* is stronger on substance than style. But Pine and Gilmore deserve rave reviews for identifying a phenomenon that companies like Commerce Bank, Anthropologie, and Potbelly Sandwich Works have turned into huge hits.

American Customer Satisfaction Index—www.theacsi.org

And now for the bad news . . . as we explained in chapter 7, the American Customer Satisfaction Index is like a heart monitor for the relationship between companies and the people with whom they do business. If you're still not convinced that there's a customer service crisis in the economy, then spend an hour on this site, reviewing more than a decade's worth of data from different industries, specific companies, even government agencies. As experiences go, reviewing ACSI data isn't all that entertaining. But it is illuminating—and it may convince your colleagues that being as good as the competition is a bad strategy for success.

A New Brand World: 8 Principles for Achieving Brand Leadership in the 21st Century by Scott Bedbury with Stephen Fenichell (Viking, 2002)

It's every marketer's dream—to help create a brand as edgy as Nike or as iconic as Starbucks. Scott Bedbury has lived both of those dreams. He spent three years as vice president of marketing for Starbucks and, before that, seven years as head of advertising for Nike. This book is a candid and canny assessment of what marketers can learn from these megabrands, and how they can put the lessons to work at their companies.

Bobos in Paradise: The New Upper Class and How They Got There by David Brooks (Simon & Schuster, 2000)

One of our main messages about maverick marketing is the power of shared values over pure economic value—the proposition that customers want to do business with companies they believe in. But what values exactly? And what do most customers believe in anyway? This painfully insightful book does a memorable job of explaining the dreams, fears, habits, and aspirations of the so-called bourgeois bohemians—well-educated, high-income consumers who believe that what they buy should reflect who they are. These are the people who drink their coffee at Starbucks, buy their board games from Cranium, and get their movies from Netflix—in other words, the customers *your* company is trying to reach.

Maverick Models: Outstanding Ways to Stand Out from the Crowd

Low-Cost *and* High-Touch—JetBlue's At-Home Reservation Agents

Who says that controlling expenses has to come at the expense of connecting with customers? Consider one small but powerful innovation by JetBlue, the low-cost, high-touch airline that has updated Southwest's business model for the Bobo generation. JetBlue replicates Southwest's rock-bottom fares and point-to-point route structure but adds colorful cabins, in-flight television, and snazzy uniforms for flight attendants. As part of its formula to impress customers, JetBlue also guarantees that travelers with questions will reach a live agent in the United States rather than an automated system or a scripted operator thousands of miles away.

How does JetBlue break the customer service mold without bankrupting its low-cost strategy? By rejecting outsourcing in favor of what founder David Neeleman calls *homesourcing*. JetBlue has more than 1,000 reservation agents in and around Salt Lake City, many of whom are stay-at-home mothers, all of whom work where they live. The company uses Internet-based telephones to route calls to available operators, who, as a group, handle more than 10 million calls per year. The lesson: delivering service that defies industry norms doesn't require huge expenses—it just requires a little imagination.

Convenience by Design—The Starbucks Card

Starbucks is a textbook case of how a company can design a customer experience so distinctive that it can charge a huge premium for its products—and watch as customers keep coming back for more. But millions of Starbucks customers aren't just willing to pay a premium—they're willing to pay *in advance,* by using the replenishable, stored-value debit card that has become an essential part of how the company does business.

Debit cards, usually in the form of gift cards, have become a familiar part of the retail landscape. (Retail analysts estimated that gift cards alone generated sales of $55 billion in 2005.) Back on November 14, 2001, though, when Howard Schultz and his colleagues introduced the replenishable Starbucks Card, it was a pretty novel idea. But the card was an immediate hit, a plastic symbol of the "psychological contract" between the company and its customers. True to form, Starbucks made sure the cards were about personality as well as convenience, designing them with colorful images (from snowflakes to pinecones to cupids to gingerbread boys) that changed with the seasons. The cards became such a sensation (5 million new cards were activated in one typical three-month period in 2005) that some customers treat them as collectibles. There's even a customer-created Web site (www.starbuckscards.com) devoted to showcasing every design of every card issued around the world. Who knew a piece of plastic could pack so much personality?

Express Yourself—Canada's Picture Postage

One way to make products and services more memorable is to make them more personal—to give users the chance to influence how a product or service performs in the marketplace. As we saw in chapter 8, that's one of the key lessons behind Jones Soda, the maverick beverage company that turns the labels on its bottles into a blank slate for its customers to express their visual take on the world.

But you don't have to be a hip brand with young fans to turn mundane products into something more emotional. A case in point: Picture Postage, a service that's been offered by the Canadian postal system—nobody's idea of a hip brand—since April 2000. (The U.S. Postal Service has authorized highly successful trials of a similar service through Internet companies such as stamps.com.) Basically, Picture Postage is to the mail what Jones is to soda. Customers submit their favorite photos to Canada Post, and 15 days later they receive a sheet of legal-tender stamps featuring their kids, their pets, or their latest vacation. The stamps are twice as expensive as normal postage, but customers love the messages they send. It's one more strategy to lick the competition: as your rivals slash costs to make their products more affordable, you add features to make your products more personal.

You Are What You Sell—AdFarm's Working Farms

You don't have to be a lifestyle company like Starbucks or a glamour brand like Apple to create a sense of shared identity in the marketplace. Consider the case of AdFarm, an award-winning advertising agency with offices in out-of-the-way locations such as Calgary, Canada, and Fargo, North Dakota. AdFarm's clients include some of the world's most powerful agribusiness companies—global giants that sell seeds, fertilizer, and equipment to farmers growing wheat, barley, soybeans, and other crops. How does a niche ad agency make an impression on its big-company clients and stay connected to the no-nonsense audience it's trying to influence? By operating two farms, encouraging rank-and-file employees to buy shares in the harvest and work the farms, and using the Web to chronicle the triumphs and setbacks that go with the territory.

AdFarm's site is called "Crazy About Farming" (www.crazyabout farming.com), and that's the message it aims to send. Online diaries offer vivid reports about the challenges of growing canola and barley on the agency's farm outside Calgary and winter wheat on the farm outside Fargo. There's talk of lousy weather, deadly pests, shifting prices. You could sense the disappointment in the North Dakota diary, for example, when employees realized that their winter-wheat crop would lose money—meaning that they, as shareholders, would lose as well.

Obviously, AdFarm's long-term success depends on the creativity of its advertising, not on the price of crops. But maintaining its farms is a creative way for AdFarm to make an impression on hard-to-impress clients. And cultivating a distinctive identity in a crowded marketplace is almost as tough as making a profit on a bushel of wheat.

REDESIGNING WORK
Essential Reading: The Best Thinking
About Great Talent

Shackleton's Way: Leadership Lessons from the Great Antarctic Explorer by Margot Morrell and Stephanie Capparell (Viking Penguin, 2001)

It's no coincidence that one of the most celebrated mavericks of the 20th century is associated with the most famous help wanted ad of all time. "Men wanted for Hazardous Journey. Small wages, bitter cold, long months of complete darkness, constant danger. Safe return doubtful. Honour and recognition in case of success." Sir Ernest Shackleton's journey to the South Pole did not end successfully, of course, but his exploits as a leader led to honor and recognition nonetheless. As this relentlessly insightful book makes clear, Shackleton deserves to be remembered not just for his bold dreams but for his dogged commitment—especially his commitment to scouting, evaluating, and bringing out the best in his crew. Shackleton was a great recruiter. Nearly 5,000 people applied for 30 spots on the ill-fated *Endurance* (although no historian has produced a verifiable copy of the renowned help wanted ad). Shackleton used all kinds of inventive techniques to probe for what made the applicants tick, such as asking hard-boiled sailors to sing (a test of whether they would boost or sap morale on a long voyage). The lessons from history are truly striking: there's almost nothing that the people-centered leaders at IBM's Extreme Blue or Southwest Airlines do to enhance the character of competition in their organizations that Shackleton didn't think of first.

"Why I Never Hire Brilliant Men," *American* magazine
(February 1924)—www.taoyue.com/stacks/articles/brilliant-men.html

History doesn't have to repeat itself. In chapter 10, we discussed this essay, published more than 80 years ago, as a classic example of a point of view in business that looks with suspicion on people of extraordinary talents. They don't get their hands dirty. They'll hog all the credit. They'll dazzle colleagues with their brains but offend them with their boasts. It's easy to look with suspicion on that out-of-date point of view, but reading this essay, which reverberates with relevance for contemporary business, drives home the crucial point that values matter as much as virtuosity—that not every great talent is a great fit with an organization. "You never sold yourself to the people with whom and through whom you had to work," the author lectures the "brilliant man" he is about to fire. "You say they were jealous, but a man of your intelligence ought to know that the answer to jealousy is modesty, hard work—and results." This is a brilliant reminder of the limits of individual brilliance.

How to Be a Star at Work: 9 Breakthrough Strategies You Need to Succeed
by Robert E. Kelley (Times Books, 1998)

If only this book had been around in 1924! Kelley, who teaches at Carnegie Mellon University, has cracked the code of how talented individuals can both stand out from the crowd and fit in with their organizations. He speaks directly to the interplay between stars and systems that we explore in chapters 10 and 11, and his book is filled with clever, grounded advice for how great people can have the greatest impact. Star performers do work and act differently from their run-of-the-mill colleagues, Kelley argues. But they operate with a "consistent pattern of day-to-day behavior" that allows them to do their best work—and bring out the best in everyone around them.

Weird Ideas That Work: 11½ Practices for Promoting, Managing, and Sustaining Innovation by Robert I. Sutton (Free Press, 2002)

There's a reason why companies with extraordinary track records in the marketplace—think of Cirque du Soleil, Pixar, and SEI Investments—have designed such out-of-the-ordinary models of the workplace. Put simply, you can't develop disruptive new ideas about how to compete if you embrace the same old ideas about how to work. This wonderfully refreshing book is one of the most creative looks at innovation we've ever read. Ultimately, though, it's a book about doing business as if people mattered—because Sutton, a popular professor at the Stanford Engineering School, understands that companies don't innovate, people do. Among his principles for building workplaces that teem with ideas: "Hire people who make you uncomfortable, even those you dislike"; "find some happy people and get them to fight"; "don't try to learn anything from people who seem to have solved the problems you face." How can any self-respecting maverick resist advice like that?

A Manager's Orientation Toolkit: Tools That Get New Employees and Transfers Productive Faster by Dr. John Sullivan (www.drjohnsullivan.com/publications/orient_ebook.htm)

The irrepressible John Sullivan loves to make big claims about the end of HR-as-usual. That's what makes him so colorful as a talent strategist. What makes him so useful is that he supplements his brash attitude with businesslike advice about how to turn bold ideas into everyday practices. This superbly valuable e-book is a case in point. It's one thing to recognize the power of orientation to make a strong first impression on new employees. It's quite another to produce a 184-page book filled with original, arresting, and downright ingenious techniques that send a clear message to everyone who joins your organization: this is the first day of the rest of your professional life. Spend a few hours with this book and we guarantee you'll reorient your whole approach to orientation.

Maverick Models: People Practices That Work

"Tell Me More" Weekends

Mike McCue, the Netscape veteran who launched fast-growing Tellme Networks, is adamant that for his company to create long-term economic value, he has to fill it with talented performers who share its values. One of his favorite techniques is called "Tellme More"—recruiting weekends that go well beyond HR norms. McCue's team starts by canvassing venture capitalists, management consultants, and colleagues in other companies for potential talent. It narrows each list of invitees from several hundred to 60 and then usually winds up with about 30 participants. On the first day, the group meets at Tellme, hears from speakers (internal and external), and splits into small groups to wrestle with big problems ("How do we make the Net as reliable as the phone?"). The most promising (and interested) participants return for a second day of conversation and debate. The idea isn't just to hire people (although Tellme hired 17 of the 30 attendees at its first weekend) but to create evangelists for the company whether or not they work there. Sure, Tellme More requires far more executive time and energy than run-of-the-mill recruiting. But that's the investment required if you don't want to add run-of-the-mill talent.

Airline on A&E

Much as they do when they struggle to cut through the clutter and connect with customers, companies that are determined to attract more than their fair of talented (and thus busy) people first have to get their attention. Southwest Airlines, true to its break-the-mold strategy in the marketplace, has broken with convention to highlight its workplace as the featured character in a reality-television series that chronicles the trials, tribulations, and triumphs of Southwest's employees and passengers at four busy airports. A typical episode of *Airline* makes you laugh, wince, and sometimes applaud. It also makes prospective employees pick up the phone or e-mail a résumé. Southwest, which already chooses from more than 90 potential candidates for every open slot, reports that the flow of job applications more than triples on Tuesdays after the show airs the night before. Not many companies are confident enough about what goes on in the workplace to broadcast it to the world. But Southwest figures that if talented people like what they see, they might see fit to join.

Whole Foods Market's Hiring Vote

In chapter 3, we described the business strategy that has allowed Whole Foods Markets to thrive in the notoriously slow-growth, low-margin grocery business. Directly connected to its strategy in the marketplace is its signature design of the workplace—in particular, its vigorous embrace of self-managed teams responsible for virtually every aspect of how the company operates. Each store is divided into roughly ten teams, and the teams have remarkable authority over purchasing, budgeting, and day-to-day execution. They also have veto power over hiring—a critical technique for Whole Foods to maintain its growth trajectory without losing its edge in productivity or quality. New hires don't join the company—they join a specific team in a specific store on a 30-day trial basis. After the trial period ends, the team votes on whether to extend a permanent job offer—and it takes a two-thirds margin to win approval. Voting on who gets to join the company may sound unusual, but the logic is simple: who better to evaluate a candidate's character and credentials than the people working alongside that candidate? You can fool some of the hierarchy much of the time, but you can't fool two-thirds of your rank-and-file colleagues any of the time.

Yahoo's Backyard

Chief People Yahoo Libby Sartain is a fervent advocate of "branding from the inside out." There is, she believes, a direct connection between the values that motivate a great Yahoo employee and what the company's best customers value about its services and brand personality. Sartain also believes that how Yahoo's HR staff interacts with the company's 10,000-plus employees should map to how Yahoo serves its 345 million users. Literally. That's why she and her colleagues redesigned Yahoo's HR intranet (known inside the company as "the Backyard") to evoke the personality and performance of the company's "YahooMaps" service. Her team launched a Web-based collection of "Guides2Yahoo" ("Guide2Working," "Guide2Paying," "Guide2Interviewing") along with a virtual "Tools for Life" series ("My Life," "My Career," "My Rewards") that focuses on how employees "grow and engage" at the company. Much like Southwest Airlines' "Eight Freedoms," which reinforced a bond between employees and customers and which she also helped devise, Sartain's Guides2Yahoo and Tools for Life demonstrate that HR can be as useful, as clever, and as playful in the workplace as Yahoo considers itself in the marketplace.

Endnotes

. . . .

M avericks at Work is not an "armchair" business book. We logged tens of thousands of miles and spent countless hours visiting, conducting interviews at, and participating in meetings, training sessions, and events inside a wide variety of organizations. Of course, we also drew on many published sources (books, articles, case studies, our own previous writings) for context, background, and statistics. These notes identify the sources we found most valuable during our work on *Mavericks at Work*.

INTRODUCTION
THE MAVERICK PROMISE

1. Alan Kay uttered his immortal words at an early meeting of the Xerox Palo Alto Research Center (PARC). He spent the 1970s at this hothouse of innovation. The full quote is even more instructive: "Don't worry about what anybody else is going to do. . . . The best way to predict the future is to invent it. Really smart people with reasonable funding can do just about anything that doesn't violate too many of Newton's Laws." For more on Alan Kay, see his organization's Web site (www. viewpointsresearch.org).
2. Pete Carril's career record at Princeton was 514–261. His teams won 13 Ivy League crowns and held their own against many powerhouse programs. See *The Smart Take from the Strong: The Basketball Philosophy of Pete Carril* by Pete Carril with Dan White (University of Nebraska Press, 2004).

3. There's more than a little mythology surrounding the origins of the word "maverick." In *The New Language of Politics* (Random House, 1968), word maven William Safire repeats a colorful (but wholly inaccurate) story about Samuel Augustus Maverick: "Old man Maverick, Texas cattleman of the 1840s, refused to brand his cattle because it was cruelty to animals. His neighbors said he was a hypocrite, liar, and thief, because Maverick's policy allowed him to claim all unbranded cattle on the range. Lawsuits were followed by bloody battles, and brought a new word to our language."

In fact, Samuel Augustus Maverick (1803–70) was a graduate of Yale, a signer of the Texas Declaration of Independence, and a fabulously successful land speculator who cared little about cattle. (Maverick County in southwest Texas is named in his honor.) When someone repaid a debt with 400 head of cattle rather than cash, Maverick's caretakers allowed them to wander unbranded. Over time, locals who saw unbranded cattle would say, "Those are Maverick's"—and a term was born that today refers to politicians, entrepreneurs, and innovators who refuse to run with the herd. (Not to mention Tom Cruise's fighter-pilot character in *Top Gun*.)

In a neat twist of fate, several of Samuel Maverick's descendants became legendary political figures in Texas with an undeniable, well, maverick streak. His grandson, Maury Maverick Sr., was a pro-FDR congressman during the New Deal and one of San Antonio's most controversial mayors. (Maury Maverick Sr. famously coined another term—"gobbledygook"—to describe his interactions with New Deal agencies.) Samuel Maverick's great-grandson, Maury Maverick Jr., was a crusading lawyer, legislator, and newspaper columnist who championed free speech and civil rights. In many respects, the Maverick tradition is to San Antonio politics what the Kennedy tradition is to Boston politics—colorful, influential, and impossible to ignore.

For accurate information on the Maverick family and the term itself, see these sources: *Turn Your Eyes Toward Texas: Pioneers Sam and Mary Maverick* by Paula Mitchell Marks (Texas A&M University Press, 1989); "Mavericks Are Texas-Grown" by Leon Hale, *Houston Chronicle,* January 23, 2004; "The Last Maverick" by Jan Jarboe Russell, *Texas Monthly* (July 2003). Another go-to source is *The Handbook of Texas Online* (www.tsha.utexas.edu/handbook/online), which has entries on multiple generations of the Maverick family as well as on the terms "mavericks" and "mavericking."

CHAPTER ONE

NOT JUST A COMPANY, A CAUSE:

STRATEGY AS ADVOCACY

1. Harvard Business School has published a case study on Arkadi Kuhlmann and his colleagues, their strategic formula, and their relationship with the bank's Dutch parent; see "ING Direct," Case 9-804-167, revised May 19, 2004; see also "Would You Like a Mortgage with Your Mocha?" by Scott Kirsner, *Fast Company* (March 2003); "ING Chief Bucks Convention" by Maureen Milford, *Wilmington News Journal,* May 30, 2004; and "Bare Bones, Plump Profits" by Amey Stone, *BusinessWeek,* March 14, 2005.

2. For an overview of the legislation and its impact on rank-and-file consumers, see "Sweeping New Bankruptcy Law to Make Life Harder for Debtors" by Michael Schroeder and Suein Hwang, *Wall Street Journal,* April 6, 2005. For a taste of Kuhlmann's full-throated opposition, see "ING Head: Bankruptcy Bill 'Dead Wrong' " by Ted Griffith, *Wilmington News Journal,* March 5, 2005.

3. *Leading the Revolution* by Gary Hamel (Harvard Business School Press, 2000). Again, we want to distinguish between the book's rhetorical excesses and its enduring substance. Hamel's insights about the emptiness

of strategy as mimicry and the power of strategic originality have shaped our perspectives on competition.

4. It's impossible to write about the power of purpose in business without paying tribute to *Built to Last: Successful Habits of Visionary Companies* by James C. Collins and Jerry I. Porras (Harper Business, 1994). What was remarkable to us during our research was seeing so vividly, in companies from GSD&M to DPR Construction, the impact of the book's ideas on how organizations compete.

5. No one explains the ideas GSD&M stands for better than the agency's cofounder and president. Still, a few articles are worth noting: "Greetings from Idea City" by Gina Imperato, *Fast Company* (October–November 1997); "GSD&M's Excellent Ad Venture" by Amy Schatz, *Austin American-Statesman,* August 26, 2001; and "Ad Libbing" by Marc Gunther, *Fortune* (October 29, 2001), which is a fascinating account of how the agency, known for its edgy language and humor, dealt with the aftermath of September 11.

6. How does a $10,000 investment become $10.2 million? See "The 30 Best Stocks" by John Birger et al., *Money* (Fall 2002). For Herb Kelleher's entertaining assessment of Southwest's growth and his performance as a leader, see "The Chairman of the Board Looks Back" by Herb Kelleher as told to Katrina Booker, *Fortune* (May 28, 2001).

7. Our discussion of Southwest's Eight Freedoms is based on interviews with Libby Sartain and her former colleague Sherry Phelps (until recently director of employment for the airline). For a more detailed description of the "internal branding" process at Southwest and Yahoo, see *HR from the Heart: Inspiring Stories and Strategies for Building the People Side of Great Business* by Libby Sartain with Martha I. Finney (American Management Association, 2003).

8. Herb Kelleher recounts the saga in his *Fortune* article. For a concise history of Muse Air, see *The Handbook of Texas Online* (www.tsha .utexas.edu/handbook/online).

9. *Hardball: Are You Playing to Play or Playing to Win?* by George Stalk and Rob Lachenauer (Harvard Business School Press, 2004).

10. Our discussion of HBO's early days and strategic innovations draws extensively on Polly LaBarre's in-depth profile of Chris Albrecht. See "Hit Man," *Fast Company* (September 2002). There is no shortage of articles dissecting HBO's far-reaching impact on the culture. Two of the best include Tad Friend's *New Yorker* essays on the network, "The Next Big Bet" (May 14, 2001) and "You Can't Say That" (November 19, 2001). *Variety* offers an exhaustive survey of HBO's programming in its August 25, 2003, special report "Showman of the Year: Chris Albrecht." In the *New York Times,* Bernard Weinraub chronicled the HBO effect in television ("HBO: The Tough Act TV Tries to Follow," September 25, 2004), while John Horn of the *Los Angeles Times* examined its growing impact on films ("HBO Emerges as a Mecca for Maverick Filmmakers," September 19, 2004). Kurt Andersen dissected the premature Schadenfreude directed at the network in "I Want My HBO," *New York* (August 1–8, 2005).

CHAPTER TWO
COMPETITION AND ITS CONSEQUENCES:
DISRUPTORS, DIPLOMATS, AND A NEW WAY
TO TALK ABOUT BUSINESS

1. For a lively discussion of the most profound and productive lessons of the Internet boom, see the interview by George Anders, "Marc Andreessen, Act II," *Fast Company* (February 2001). Another valuable interview is "On the Record: Marc Andreessen," *San Francisco Chronicle,* December 7, 2003. For helpful background on Tellme, see "A Telemarketer You Can Talk To" by Steve Rosenbush, *BusinessWeek,* June 22, 2004, and "Tech IPOs: Here Comes the Next Wave" by Justin Hibbard, *BusinessWeek,* March 7, 2005.

2. For a soft-spoken guy who doesn't seek attention, Craig Newmark attracts plenty of it. Here is our list of the best writing about the company:

"Craig$list.com" by Ryan Blitstein, *San Francisco Weekly,* November 30, 2005; "Guerilla Capitalism" by Adam Lashinsky, *Fortune* (November 29, 2005); "Web Board Craigslist Makes a Name for Itself" by Janet Kornblum, *USA Today,* September 28, 2004; "Craig's To-Do List: Leave Millions on the Table" by Matt Richtel, *New York Times,* September 6, 2004; and "The Craigslist Phenomenon" by Idelle Davidson, *Los Angeles Times Magazine,* June 13, 2004.

3. For an unblinking assessment of the turmoil facing the toys and games business, see "More Gloom on the Island of Lost Toy Makers" by Constance L. Hays, *New York Times,* February 23, 2005. For a case study on the birth and growth of Cranium, see "Inside the Smartest Little Company in America" by Julie Bick, *Inc.* (January 2002). For some philosophy on fun, families, and the Cranium formula, see "The Play's the Thing" by Clive Thompson, *New York Times Magazine,* October 28, 2004.

4. The *Wall Street Journal*'s Jim Carlton revels in the company's Silicon Valley sensibilities in "Taking Lessons from a Tech Book," June 2, 1999. In "Building the New Economy" (*Fast Company,* December 1998), Eric Ransdell offers a must-read for anyone interested in DPR. After the company won a Sacramento Workplace Excellence Award, the *Sacramento Bee* provided a smart take on how DPR works in "Looking Up" by Loretta Kalb (April 1, 2004).

CHAPTER THREE

MAVERICK MESSAGES (1):

SIZING UP YOUR STRATEGY

1. *The Innovator's Dilemma: When New Technologies Cause Great Firms to Fail* by Clayton M. Christensen (Harvard Business School Press, 1997). See also *The Innovator's Solution: Creating and Sustaining Successful Growth* by Clayton M. Christensen and Michael E. Raynor (Harvard Business School Press, 2003).

2. For more background on the distinctive sense of purpose at Whole Foods, see two articles by Charles Fishman ("Whole Foods Is All Teams," *Fast Company,* April–May 1996, and "The Anarchist's Cookbook," *Fast Company,* July 2004), along with "The Virtue in $6 Heirloom Tomatoes" by Jon Gertner, *New York Times Magazine,* June 6, 2004. The company's Web site offers a presentation by CEO John Mackey called "Creating a New Business Paradigm," which explains his mind-altering perspective on the ideas that drive the company, from the "paradox of shareholder value" to the power of "creative love" in business (www.wholefoodsmarket.com/investor/presentation_SAR.html).

3. See "Banking on America" by Richard Tomlinson, *Fortune* (November 24, 2003).

CHAPTER FOUR
IDEAS UNLIMITED:
WHY NOBODY IS AS SMART AS EVERYBODY

1. See "Open Wallets for Open-Source Software" by Gary Rivlin, *New York Times,* April 27, 2005.

2. The Goldcorp Challenge turned McEwen into a celebrity in his native Canada and a symbol of innovation around the world. Here are some of the best sources of information on him, the company, and the Challenge: "Strike It Rich: The Goldcorp Gold Mine" reported by Serena Altschul, *CBS Sunday Morning,* May 15, 2005; "Right Play, Right Time" by Katherine Macklem, *Maclean's,* June 23, 2003; "He Found Gold on the Net (Really)" by Linda Tischler, *Fast Company* (June 2002). For background on the Red Lake region, see "Red Lake—Mining Area That Just Keeps on Giving" by David Mason, *Investor's Digest of Canada,* February 7, 2003.

3. "In Secret Hideaway, Bill Gates Ponders Microsoft's Future" by Robert A. Guth, *Wall Street Journal,* March 28, 2005. It's important to

note that there is a strong participatory element to Gates's go-it-alone weeks. The strategy papers and technical memos he reviews are submitted by Microsoft staffers, and those papers are posted to an internal Web site open to company employees.

4. For the personal saga behind Linux, see *Just for Fun: The Story of an Accidental Revolutionary* by Linus Torvalds and David Diamond (Harper Business, 2001). For a collection of essays on the technical performance and entrepreneurial potential of open-source architectures, see *Open Sources: Voices from the Open Source Revolution,* edited by Chris DiBona, Sam Ockman, and Mark Stone (O'Reilly Media, 1999).

5. See *The Pro-Am Revolution: How Enthusiasts Are Changing Our Economy and Society* by Charles Leadbeater and Paul Miller (Demos, 2004, www.demos.co.uk).

6. See "The Power of Us" by Robert D. Hof, *BusinessWeek,* June 20, 2005. For more smart thinking on how the mass-participation mind-set is reshaping science and technology, see two essays in *Wired* ("Open Source Everywhere" by Thomas Goetz, November 2003, and "We Are the Web" by Kevin Kelly, August 2005).

7. For a good introduction to the barely controlled chaos of the Edinburgh Fringe Festival, see "Drama as Sport for Culture Die-Hards" by Jesse McKinley, *New York Times,* August 26, 2004. See also "Why the Fringe Matters" by Rebecca Thomas, *BBC News Online,* August 1, 2002. For a sense of the career-changing impact of awards at the Fringe, see "Top Prizes at Edinburgh Fringe" by Karla Adam, *New York Times,* August 29, 2005.

CHAPTER FIVE

INNOVATION, INC.:

OPEN SOURCE GETS DOWN TO BUSINESS

1. Raymond's book, *The Cathedral and the Bazaar: Musings on Linux and Open Source by an Accidental Revolutionary* (O'Reilly, 1999), is a

foundational text for the rise of grassroots innovation. For more of his writings and rants, visit his Web site (www.catb.org/~esr). See also "Inspired by Work" by William C. Taylor, *Fast Company* (November 1999).

2. For an overview of the far-reaching changes at Procter & Gamble, see "P&G: Teaching an Old Dog New Tricks" by Patricia Sellers, *Fortune* (May 31, 2004), and "P&G Chief's Turnaround Recipe: Find Out What Women Want" by Sara Ellison, *Wall Street Journal,* June 1, 2005. For background on Connect + Develop, see "Innovation Inside Out" by Gary H. Anthes, *Computerworld* (September 13, 2004), "Outsourcing Innovation" by Erick Schonfeld, *Business 2.0* (May 30, 2003), and "Grand Opening" by Kenneth Klee, *IP Law and Business* (February 25, 2005).

3. In "Diary of a Gold Digger," Nick Rockel tags along as O'Dea provides a guided tour of the Red Lake region and his own history in the mining business (*B.C. Business Magazine,* January 2003).

4. For a rigorous grounding in the theory and practice of InnoCentive, see "Complexity Theory and Pharmaceutical R&D," a presentation by Alph Bingham to the 2003 CSFB Thought Leaders Forum (www.csfb.com/ thoughtleaderforum/index.shtml), and "The Power of Innomediation" by Mohanbir Sawhney et al., *MIT Sloan Management Review* (Winter 2003).

5. For a succinct take on one of advertising's most enduring mavericks, see "America's 25 Most Fascinating Entrepreneurs: Dan Wieden" by Warren Berger, *Inc.* (April 2004). Richard Read offers a helpful survey of Wieden + Kennedy's boundary-pushing approach in "Embedded Advertising," *The Oregonian,* September 13, 2004.

6. Ron Lieber draws a vibrant picture of W+K's workplace in "Creative Space," *Fast Company* (January 2001). See also "Home Court Advantage" by Polly LaBarre, *Fast Company* (October 1998).

7. To find a copy of "12"'s ingenious monograph, visit the school's equally inventive Web site and start searching (www.wk12.com).

Good luck! For a glimpse of the free spirit and restless mind of "12" founder Jelly Helm, visit the Web for a collection of his essays, speeches, and rants (www.ciadvertising.org/sa/spring_03/382j/panaboy/Jelly.htm). For a nice profile of him, see "Jelly's Dozen" by Joseph Gallivan, *Portland Tribune,* August 3, 2004.

CHAPTER SIX
MAVERICK MESSAGES (II):
OPEN-MINDING YOUR BUSINESS

1. For the definitive account of the origins of the initiative, see "The World Bank's Innovation Market" by Robert Chapman and Gary Hamel, *Harvard Business Review* (November 2002).

2. See *The Ten Faces of Innovation* by Tom Kelley with Jonathan Littman (Doubleday Currency, 2005) and "The Power of Design" by Bruce Nussbaum, *BusinessWeek,* May 17, 2004.

3. For all you need to know about Jeff Selis, his art, and his passion for man's best friend, visit www.dogblessamerica.com.

CHAPTER SEVEN
FROM SELLING VALUE TO SHARING VALUES:
OVERCOMING THE AGE OF OVERLOAD

1. Vernon Hill's unconventional business practices are the subject of a Harvard Business School case study, *Commerce Bank,* case 9-603-080, revised March 18, 2003. This case study draws extensively from a profile of the bank by Chuck Salter ("Best of the Best: Customer Service") in *Fast Company* (May 2002). *Barron's* has written extensively about Commerce: see "Service Master" by Jay Palmer, January 28, 2002, and "Bank Interrupted" by Jonathan R. Laing, July 26, 2004. For a skeptical perspective on the company, see "An 'Oops' at the Bank of 'Wow'" by Gretchen Morgenson, *New York Times,* August 1, 2004.

2. The ACSI offers much of its data online (www.theacsi.org). ACSI founder Claes Fornell has written a valuable analysis of customer service trends and their implications for the economy, the stock market, and management; see *The American Customer Satisfaction Index at Ten Years* by Claes Fornell et al., available on the ACSI site.

3. See the truly memorable article "In Search of a Real, Live Operator: Firms Spend Billions to Hide Them" by Jane Spencer, *Wall Street Journal,* May 8, 2002.

4. For an overview of the oversupply, overcapacity, and sensory overload that grip the economy, see two important books: *Funky Business: Talent Makes Capital Dance* by Jonas Ridderstråle and Kjell Nordström, 2nd ed. (Financial Times Management, December 2002), and *The Paradox of Choice: Why More Is Less* by Barry Schwartz (Harper Perennial, 2004).

5. The chairman of Starbucks has written a surprisingly caffeinated account of the theory and practice behind the company; see *Pour Your Heart into It: How Starbucks Built a Company One Cup at a Time* by Howard Schultz (Hyperion, 1999). See also "Hot Starbucks to Go" by Andy Serwer, *Fortune* (January 26, 2004). And be sure to check out the indispensable and entertaining blog Starbucks Gossip (www.starbucksgossip.com).

6. For more background on Maveron, see "How to Find a Hit as Big as Starbucks" by Jeremy B. Dann, *Business 2.0* (May 2004). For details on Potbelly, see "Potbelly's Leader: People Stoke Growth" by Ann Meyer, *Chicago, Tribune,* May 9, 2005.

7. On the political scandal that embroiled two company executives (but not the bank itself), see "As Banks Bid for City Bond Work, 'Pay to Play' Tradition Endures" by Mark Whitehouse, *Wall Street Journal,* March 25, 2005, and "Jury Convicts Kemp, Bankers in Pay-to-Play Scheme," *Philadelphia Inquirer,* May 9, 2005.

8. Our discussion of Anthropologie's origins and strategy draws extensively on Polly LaBarre's article "Sophisticated Sell," *Fast Company* (December 2002). For details on Urban Outfitters, see "Urban

Cowboy" by Heidi Brown, *Forbes* (November 1, 2004). Laura Compton provides a nice account of the customer loyalty that Anthropologie inspires in "Seducing Softly Us: Why Women Anthropologie," *San Francisco Chronicle,* September 12, 2004. For a discussion of the Anthropologie difference in Glen Senk's own words, see a write-up of his speech to the annual *WWD* CEO summit, "A Lesson in Anthropologie" by Jean E. Palmieri, *WWD* (November 17, 2004).

CHAPTER EIGHT

SMALL GESTURES, BIG SIGNALS:

OUTSTANDING STRATEGIES TO STAND OUT

FROM THE CROWD

1. *Training* magazine selected DPR Construction as one of its Top 100 companies for workforce development in 2003. Holly Dolezalek's article in the February 2003 issue offers some good insights into how DPR's workplace culture shapes its customer connections. For details on the Oceanside complex, see "To Cut Costs, Biogen to Sell Facility for $408 Million" by Jeffrey Krasner, *Boston Globe,* June 17, 2005.

2. See *Lovemarks: The Future Beyond Brands* by Kevin Roberts (power-House Books, 2004). Ever the marketer, the Saatchi & Saatchi CEO published a sequel, based on the emotional reaction to his first book, called *The Lovemarks Effect: Winning in the Consumer Revolution* (power-House Books, 2006).

3. Both Julie Bick's article in *Inc.* ("Inside the Smartest Little Company in America," January 2002) and Clive Thompson's *New York Times Magazine* piece ("The Play's the Thing," November 28, 2004) offer nice glimpses of the product development process at Cranium. See also "Games on the Brain" by Stephanie Dunnewind, *Seattle Times,* February 28, 2004.

4. For more insights into the truly inspiring Children's Hospital at Montefiore, see Polly LaBarre, "Best of the Best: Strategic Innovation," *Fast Company* (May 2002). For more head-spinning details on

the truly outlandish Mohegan Sun casino, see the resort's Web site (www.mohegansun.com). For background on the designer himself, see "The People's Architect" by John H. Richardson, *Esquire* (March 2002); "David Rockwell Has a Lot of Nerve" by Bill Breen, *Fast Company* (November 2002); and "Inventive Optimism" by Fred Bernstein, *Oculus* (Winter 2004–05).

5. Peter van Stolk and his company have been a source of fascination for entrepreneurs interested in branding, marketing, and the youth market. See "Small Companies, Big Impressions" by Dave Fusaro, *Food Processing* (May 18, 2004), and "Gen Y: A Tough Crowd to Sell" by Bruce Horovitz, *USA Today,* April 22, 2002. In "Soda Jerk," Christopher Steiner chronicles van Stolk's setbacks and comebacks (*Forbes,* April 11, 2005). For a glimpse into the life of a 49-pound celebrity endorser, see "7-Year-Old Skateboarder Rides Extreme Marketing Wave," *Seattle Times,* May 2, 2004. Jones began working with the skateboarder when he was four years old.

6. Operating at the intersection of movies and the Internet, Netflix has generated A-list attention—much of it with a manic-depressive quality that reflects the ups and downs of its stock price. But there are some levelheaded sources on Netflix. In "On a Mission to Change the Economics of Hollywood," *Los Angeles Times* writer Jon Healy conducts a savvy Q&A with Hastings (April 10, 2004). Gary Rivlin's February 22, 2005, article in the *New York Times,* "Does the Kid Stay in the Picture?" sizes up the promise and peril of its meteoric growth. Hacking Netflix (www.hackingnetflix.com) has become a must-see blog on the inner workings of the company.

CHAPTER NINE
MAVERICK MESSAGES (III):
BUILDING YOUR BOND WITH CUSTOMERS

1. When the *Boston Globe* wrote an article on Paul English and his 1-800 customer cheat sheet, the reaction was immediate and intense. English

wound up giving more than 100 radio, TV, and print interviews and achieved the ultimate in public attention—an appearance in *People* magazine. See "Sick of Automation? Dial 0 for Human" by Bruce Mohl, *Boston Globe,* November 6, 2005, and "Executive Has an Answer to Phone System Cheat Sheet" by Bruce Mohl, *Boston Globe,* December 2, 2005. To peek at the cheat sheet yourself, visit the Web (www.gethuman.com).

2. Our data on the publishing industry comes from several sources: "Quest for a Best Seller Creates a Pileup of Returned Books" by Jeffrey A. Trachtenberg, *Wall Street Journal,* June 3, 2005; "Expo Week Arrives, and Books Are Back" by Edward Wyatt, *New York Times,* June 2, 2005; and "The Never-Ending Stories: Publishers Are Cranking Out More Books Than Ever" by David Mehegan, *Boston Globe,* June 4, 2005.

3. The expansion of Starbucks as a brand and an employer has made it an occasional (and occasionally amusing) target for organized labor. In New York City, activists from the Industrial Workers of the World (the "Wobblies" of anarcho-syndicalist fame) tried to organize several shops. Their slogan: "No latte, no peace." See "Union Steps up Drive to Organize Starbucks" by Anthony Ramirez, *New York Times,* November 26, 2005; see also "A Union Shop on Every Block" by Philip Dawdy, *Seattle Weekly,* December 7–13, 2005.

4. See "They're Off to See the Wizards" by Katie Hafner, *New York Times,* January 27, 2005.

CHAPTER TEN

THE COMPANY YOU KEEP: BUSINESS AS IF PEOPLE MATTERED

1. For more information on IBM's Extreme Blue program, visit the Web (www-913.ibm.com/employment/us/extremeblue/). See also "IBM Interns Are a Breath of Fresh Air" by Mike Cassidy, *San Jose Mercury News,* August 24, 2004. Jane Harper has easily held a dozen jobs in her 25-year career at IBM. In each one, she has been a change dynamo.

For more on her singular leadership track, see "Faster Company" by Scott Kirsner, *Fast Company* (May 2000).

2. Extreme Blue is a small but vital component of IBM's aggressive push to embrace the future. Further reading on the company's agenda includes "Leading Change When Business Is Good," an interview with CEO Sam Palmisano by Paul Hemp and Thomas A. Stewart, *Harvard Business Review* (December 2004); "Beyond Blue" by Steve Hamm and Spencer E. Ante, *BusinessWeek,* April 18, 2005; and "The Information Puzzle" by Sam Palmisano, *Newsweek,* December 2, 2005.

3. See *The War for Talent* by Ed Michaels, Helen Handfield-Jones, and Beth Axelrod (Harvard Business School Press, 2001), and "The Talent Myth" by Malcolm Gladwell, *The New Yorker,* July 22, 2002. Thanks to Randall Cross for pointing out the essay, "Why I Never Hire Brilliant Men."

4. Two of the most provocative and useful essays on John Sullivan's Web site are "The 20 Rules for Great Recruiting" (March 26, 2001) and "Is Your HR Department Unwittingly a 'Socialist' Institution?" (November 28, 2004). Visit www.drjohnsullivan.com to find them.

5. Jane Harper and the Extreme Blue team contributed to the ideas in the "Staying Extreme" manual. John Wolpert, former lab director for Extreme Blue in Austin, deserves credit for producing the original draft in 2002.

6. We discussed Marc Andreessen's savvy take on hiring during our interviews with him. He also explained the Rule of Crappy People to George Anders in "Marc Andreessen, Act II," *Fast Company* (February 2001).

7. Southwest's culture has been endlessly dissected in books and case studies. For a good overview of the airline's approach to recruiting and training, see "How Fun Flies at Southwest Airlines" by Brenda Paik Sunoo, *Personnel Journal* (June 1995). For a sober-minded perspective on

Southwest's fun-loving culture, see *The Southwest Airlines Way: Using the Power of Relationships to Achieve High Performance* by Jody Hoffer Gittell (McGraw-Hill, 2003).

8. Yahoo's fortunes have changed dramatically since the dark days of the dot com crash. Michael S. Malone chronicles the new realities in "The UnGoogle (Yes, Yahoo!)," *Wired* (March 2005). Many thanks to Tim Sanders, bestselling author and former chief solutions officer at Yahoo, who generously gave of his time and insight during our several visits to the company.

9. She has published a book on the subject. See *Brand from the Inside: Eight Essentials to Emotionally Connect Your Employees to Your Business* by Libby Sartain and Mark Schumann (Jossey-Bass, 2006).

10. The Cirque du Soleil story, with its blend of creativity, glamour, and powerhouse results, is catnip to business writers and academics alike. The key articles include "Blue Ocean Strategy" by W. Chan Kim and Renée Mauborgne, *Harvard Business Review* (October 2004); "The Phantas-magoria Factory" by Geoff Keighley, *Business 2.0* (January-February 2004); "The $600 Million Circus Maximus" by Christopher Palmeri, *BusinessWeek,* December 2, 2004; "Lord of the Rings," *The Economist,* February 5, 2005; and "Join the Circus" by Linda Tischler, *Fast Company* (July 2005).

11. There's no shortage of in-depth media coverage on the brutal competition among Google, Yahoo, and Microsoft for the technology world's best-and-brightest players. See, "Google Ignites Silicon Valley Hiring Frenzy," *Wall Street Journal,* November 23, 2005, as well as "Revenge of the Nerds—Again," *BusinessWeek*, July 28, 2005. *BusinessWeek* also had an informative cover story on the new battle for talent. See "Star Search," by Nanette Byrnes, October 10, 2005.

12. You can find John Sullivan's in-depth case studies and essays about Google, Starbucks, and other companies on a valuable Web site called Electronic Recruiting Exchange. Visit www.ere.net.

CHAPTER ELEVEN
PEOPLE AND PERFORMANCE: STARS, SYSTEMS, AND WORKPLACES THAT WORK

1. *Cirque du Soleil: 20 Years Under the Sun: An Authorized History* by Tony Babinski and Kristian Manchester (Harry N. Abrams, 2004) relates Natasha Hallet's story and chronicles Cirque's history from its earliest street-busking days.

2. For more background on Pixar, see "Welcome to Planet Pixar" by Austin Bunn, *Wired* (June 2004); "All Too Superhuman" by Richard Corliss, *Time,* October 25, 2004; "Talk of the Toon" by Charles Gant, *The Times* (London), November 8, 2003; and "Pixar's New Digs Coddle Animators, Writers, and Tech Heads" by Rick Lyman, *New York Times,* June 11, 2001. A collection of profiles on Pixar's leadership triumvirate of Steve Jobs, Ed Catmull, and John Lasseter sheds more light: "Pixar's Unsung Hero" by Peter Burrows, *BusinessWeek,* June 30, 2003; "Pixar's Mr. Incredible May Yet Rewrite the Apple Story" by Randall Stross, *New York Times,* October 24, 2004; and "The Man Who Built Pixar's Incredible Innovation Machine" by Brent Schlender, *Fortune* (November 15, 2004).

3. *Composing Pictures* by Donald W. Graham (Van Nostrand Reinhold Co., 1970).

4. SEI has landed near the top of *Fortune*'s "100 Best Companies to Work For" list for five years in a row (2001–2005). See also "Total Teamwork: SEI Investments" by Scott Kirsner, *Fast Company* (April 1998), and "From Fried Chicken to Seared Fund Managers" by Debbie Harrison, *Financial Times,* July 5–6, 2003.

5. Rich Karlgaard tells Dick Resch's personal and business story in *Life 2.0: How People Across America Are Transforming Their Lives by Finding the Where of Their Happiness* (Crown Business, 2004). For a sense of the KI chief's presence in Green Bay, see "KI President Dick Resch" by

Richard Ryman, *Green Bay Press-Gazette,* January 5, 2003, and "Arena Complex Is Likely to Be Big Tourist Draw" by Nathan Phelps, *Green Bay Press-Gazette,* August 18, 2002.

CHAPTER TWELVE
MAVERICK MESSAGES (IV): PRACTICING YOUR PEOPLE SKILLS

1. Thanks to John Battelle for pointing out the glaring contrast between Google's top ten list and the (now disappeared) MSN Search top ten list in a post on his SearchBlog, January 7, 2004 (http://battellemedia.com/). Google's list is available on the Web (www.google.com/jobs/reasons.html).

2. Visit Southwest Airlines on the Web for a gallery of advertising from the last three decades (www.swamedia.com). Google outflanks most companies when it comes to the sheer inventiveness of its employment ads. Silicon Valley commuters curious (and smart) enough to figure out a cryptic billboard (it read "{first 10-digit prime found in consecutive digits *e*}.com") found a Web site containing an even harder problem—and a shot at an interview. Google has even crafted its own version of a standardized test: the Google Labs Aptitude Test (or GLAT). The test is a quirky mix of equation solving, multiple choice, and essay writing. For a copy, visit the Web (http://googleblog.blogspot.com/2004/09/pencils-down-people.html).

3. "Story art" even seeps into Pixar's presence on the Web. The company's site features an "Artist's Corner" with profiles and portfolios of Pixarians' art (www.pixar.com/artistscorner/index.html).

Acknowledgments
. . . .

M avericks at Work is rooted in a decade-long conversation about
competition, leadership, and the true meaning of success—a
conversation we've been having with a network of friends,
associates, and business thinkers who've been gracious enough to take
our ideas seriously and share their ideas with us. We own all the mistakes in this book. But we owe a debt of gratitude to so many people
for making it possible.

First and foremost, we must acknowledge Alan M. Webber, who's
been a cherished friend and indispensable colleague for more years than
any of us care to disclose. Alan is smart enough to plead not guilty, but
he is a partner-in-crime in whatever we think and write about the
changing world of business. Thanks for everything, Alan.

Richard Pine of Inkwell Management is more than a literary agent.
He's a force of nature, a source of quiet confidence, and an all-around
mensch. He shaped our early ideas, smoothed over the inevitable rough

patches during the writing, and never lost his enthusiasm. The world needs more people like Richard.

Thanks to Jane Friedman, Michael Morrison, Lisa Gallagher, David Highfill, Dee Dee De Bartlo, Lynn Grady, Carl Lennertz, Debbie Stier, and the high-energy crew at HarperCollins and William Morrow. We're thrilled that *Mavericks at Work* is in the hands of such a maverick group.

Many other thinkers, writers, and leaders have shaped our perspectives on where business can and should be going. Here's to those from whom we've learned so much: Colleen Aylward, Scott Bedbury, John Seely Brown, Marcus Buckingham, Pip Coburn, Jim Collins, Laurie Coots, John Ellis, Seth Godin, Gary Hamel, David Kuehler, Tim O'Reilly, Tom Peters, Dan Pink, Ron Pompei, Feargal Quinn, Ivy Ross, Rusty Rueff, Andy Stefanovich, Bob Sutton, Keith Yamashita.

The most rewarding part of this project was the chance to immerse ourselves in so many amazing organizations and meet so many truly remarkable leaders. Thanks to all of the executives and entrepreneurs who opened their companies to us. Special thanks to the unsung heroes who helped us get access, didn't object when we asked to come back (again and again), and made sure we got our facts right. You're too numerous to list, but you know who you are. We couldn't have done this without you.

How could we not acknowledge the brains, camaraderie, and enduring friendship of the *Fast Company* gang? Many of us have moved on to the next adventure, but none of us, it's fair to say, will forget the thrill of our adventure together. All of you have had a hand, directly or indirectly, in the making of this book. Thanks for being such great colleagues and friends.

Finally, a few personal acknowledgments.

Bill would like to thank his parents, brothers, and sister for their unconditional support and endless supply of good cheer. I also want to thank Carl Mayer and Eliot Spitzer for nearly 30 years of friendship—egging me on, keeping me honest, never missing a chance to bust my chops. As for Chloe Mantel—well, who can explain your willingness to put up with me for so long? Thanks for setting the bar so high.

Polly would like to thank her family—her sister, Melissa, especially—for their unstinting love and general enthusiasm over a lifetime. So many dear friends have cheered me on and set me straight time after time. Thank you Dede Welles, Mark Gimbel, Gordon Gould, Zeke Brown, Tracy Schlapp, and Paula Chauncey. Two people, in particular, lived through every wrinkle of writing this book with me. Anna Muoio's friendship is precious beyond words. Her spirit, curiosity, and compassion raise me up on a daily basis—and, I'm sure, will continue to do so until we both land in our rockers. Fergus Kinnell, thank you for not only providing me with a room of my own but also for making me a home in your heart.

Index

....